Trans Narrators

# Gender and the Body in Literature and Culture

Series editors: Ruth Heholt and Joanne Ella Parsons

**Recent books in the series:**
*Consuming Female Beauty: British Literature and Periodicals, 1840–1914*
Michelle Smith

*Dissident Gut: Technologies of Regularity, Politics of Revolt*
Jean Walton

*Trans Narrators: First-Person Form and the Gendered Body in Contemporary Literature*
Chiara Pellegrini

**Forthcoming**
*Vladimir Mayakovsky, Poetics of Virility and Masculine Style*
Connor Doak

*The Drunkard in Victorian Fiction and Culture: From Conviviality to Cursed Thirst*
Pam Lock

*Medicine and Women's Fiction: Hysteria, Bodies and Narratives, 1850s to 1930s*
Louise Benson James

*Masculinities in Contemporary Nigerian Fiction: Receptivity and Gender*
Uchechukwu Peter Umezurike

# Trans Narrators

First-Person Form and the Gendered
Body in Contemporary Literature

Chiara Pellegrini

**EDINBURGH**
University Press

Edinburgh University Press is one of the leading university presses in the UK. We publish academic books and journals in our selected subject areas across the humanities and social sciences, combining cutting-edge scholarship with high editorial and production values to produce academic works of lasting importance. For more information visit our website: edinburghuniversitypress.com

© Chiara Pellegrini, 2025

Edinburgh University Press Ltd
13 Infirmary Street
Edinburgh EH1 1LT

Typeset in 11/13 Adobe Sabon
by Cheshire Typesetting Ltd, Cuddington, Cheshire

A CIP record for this book is available from the British Library

ISBN 978 1 3995 2694 4 (hardback)
ISBN 978 1 3995 2696 8 (webready PDF)
ISBN 978 1 3995 2697 5 (epub)

The right of Chiara Pellegrini to be identified as the author of this work has been asserted in accordance with the Copyright, Designs and Patents Act 1988, and the Copyright and Related Rights Regulations 2003 (SI No. 2498).

# Contents

Acknowledgements vi
Series Preface viii

Introduction: From Narrating Trans to Transing Narration 1

1. Trans Narrators and the Politics of Form: Toward a Trans Narratology 28
2. Trans Narrators and Temporality: Time Beyond Transition, Truth Beyond Memoir 66
3. Trans Narrators and Embodiment: Textual Corporeality and Gender Multiplicity 102
4. Trans Narrators and Reliability: Claiming Authority in Marginalised Realities 138

Conclusion: More than I 174

Bibliography 182
Index 193

# Acknowledgements

The research for this book first began during my PhD at Newcastle University, and I have many colleagues to thank for making this possible. My first thanks go to Stacy Gillis, excellent mentor and friend. I am very grateful to Kate Chedgzoy and Susan S. Lanser for their generous and rigorous advice during the examination of my thesis and beyond. The School of English Literature, Language and Linguistics has supported my participation in conferences and other activities that have helped shape my ideas, and has provided a wonderful environment for my development as a researcher. Within the School, I want to especially thank Ruth Connolly and Neelam Srivastava for their advice and guidance over the years.

The International Society for the Study of Narrative has been a home for countless conversations with colleagues that have enriched my approach to narrative. In particular, the panels on Trans/Forming Narrative Studies at recent Narrative conferences have provided wonderful opportunities for collaboration with others who share the goal of developing a trans narratology, as has the Trans/Queer Gender and Narrative Form symposium that I organised in 2021. The ideas exchanged at the Summer Course in Narrative Studies at Aarhus University in 2017 still influence my thinking now.

The advice of brilliant and empathetic researchers and friends has helped me navigate the complexities of writing this book, both intellectually and practically. I especially want to thank Stephanie Davies, Joey Jenkins, Helen King, Lena Mattheis, Marco Medugno, Cody Mejeur, Chris Mowat, Gráinne O'Hare, Caroline Rae, Damiano Sacco, Joonas Säntti and Sven Van den Bossche.

I am also grateful to my new colleagues at Canterbury Christ Church University for welcoming me and valuing my ideas.

The support of my family and other loved ones, who only have a vague sense of what this book is about but are always ready to encourage me, also deserves to be acknowledged.

Finally, special thanks go to queer and trans friends, colleagues, writers and campaigners, who are an endless source of inspiration.

# Series Preface

This series has a dedicated focus on gender and the body. With pressing questions about embodiment, gender identity, race, the Anthropocene and the post-human being played out in academia and wider society, this series provides space for full and detailed scholarly discussions in the form of collections and monographs. Encouraging interdisciplinarity and crossovers in subjects, time periods and genres, the series challenges and expands discussions around LGBTQI embodiments, race and racialisation, and the changing nature of masculinity, as well as opening up old and new debates around femininity and feminism. Looking at narratives from different periods and cultures, the series is committed to publishing pioneering research that will enhance many disciplines.

Series Editors: Ruth Heholt and Joanne Ella Parsons

# Introduction: From Narrating Trans to Transing Narration

I am interested in narrators who say 'I' for two ostensibly antithetical reasons: because they tend to resemble an embodied person, and because this pronoun tells us little about how, where, and when this person might be embodied. The I has no predetermined gender, and it designates simultaneously the one who tells the story, the one who is in the story, and the one who exists after, before, and during the story. At the same time, trans narrators are anchored in a definable reality, representing and reflecting voices that are elsewhere repeatedly silenced. Trans narrators, strictly speaking, are textual entities who produce a narrative about themselves; who, at least to some extent, construct an embodied identity about which there is something to tell; and who name this identity as trans, either avowedly or implicitly through reference to cultural codes established by other trans writing. While attending to the characteristics of these narrators in contemporary texts specifically, I want to make two broader suggestions: (1) narrators are trans: the way in which narrators operate and exist in a text resonates with how trans scholars have theorised the meaning of this term; (2) trans subjects are narrators: they are placed, more than is the case for cis people, in a position in which they have to continually produce an account of themselves that follows certain patterns of intelligibility, be it to obtain legitimation, satisfy curiosity, or combat erasure. Therefore, I occasionally use 'trans narrators' to designate agents that exist beyond the text (authors and other people who communicate) or to designate textual speakers that are trans in a more abstract sense of the term. As I approach trans narrators, I combine the insights and methodologies of two fields of analysis – narrative studies and trans studies – to examine three key areas of inquiry: temporality, embodiment, and reliability. Fostering an encounter between narrative studies and trans studies allows me to show how matters of temporality, embodiment, and reliability are formal aspects of narrative as much as they are urgent political concerns for marginalised people. My aim, whatever the results may be, is unequivocally to do justice to trans people and amplify their stories, their perspectives, and their material concerns, against voices that wish to deny their rights and existence.

The trans narrators I discuss in this book are first-person narrators. Gérard Genette's objection that the term 'first person' is 'inadequate' (243) is legitimate: any narrator, by definition, refers to themselves as 'I' (speaking in the first person) and to others as 'he', 'she' or 'they' (speaking in the third). However, I continue to use this word to designate what Genette would call homodiegetic and autodiegetic narrators: narrators who are in the story they tell, and whose story is about themselves. The term 'first person' allows me to imply that a producer of narrative is a 'person' who speaks 'first'. Trans scholar Talia Mae Bettcher argues that 'trans politics ought to proceed with the principle that transpeople have *first-person authority* (FPA) over their own gender' ('First Person Authority' 98). If a subject has first-person authority, their statements about themself occupy 'a superior epistemic position' compared to those of another person about them (100). This is an ethical and political necessity when considering a group who has been 'historically relegated to objects of investigation, where any capacity to avow has been disabled under the socially recognized authority of the medical scientist' (114). The 'capacity to avow' as narrator, then – to speak first about one's person – becomes a way in which, through narrative, trans subjects have the opportunity to redress an unjust history that has robbed them of the possibility to articulate a discourse about themselves. Allowing audiences to hear trans voices directly without mediation is ethically bound up with recognising the authority of these voices over their own experience. A shift can then occur from being positioned as (solely) the object of narrative to becoming the subject that produces that narrative. When trans authors write trans narrators, this agency is doubly claimed. Despite any questioning that may arise as to the extent to which a narrator is a 'person' and narrating in print constitutes 'speaking', the textual constructs that say 'I' in the texts I consider function in part because they resemble speaking people – speaking people belonging to groups whose capacity to speak and whose rights as people are continually denied.

At the same time as they obtain hard-fought epistemological and discursive control, 'speaking people' in narrative can also enjoy a freedom from temporal and spatial boundaries, as well as an ambiguity, transformability, and multiplicity of presence that is not possible when one is embodied in the extra-textual world. Narrative studies has introduced the notion of distinct diegetic levels: the level at which the elements of the story exist and the level outside of it, where the narrator perceives and presents them as discourse. Naming these levels allows us to see that the referent of the deictic word 'I' is in multiple times and places at once. The I can designate both the narrator outside the story (*I* tell you I was there) and its counterpart as character in the diegetic level where the story takes place (I tell you *I* was there). Trans writers reveal how the capacity that narrators have for movement, for different degrees of definition, and for plurality of signification also characterises gender. The pronoun I in English can suspend gender, designating he, she, and/or the singular they, successively or simultaneously or stably or not at all. Both as regards narrative and as regards gender, the I is able to exist ambiguously, to cross the borders that order language and identity, and to designate multiple selves. While it does this, the I also offers a subject position for speaking first, for controlling one's own visibility, and for constructing one's own temporality. The encounter I want to foster here between trans studies and narrative studies is crucial to understanding the textual, ethical, and social functions of narrators who say 'I'. In the rest of this introduction, I give an overview of key insights and perspectives from these two fields that are necessary in order to understand the methodology I develop for studying trans narrators in contemporary trans literature. This methodology may prove useful for studying trans narrators across a range of fictional and non-fictional texts, historical periods, and cultural contexts. Here, I employ it to investigate contemporary trans literature in English, and it is therefore attuned to this specific context.

## Contemporary trans literature

Like any gesture of canon formation, attempting to define contemporary trans literature entails exclusions, tensions, and simplifications. In this book, I have chosen to focus closely on nine texts from the past ten years that illustrate trans authors' negotiations with first-person voice, personal and collective time, the representation of bodies and genders, and the act of telling the truth. A description of contemporary trans literature could begin by listing these nine texts alongside the ones that are left out: the ones I mention but analyse less closely, the ones I have not mentioned, the ones I have not read, the ones released while this book is being prepared for publication. In her comprehensive analysis of the emergence of twenty-first-century American transgender writing, Trish Salah makes one of these lists, occupying a page with names of authors and presses, titles of collections and scholarly panels (175). Generally, lists constitute a fundamental way in which trans literature is introduced, promoted, and popularised. The proliferation of online articles and posts called 'Ten Transgender Poets You Should Know', 'Must-Read Trans Sci-Fi and Fantasy Books', or '28 YA Books with Trans and Nonbinary Characters' offers an array of canons from the most general to the most specific. In lieu of such a list, over the course of this book I touch on a variety of texts and authors that fit the scope of this study, knowing and hoping that others will find more. The fact that no list could ever be complete but that lists can be attempted signals that trans literature is a category of recent and still active formation, beginning to be named just when it becomes impossible to circumscribe. The increasing visibility of trans stories over the past couple of decades prompts desires to trace a history and define a category into which these stories would fit, be it as a genre to be marketed, a reading list to complete, or an object of academic analysis. Here, I want to give an overview of some of the questions raised by these attempts at canon formation, together with tracing some twentieth-century forms and genres that shape what trans literature looks like today.

In this book, I focus on texts by authors who are (out as) trans. The question of what counts as a trans text is, however, not always as simple as a correlation with authorship. In an article that sets out to investigate 'what counts as transgender literature', Gabrielle Bellot obtains a range of views from interviewing trans authors and publishers. Her conclusion, not unlike that of other articles on this topic, is fairly definitive while leaving room for nuance:

> it seems that many of us would agree trans people are usually the ones who will know best what it's like to be trans, so we *should*, ideally,

be the ones writing our literature, even if it's *possible* for someone non-trans to.

The opinions she collects range from considering only texts 'connected really explicitly to transgender authorship' to including 'work that resonates with or illuminates or otherwise serves transgender communities'. On the one hand, it seems important to make a distinction between texts in which those who are marginalised for their gender speak for themselves and texts in which their stories are used (however respectfully) by someone who considers themself external to this experience. On the other, defining too rigidly what counts as trans literature is never too far from defining what counts as 'proper' trans, a gesture that, as Travis Alabanza argues, is characteristic of a 'cisgender world' doing 'what an often colonial gender project knows how to do: divide and regulate' (48). Would authors who may not be out as trans or may not recognise trans as a label for their gender variance count as trans authors? And what to make of the work of authors who are not trans that nonetheless resonates with a large number of trans people?[1] Bellot's 2016 article is one example of how an increased public interest in reading, naming, and discussing trans texts immediately entails questions about the ethics of representation, the fixity of identity categories, and the issue of cultural marginalisation. This is the environment in which the authors I discuss in this book operate, making a self-conscious intervention into an emergent canon.

In beginning a discussion of trans literature with the question of authorship, I follow the voices in narrative studies who argue for 'according a special value to the historical author and especially to the historically minoritized author, whose agency as a strategic creator of a text we should be at pains to restore' (Halpern 57). As will become clear, the fact that the trans narrators I analyse are constructed by trans authors (whether more or less autobiographically) comes to matter in a number of ways when interpreting textual temporality, embodiment, and reliability. The question of trans readers as makers of trans literature also deserves some attention. At the same time as there seems to be increasing popular demand for trans narratives, which publishers are keen to meet, discussions about decentring cisgender audiences have also become more common. In the afterword to *Meanwhile, Elsewhere: Science Fiction and Fantasy from Transgender Writers*

(2017), Cat Fitzpatrick and Casey Plett explain their goal in collecting speculative short stories from trans authors: 'we wanted to make a book by trans writers that centred a trans reader as much as possible, that dispensed with the worry of explaining ourselves to cis people, and that would allow us to talk to each other' ('Afterword' 439). Similarly, in discussing her bestselling novel *Detransition, Baby* (2021), Torrey Peters describes the liberating feeling of 'trans women writing for other trans women': 'you never slowed down to explain anything because trans women already know' ('Seeing through a Trans Lens'). In these moments of canon formation – editing an anthology, being interviewed about a bestseller – trans authors make clear that a trans authorial audience affects the quality of a text: for Fitzpatrick and Plett, its 'intimacy' ('Afterword' 439), for Peters its 'speed'. This will become relevant especially in Chapter 4, as an exploration of reliability requires discussion of extra-textual participants like authors and audiences. For now, I want to note that I am a cis reader myself: I owe my understanding of transness to the self-representations and theorisations of trans people, who should always be at the centre of defining what trans literature is.

Within the broader field of contemporary trans literature, I focus on first-person narrators in mainstream anglophone prose. In order to understand hegemonic paradigms for writing trans identity, I examine authors who have achieved some degree of commercial and/or critical success, who are based in North America or the UK, and who write short stories, novels, or memoirs. The texts I discuss, however, are not simply the most visible ones; they are also ones that openly confront the audience expectations that come with this visibility. While operating at the centre of trans literature in one sense (compared, for instance, to non-Western authors or unpublished authors), these writers occupy a speaking position that is always at risk of being dismissed, pigeonholed, or reduced to its most palatable features. I find prose to be the most apt venue for analysing these tensions, but trans cultural production negotiates temporality, embodiment, and reliability in many other forms. For instance, Marquis Bey argues that poetry is 'the genre, the discursive avenue, through which many black and trans and femme people have chosen to write' (29), in opposition to 'a fictionalized account used to illustrate what it's like to be black and/or trans and/or femme' (30). Broader trans artistic production is explored in books like micha cárdenas's *Poetic Operations:*

*Trans of Color Art in Digital Media* (2021) and Jian Neo Chen's *Trans Exploits: Trans of Color Cultures and Technologies in Movement* (2019). In comparison with North America, there is a notable absence of scholarly attention paid to trans authors in the UK. This is no doubt due to the fact that trans studies, as Ezra Horbury and Christine 'Xine' Yao argue, 'has remained a minority discipline in the United Kingdom' (446). Together with the 'institutional ignorance, if not outright suppression, of Black and women of colour feminisms' (448), UK academia permits transphobic scholarship by employing a 'strategic amnesia' about the available expertise of trans scholars and writers, who are rarely cited or consulted on matters of gender (446). Despite their differences, however, the UK and North America form a shared context for the production and contestation of narrative models for understanding trans identity.

In this transnational context, first-person voices in contemporary trans literature have been shaped by a tradition of writing gender transgressions and transitions. At the start of the twentieth century, medical case histories provided a model for narratives of sexual identity that deviated from societal norms, including cases of 'uncertain sex' and 'the desire to change sex' (Funke 136).[2] As Jana Funke argues, 'narratives of the self influenced how sexologists came to understand human sexuality and were, in turn, regulated by the sexological scripts of sexual development' (136). The mutually constitutive relationship between medical case histories and trans autobiography shaped the memoirs that were published in this century under the label of 'transsexual' narratives, which for a long time constituted the only widely available texts authored by trans people who were out as trans. Books like Christine Jorgensen's *A Personal Autobiography* (1967), in the US, and Jan Morris's *Conundrum* (1974), in the UK, helped codify the narrative of a woman born in the 'wrong body' who undergoes medical transition and surgery to move toward happiness and social acceptance. Contemporary trans authors still have to contend with this narrative as the archetypal literary representation of transness, which is often regarded as having overshadowed and curtailed more expansive imaginative possibilities, including the possibility of writing fiction. Trans writer Kuchenga Shenjé explains that '[t]rans people were not given the freedom to write fiction about our place in society because we were so occupied with the toil of proving that we, as people, were not a fiction'.

8   Trans Narrators

The current ambivalence toward autobiographical forms can also be accounted for by their proximity to the discourse of medical establishment, invested in validating gender variance only to the extent that it could be controlled and giving trans people a voice to prove their existence and no more. The whiteness of transsexual memoirs also prompts the search for other literary histories: Shenjé centres Black cis authors as producing the narratives out of which she 'blended a sense of belonging'. Modes of articulating identity and resistance in the face of erasure provided by Black, indigenous, and postcolonial literatures overlap and interlink with trans canons in ways that are now beginning to be explored more widely.

Forming an intersecting genealogy, narratives of transmasculine identity from Radclyffe Hall's *The Well of Loneliness* (1928) to Leslie Feinberg's *Stone Butch Blues* (1993) engage to different extents, like the memoirs of trans women, with available medical models in order to articulate gender variance. Representations of transmasculinity, however, have also often been either interpreted or explicitly presented as narratives about lesbian sexuality and/ or the transgression of patriarchal norms. Rachel Carroll traces a tradition of writing and reading 'female-to-male gender crossing as an important metaphor for feminist subversion' or as 'claimed for a larger history of female same-sex desire' (11). Therefore, even the most straightforward history of trans writing involves not only considering the self-representations of subjects explicitly publishing under the sign of a trans- prefix, but also, as Jay Prosser influentially argued in relation to *The Well of Loneliness*, 'performing retroactive readings of figures and texts that have been central to the lesbian and gay canon' (167). While it has been important to assert trans identity as amounting to something more than feminist transgression or queer desire, trans texts often represent a complex tangle of circumstances and investments. Feinberg's semi-autobiographical novel, for instance, articulates a narrative of identity shaped variously by patriarchal pressures, the world of butch and femme communities, and the trajectories of medical transition (among other forces). Unlike conventional transsexual narratives, *Stone Butch Blues* interrupts medical transition, embraces gender outside the binary, and rejects social assimilation with a call for anti-capitalist organising. This type of story marked a turn in trans representation. In their pamphlet *Transgender Liberation: A Movement Whose Time Has Come*

(1992), Feinberg advocated for the term 'transgender' to name the range of gender-nonconforming identities of a community united by the demand to 'choose our own self-definitions' (6). Over the course of the 1990s, trans studies also began to emerge as an academic field, and alongside it new narratives of identity gained prominence, embracing unstable gender categories, disruptions of established orders, contradictions, and ambiguities as strategies for representing the trans body in defiance of medical authorities, which had demanded assimilation into patriarchal and heteronormative models of man and woman.

While I continue to follow this history below, when I discuss the development of trans studies, another strand worth pursuing in order to trace the roots of current forms of trans writing is the questioning of binary gender in twentieth-century feminist fiction. Novels like Ursula K. Le Guin's *The Left Hand of Darkness* (1969), Marge Piercy's *Woman on the Edge of Time* (1976), and Octavia Butler's *Xenogenesis* trilogy (1987–89) invent social and biological arrangements, on other planets or in the future, with participants who are other than male or female. This kind of speculative fiction did not always have explicit links to a community of gender-variant people who, on the same planet and in the same present in which these novels were being published, were articulating the reality of their own experience – but it often spoke to this experience. Trans author Kate Bornstein explains turning to science fiction in the 1960s 'searching for characters like myself', being drawn to stories of 'men who were magically or technologically turned into women, women who rightly assumed themselves to be men, alien races that have more than two genders' (*Queer and Pleasant Danger* 40). Decades later, trans-authored science fiction draws on this tradition and aims to challenge not only the same patriarchal limitations that were exposed by feminist science fiction, but also the way in which, for the latter, gender variance remained an otherworldly possibility, meaning that 'trans people have been treated [...] as part of the spectacle' (Fitzpatrick and Plett 440). Twentieth-century authors invested in articulating androgyny or non-heteronormative sexuality have similarly employed non-gendered or multiply gendered characters that resonate with fiction by trans and non-binary authors in the twenty-first century. The magically gender-shifting protagonist of Virginia Woolf's *Orlando* (1928) can be traced as a precursor of shapeshifting Paul in Andrea Lawlor's *Paul Takes the Form of a*

*Mortal Girl* (2017), and the never-gendered narrator of Jeanette Winterson's *Written on the Body* (1992) is a technique adopted in Sara Taylor's *The Lauras* (2016) to voice a gender-nonconforming teenager.

Operating against the background of the gender-variant voices that gained visibility before current understandings of trans, contemporary trans narrators negotiate temporal orders, non-normative or ambiguous embodiments, and truth and authority. In the chapters that follow, I often return to speculative feminist genders, fluid narrators, and histories of trans autobiography, following links that form an always incomplete canon of trans literature. Some of these topics have been pursued in a number of other works in much more detail than I can provide here. Books like Prosser's *Second Skins: The Body Narratives of Transsexuality* (1998), on autobiographical narratives, and Carroll's *Transgender and the Literary Imagination: Changing Gender in Twentieth-Century Writing* (2018), on representations of gender change, help explore further the twentieth-century precursors of contemporary trans narratives. Pursuing even earlier iterations of these narratives, Kit Heyam's *Before We Were Trans: A New History of Gender* (2022) illuminates a number of culturally specific articulations of gender-variant identity that expand canonical understandings of transness. C. Riley Snorton's history of Blackness and transness, *Black on Both Sides: A Racial History of Trans Identity* (2017), addresses the narrative 'shadows' that appear 'by way of obstruction' beyond the presence of figures like Jorgensen (143). Finally, Salah's 'Transgender and Transgenre Writing' (2021) names trans voices in community magazines, newsletters, performance art, and unpublished manuscripts that risk being erased in the current boom of trans cultural production. She asks,

> we write literary histories that exclude our folk forms, our obscene, erotic, and illicit forms, our woodworked and transsexual writers, non-Anglo European and/or non-university educated writers, and/or nominate only worthy, canonical progenitors for the current moment of flourishing. Do we catalog our work in terms that reify national traditions, period, or generic boundaries? (186)

Any act of circumscribing and ordering trans literature should prompt reflection on our citational practices and on the political conditions that bring some texts to the surface, suppress others, mark some as central and others as peripheral, and direct the search for roots toward particular genres and media. These trans literary histories and the questions raised by the efforts to name them form the shifting intertextual terrain on which contemporary trans narrators come to produce a textual subjectivity.

## Trans studies and narrative

Since its emergence in the early 1990s, trans studies has fought on narrative ground.[3] A key impetus behind the formation of this discipline was the need to reclaim first-person authority over bodies and language, allowing trans people to challenge the way they are narrated by others by displacing sensationalist media language and the categories of medical science as the primary paradigms for understanding trans identity. Feinberg's *Transgender Liberation* pamphlet identified a need to combat the historical oppression of 'people who defy the "man"-made boundaries of gender' (5), and popularised the term 'transgender' (now most commonly subsumed under 'trans') to define this group. Naming this community, situating them in a longer history of gender variance, and identifying a future to fight for are narrative operations employed by Feinberg to build solidarity among those punished for transgressing gender norms. A decade later, Susan Stryker and Stephen Whittle's *Transgender Studies Reader* (2006) defined the field inaugurated by work like Feinberg's as an interdisciplinary range of investigations of how gender is 'more complex and varied than can be accounted for by the currently dominant binary sex/gender ideology of Eurocentric modernity', clarifying that this field is 'as concerned with material conditions as it is with representational practices' (Stryker, 'Knowledges', 3). Any analysis of literature that takes place in trans studies rubs shoulders with scholarship in history, law, philosophy, health, and medicine, as well as with the political activism that originates and grounds this scholarship. Opening up narrative studies to trans studies, therefore, means welcoming a plurality of methodologies and applications, one to which, after all, narrative studies has declared itself open since David Herman defined its 'postclassical' phase (2). Contextual elements of narratives that may have traditionally been excluded from the purview of this discipline – the bodies and identities of authors and readers, the historical and ideological circumstances of production and reception, the material conditions of narrative communication – have long been recognised as inseparable from the formal operations of texts. In what follows, I show how narrative appears in trans studies as an object of investigation, a tool for legitimisation, a political strategy, and a model to disrupt.[4]

Sandy Stone's 'The Empire Strikes Back: A Posttranssexual Manifesto' (1992), a foundational text of trans studies, begins by noting that popular trans narratives are constructed to show their protagonists' surgical transformation from 'unambiguous men, albeit unhappy men, to unambiguous women' (156). Stone conceives of the assimilation of gender-variant individuals into the psychopathological identity of the transsexual as a demand to complete this transformation in order to erase the very evidence that it has taken place. After surgery, the trans individual is instructed to 'fade into the "normal" population as soon as possible' by '*constructing a plausible history*' about a stable and coherent gender; against this pressure, Stone urges instead to reveal 'the complexities and ambiguities of lived experience' (164). The act of constructing a plausible history, taking for granted that hormonal and surgical interventions have taken place, would entail disavowing a pre-transition past and embracing the future offered by doctors, one in which mind, body, behaviour, and appearance form a coherent whole clearly locatable on one side of the male/female binary. Stone's call to pull at the seams of this narrative is taken up by books like Bornstein's memoir/essay/textual collage *Gender Outlaw* (1994). In the book, Bornstein explains, 'I was told by several counselors and a number of transsexual peers that I would need to invent a past for myself as a little girl' (76). As an explicit rejection of this suggestion, *Gender Outlaw* reveals a discontinuous and multiply gendered self. For instance, chapter 3 reproduces an interview in which Bornstein is asked about the surgical process of 'men becoming women' (20) but ends with an old photograph of the author at her Bar Mitzvah with the caption: 'Today I am a man' (24). The transmedial and anti-chronological juxtaposition of moments representing becoming a man and becoming a woman signals the refusal to provide a history that smooths out the contradictions of being trans. Theorising a 'posttranssexual' and transgender identity, for these authors, is about presenting an account of gendered embodiment and subjectivity that differs from canonical narratives, including those constructed by trans subjects themselves in order to provide a 'plausible history' that would allow them to blend in.

In the third decade of the twenty-first century, a multiplicity of alternatives to the model Stone and Bornstein were critiquing has emerged and, to some extent, has expanded popular understandings of trans identity. At the same time, new visibility has produced new norms, making certain identities, embodiments, and lives intelligible at the expense of others. Already in 2013, *The Transgender Studies Reader 2* noted that a 'second iteration of the field' had to contend with 'new imperatives and opportunities for "transgender normativity" […] that secure citizenship for some trans bodies at the expense of others, replicating many forms of racism, xenophobia, and class privilege' (Stryker and Aizura 3). Trans identities become accepted in cisnormative society the more they are aligned with the values, interests, and lifestyles of privileged groups. For instance, Dan Irving notes that social recognition for trans subjects hinges on the ability of their body to 'constitute a productive working body, that is, […] capable of participating in capitalist production processes' (40). The assimilation into normalcy that awaits at the end of transition entails being able to function as a worker: Irving argues that dominant discourses for either medically evaluating successful transition or seeking to obtain legitimation for trans individuals focus on employability and contribution to society through labour. Jake Pyne also adds to the 'list of the costs' for normative belonging 'an incitement to able-mindedness' ('Autistic Disruptions' 344). He analyses 'autistic-trans stories' as offering 'a possible way out of the new traps of trans identity' through their acts of 'scrambling transgender's narratemes' (345). Neuronormativity and participation in capitalist production are only some of the goals to be secured at the 'end' of transition. Crucially, as will become particularly clear in my discussion of texts by non-binary authors, the demand for transition to both occur in the first place and then settle itself on one side of the gender binary powerfully shapes which narratives of identity are most acceptable and intelligible.

The concern that avenues for legitimisation and incorporation into mainstream liberal discourses are offered at the price of participating in power structures that harm marginalised people echoes across contemporary trans studies. In *Black Trans Feminism* (2022), Bey argues that our identity categories are already 'hegemonic bestowals, and will thus have diminished liberatory import' (4). While finding it necessary to 'centre the needs, experiences, and material concerns of trans women, trans femmes, and nonbinary femmes' (11), Bey views transness and Blackness as 'inflections of mutinous subjectivities that have been captured and consolidated into bodily legibilities' (9). Naming identities is a form of narrative sense-making which, like all such operations, can be both enabling and limiting. Bey explores a history in which 'ways of adorning oneself as a mechanism for identification took on a potency that needed to be made as immutable and categorical as physiognomy', leading to the twentieth-century moment in which 'medico-juridical practitioners invented medicalized notions of gender *as* a form of race, as a phenotype' (21). Taxonomies for fixing embodiments through a white gaze show their coercive legacies today. Introducing *Trap Door: Trans Cultural Production and the Politics of Visibility* (2017), a collection of trans of colour critiques of visibility, Reina Gossett, Eric A. Stanley and Johanna Burton explain 'the paradox of trans representation', by which

> trans people are offered many 'doors' – entrances to visibility, to resources, to recognition, and to understanding. Yet [...] these doors are almost always also 'traps' – accommodating trans bodies, histories, and culture only insofar as they can be forced to hew to hegemonic modalities. (xxiii)

As some trans, non-binary and gender-nonconforming individuals are increasingly accepted in mainstream culture, the narratives that are most visible still remain white, binary, middle class, neoliberal – in other words, those most intelligible according to a cis standard, with ordered temporalities, sortable bodies, and reliable narrators. Meanwhile, all trans people experience the 'traps' of being seen, standing out, being singled out: objectification, violence, invasive curiosity, and the responsibility to represent others.

Trans of colour critique reveals that the formation of 'transgender studies' may itself be a narrative in need of disruption. As Snorton writes, 'the condensation' of transness into the category of transgender is a racial narrative' (8). Reducing the destabilising potential and fugitivity of transness to a movement between genders is seen by scholars like Snorton to undermine a critique of gender identities as instruments of white violence. Trans studies has become increasingly concerned with recognising that the most visible trans movements, especially if invested in affirming and achieving recognition through medicolegal systems, have often been white-centric. Chen makes this argument in relation to 1990s trans activism:

> These legal frameworks [...] often presumed the possibility and desirability of a productive relationship with the U.S. state without addressing the impact of state divestment, policing, imprisonment, militarization, and direct and administrative violence on the lives of low- and survival-income trans people of color and immigrant communities. (7)

New trajectories for trans studies are opened up by attending to entanglements between race and gender, such as how anti-trans bathroom legislation in the United States is a form of gender segregation that 'cannot be disimbricated' from 'the legacy of racial slavery' (Gossett 184). In this way, the project of trans studies as an unfixing of gender can be traced back to Black feminist thought, which has revealed that '[i]n the historic outline of dominance, the respective subject positions of "female" and "male" adhere to no symbolic integrity' (Spillers 66). As these debates show, trans studies is not only dedicated to examining narratives but is always in the process of narrating itself, uncovering new genealogies and setting new goals.

While counter-narratives about trans studies as a discipline centre on North America, as this is the location of first emergence and institutionalisation of the field, trans political discourse in the UK is also in the process of being reshaped. The publication of Shon Faye's bestselling book *The Transgender Issue* (2021) intervened in a polarised landscape rife with misinformation and called for a change of narrative: while 'Britain is immersed in a deafening conversation about trans people' (8), Faye notes, there is no discussion of the 'systemic issues affecting trans people's lives' (9). Attention in the media is directed away from not only the needs of trans people but also misogynistic violence, rising poverty, inhumane anti-immigration policies, and an underfunded healthcare system, toward the supposed threat that already marginalised groups pose to the general population. Anti-trans writers and organisers claiming to work in defence of women's rights appeal to biological and essentialist notions of maleness and femaleness to cast trans men as brainwashed by a patriarchal culture that convinces them to renounce their womanhood, trans women as predators wanting to violate women's spaces, and non-binary people as confused about biological facts. Descriptions of trans people as dangerous, as Ruth Pearce, Sonja Erikainen and Ben Vincent highlight, particularly rely on some unexamined gendered and racial power structures:

> One's ability to be recognised or awarded a position as 'vulnerable' is conditioned by whiteness and gender normativity. It is often trans women and non-binary people, especially trans women and non-binary people of colour, who are most vulnerable to gender-based violence in women-only spaces in material terms. (680)

The complicities of anti-trans discourse with broader patriarchal logics that harm most women remain unaddressed by British feminism when it is led by the concerns of white middle- and upper-class women. Irish feminists have also positioned themselves vocally against trans-hostile discourse, which is viewed as just another export from the colonising country (Faye 234). Given this context, it is perhaps unsurprising that the reframing of gender and transness through the lens of race and anti-colonial thought that has been taking place in the US struggles to gain purchase in British academia and public discourse.

As questions of space are central to these debates, the self-narrating of trans studies is also often a spatial one. I have used spatial metaphors myself to describe how disciplines and methodologies interact ('opening up', 'welcoming in', and even the very word 'field'). This tendency toward these metaphors can be seen, for instance, in Stryker's assertion that 'queer studies remains the most hospitable place to undertake transgender work', as the latter can offer an 'in-house critique' while sometimes 'setting out to make a home of its own' ('Evil Twin' 214). Since its inception, trans studies has positioned itself in relation to queer studies through various degrees of proximity and distance. Some trans scholars have questioned queerness as a paradigm through which to understand transness due to the former's emphasis on sexuality and desire rather than embodiment and identity. Prosser, for instance, noted in 1998 that queer theory tends toward an 'enmeshing of homosexual desire with transgender identification' (22). The queer politics of identity, for Prosser, entail an emphasis on mobility, flux, traversing, and deviating that is at odds with some trans subjects' desires for stability, permanence, belonging, and coinciding as they seek 'the recognition of our sexed realness;

acceptance as men and women; fundamentally, the right to gender homes' (204). Writing at the same time as Prosser, Henry Rubin similarly argues that 'trans desires for realness and legibility' may be '"unseemly" to queer theory' (186). For these scholars, queer names an ongoing disruption of stable identity that is incompatible with wanting to 'stay' (be 'at home') in/as an intelligible gender. On the other hand, the links between trans and queer scholarship and activism are seen by others as being too readily dismissed, with the consequence of excluding those who find value in their intersection. Jack Halberstam, while opposing the idea that 'fluidity and flexibility are always and everywhere desirable', responds to Prosser by noting that '[s]ome bodies are never at home [...] some bodies recognize and live with the inherent instability of identity' (164). Just a few years after Stone and Feinberg's first positing of a transgender and posttranssexual community and politics, the identity of trans studies was already a contested narrative.

Starting in the 2010s, voices contributing to *Transgender Studies Quarterly* – the journal that confirmed the status of trans studies as an established academic discipline – continue to offer differing perspectives on the extent to which queer and trans overlap. Kadji Amin notes that, if a distinction between gender and sexuality is reified, 'the self-understandings of those gender-variant subjects who do not experience their gender as separate from their sexuality are increasingly dismissed' (221). At the same time, considering gender and sexuality together does not mean that queer and trans studies would coincide. In a dialogue with Emmett Harsin Drager that sparked much controversy in subsequent issues of the journal, Andrea Long Chu provocatively claims that, despite Prosser's interventions, 'the working definition of trans is just "queer, again"' (Chu and Harsin Drager 105). Like all fields, trans studies contains discordances and at times irreconcilable views on methodologies, objects, aims, and ontologies. In developing the concepts I use in this book to analyse trans narrators, I aim to keep these tensions and incompatibilities alive rather than attempting to resolve or simplify them – attachment to gender and discarding of gender, distinctions between identities and enmeshing of identities, concerns with reasserting the materiality of the body and concerns with transcending it. In a recent interview, Stryker explains,

> I really feel like part of what I think of as a trans aesthetic, or a trans critical method, is to always say, 'it's *both and* and *neither nor* and

*either this or that*'. It's like all three logical operations happening at the same time. ('Trans Studies, Trans Feminism' 797)

Different logical operations happening at the same time is an apt way to describe how temporality, embodiment, and reliability take shape in contemporary trans narratives – and the questions of time, space, visibility, and voice raised here inform the theoretical framework I develop in the following chapter. The existing investment of trans studies in constructing, contesting, analysing, and multiplying narratives prepares the terrain for an encounter with narrative studies. But how does the latter move toward questions of transness?

## Narrative studies and trans

In line with other contemporary approaches that examine what narrative form does for real subjects and, in turn, how social and political contexts shape narrative form, the theoretical framework I employ issues from the premise that trans lived experiences and knowledges can be put into conversation with how narrative studies thinks of narratorial acts such as constructing a temporality, representing the narrator's body, signalling a reliable voice, presenting the narrating agent as a unified consciousness, or revealing and withholding information about the storyworld. Just as gender is discussed in multiple, overlapping, and sometimes mutually exclusive locations (under 'feminist', 'queer', 'trans', 'Black', and more), a unified field of inquiry into narrative form is equally difficult to circumscribe. Over the course of this book, I draw on works of narrative studies or narratology in a deliberately ad hoc manner. For instance, some categories for defining narrative time come from structuralist approaches; some reflections on embodiment come from cognitive ones; some notions of reliability come from rhetorical perspectives; and some ideas about how gender is encoded in narrative form have first been suggested by feminist and queer narratologies. To start with, I focus mostly on the latter, especially attending to the sites in which the insights from these narratologies are on the verge of constituting – though they never definitively become – a trans narratology. Approaches to narrative form are manifold, shifting, and heterogeneous, in the way that discourses about gender, and genders themselves, also are. Borrowing, transforming, and repurposing tools of analysis, letting methodologies touch and enrich each other, is the only way in which the multifaceted formal, political, and ethical implications of trans first-person narration can be adequately addressed. But even as I show what some trans narrators have in common, I do not aim to propose a universal or comprehensive model. The concepts I devise in the next chapter – re-narration, trans-inhabitation, and renounced reliability – are hybrid concepts, blending the textual taxonomies of narrative studies and the political concerns of trans studies, with the awareness that the textual and the political, in the current iterations of both fields, are inextricably linked.

The position I take on narrative could not be articulated without a tradition, established by feminist narratology, of examining how narrative structure, language, and textual features entail ideological positions. In the 1980s, feminist perspectives like the ones collected in *The Poetics of Gender* (1986) began to question supposedly impartial literary theories, in a 'common interrogation' of the universalisation of masculine experience and norms 'as they inhere in all diacritical and interpretive acts, including the workings of grammar itself' (Miller xii). Rachel Blau DuPlessis's *Writing Beyond the Ending* (1985) similarly argued that '[a]ny literary convention – plots, narrative sequences, characters in bit parts – as an instrument that claims to depict experience, also interprets it' (2). Both claims, although not yet naming a feminist narratology, point to how the production and interpretation of literary forms is always conducted from specific embodied and political positions. Susan S. Lanser's 'Toward a Feminist Narratology' (1986) first theorised an encounter between structuralist narrative theories and feminist criticism, suggesting that narratology would benefit from considering 'women as both producers and interpreters of texts' (343). I now take up this question and shift its focus: how does an attention to trans, non-binary, and gender-nonconforming authors and readers change how narrative form can be both constructed and analysed? The title of Chapter 1 explicitly echoes Lanser's, the 'toward' intending to inaugurate, rather than impose a definitive shape on, the encounter between 'trans' and 'narratology'. After Lanser's article, Robyn R. Warhol explicitly described the subject of her book *Gendered Interventions* (1989) as a problem that could be addressed by a 'feminist narratology' (3). Warhol urges feminist critics to move beyond 'the study of how women are portrayed in texts', which occurs at 'the level of story', in order to take 'a detailed look into gender's effect on the level of discourse'

(6). Similarly, looking not only at trans stories but at the shapes that these stories take reveals that formal choices can reinforce or challenge gender categorisations, structural marginalisations, and models of selfhood.

Despite gender having remained central to narrative studies in the last three decades, an explicit consideration of genders that are other than binary or fixed has been persistently absent in this field: individuals who are not men or women, or who are trans, are almost never imagined as possible readers or authors. Just as feminist narratology proposed to address 'the gaps in models that are based almost exclusively on men's writing' (Warhol 14), by discussing trans narrators I extend this challenge to models that are based almost exclusively on the writing of cis authors. The question 'what narratives are excluded?' can in fact be posed to feminist narratology itself, in response to its own call for intersectional approaches. In her 2006 book on feminist narratology, Ruth Page recognises that it 'seems less easy now to pose "texts by women" as a simple, homogenous category, and important differences between women need also to be recognized' (15). A desire to nuance categories of gender is also expressed in Warhol and Lanser's *Narrative Theory Unbound* (2015), the first collection to explicitly include interventions in 'queer narratology'. Warhol and Lanser show awareness of the risk that the 'rich multiplicity not just of genders and sexualities but also of narrative practices could indeed get reduced into essentialist and universalizing generalizations' (2). Like in this mention of a 'multiplicity of genders', a tendency to gesture toward naming trans without quite reaching it has appeared throughout theorisations of feminist narratology. For instance, Page acknowledges that 'other gendered alternatives may be possible that go beyond this two-way distinction [men and women], for example, through gender blending or in cyborg imagery' (15). A dialogue with trans studies can tell us more precisely what these 'other gendered alternatives' are. A similar gesture toward the remit of trans studies can be found in Tory Young's introduction to a special issue of *Textual Practice* on 'Futures for Feminist and Queer Narratology' (2018), which notes a connection between narratological work on the ambiguity of pronouns and, in the wider world, 'the deliberate deployment [...] of the pronouns "they" and "them" to refer to a single subject' (916). These kinds of links are precisely the ones I want to foster here.[5]

In the context of the entanglement between 'queer' and 'trans' that I have outlined above, trans narratology does not develop separately from queer narratology, but it does add a new emphasis to it. Twenty years before the *Narrative Theory Unbound* collection – which dwells at length on the relationships between feminist, queer, gender, sexuality, and narrative – Lanser's article 'Sexing the Narrative' (1995) suggested the possibility that 'there might [...] be a queer narratology in which questions of sexuality become a telescope through which to seek narrative elements not before attended to' (93). From its inception, queer narratology takes as its object not only sexuality but also gender. Through a reading of the first-person narrator of Winterson's *Written on the Body*, who is never gendered, Lanser argues that the gender and sexuality of a narrator are 'narratologically significant elements' (90) and that, as they are unmarked in this novel, they create two possible 'narrative scenarios' – the narrator is male and in a heterosexual relationship, or is female and in a lesbian relationship (89). An alternative beyond the 'two' is opened up when looking at this through the lens of trans studies. Critics' attempts to decode the narrator of *Written on the Body* over the years – a narrator whose gender is deliberately obscured through omissions – can be shown to derive from a cisnormative anxiety to assert a stable and biologically anchored binary. Even Jennifer A. Smith, who first suggests reading this narrator as a 'trans-subject position', argues that this allows the reader to situate 'him/herself in relation to the text' (425). Identities that are neither 'him' nor 'her' remain excluded, and even if the narrator can be imagined to be trans or non-binary, the reader is not. This is repeated with contemporary texts like Taylor's *The Lauras*, which is viewed as 'frustrating' in leaving one reader 'continuously trying to figure out if Alex, the main character, was a teenage boy or girl' (Jordan).[6] Trans studies would help us take seriously a narrator's assertion that 'I like to keep my body rolled up away from prying eyes' (Winterson 89), which resonates with trans people's own frustration at the demand to be visible and intelligible to a cis audience.

Lanser's most recent development of the queer narratological approach comes to overlap significantly with what we could call a trans narratology. In 'Queering Narrative Voice' (2018), she focuses on the 'sexual indeterminacy' of heterodiegetic narration (933) and draws attention to some students' habit of using the pronoun 'it' when referring to a third-person narrator ('it says...').

The discussion begins to link the notion of queer voice to trans identity: 'In this sense, "it" resembles the neutral pronoun "they" currently chosen by persons who reject the binary of he or she' (933). If we continue to follow this thread, we can imagine that, as non-binary identities and the pronouns associated with them gain visibility, readers could begin referring to a non-gendered narrator as 'they' as a matter of course (as in fact I already hear some students do). Additionally, being neither male nor female is a characteristic of not only disembodied heterodiegetic narrators but also some autodiegetic narrators who represent real people: existing beyond the binary is a possibility not only for an abstract narrative voice but for an embodied character too. Alongside these allusions to it, Lanser explicitly names transness in this article. She describes a situation called 'narrative "cisgender" – a state in which the author's and the heterodiegetic narrator's genders both coincide with a normative body' (932). If narrative cisgender is a match between the gender of the author and that of the narrator, narrative transgender would then be a disidentification across narrative levels, in which the gender of the narrator is different from that of the author. How do we deal, then, with a disidentification within narrative levels, where it is the narrator who is trans and their trans gender may or may not match that of the author? Further, do we have a 'narrative transgender' when the genders of the narrator are multiple? On these topics and many others, an engagement with trans studies can develop already existing insights by feminist and queer narratologists to new conclusions.

A generative site for these developments also emerges when trans narratives become the object of queer narratology. For instance, Teagan Bradway's discussion of Paul Preciado's *Testo Junkie* (2008) focuses on elements that are significant for a trans narratology, such as a 'queer-trans wedding plot' (717). Bradway discusses transness and queerness together as having the capacity to disrupt dominant orders and teleologies while at the same time taking forms that 'figure and sustain queer relations of belonging in and across time' (723). This indissoluble coupling of trans and queer is productive, as are many other queer works that examine trans narratives. There are, however, benefits to defining trans narratology as having its own history, focus, and aims. For instance, Bradway confronts the 'antinarrativity' that is 'foundational to queer literary studies' (711) and considers how, instead, 'narrative affords important agencies for queerness' (712). Compared to queer, trans has been less persistently associated with unruliness, disruption, interruption, and, above all, anti-narrative; therefore, it needs less rescuing from this association. If trans is sometimes aligned with these operations, it is also the case that it has been linked (precisely as opposed to queer) to normativity, linearity, reintegration, and narrative. A shift in focus from how narrative studies has so far regarded gender is ultimately needed to align it with trans studies, and this shift is beginning to happen. The 2024 special issue of *Narrative* on trans narratologies that I co-edited with Cody Mejeur contains a number of interventions that effect a refocusing of textual elements like plot, genre, narrative voice, metaphors, and paratexts as trans. Vera Nünning and Corinna Assmann's *Palgrave Handbook of Feminist, Queer and Trans Narrative Studies* (2024) is the first volume to include interventions that name themselves as trans narrative studies, pointing to the areas of narrative studies that stand to gain new categories, relevance, and stakes in the context of trans studies, a field already deeply invested in narrative. The tools of narratology, as they are developed and applied from a range of perspectives and in a variety of domains, can be invaluable for analysing with rigour and precision the textual workings of time, the body, and voice. Narrative studies has the capacity to play a key part in analysing how trans narrators operate in contemporary literature; by doing so, it can extend into a new direction that is both intellectually compelling and politically urgent.

## Structure of the book

In bringing together trans studies and narrative studies, the model I propose for analysing trans narrators will not constitute a perfectly symmetrical encounter of these two fields, as my emphasis shifts across a wide range of questions – from syntactical distinctions between subject and object to paratextual commentaries about trans-related legislation, from hypothesising about whether the author is anticipating a hostile audience to reconstructing the sequence of events in their storyworld. Each of my areas of inquiry – temporality, embodiment, and reliability – is a site of transformation in which categories and tools for the study of narrative acquire new political and affective meanings and, in turn, trans theory and lived experience illuminate new textual strategies. After outlining the system of metaphors and linguistic conventions that structure how trans identity is understood in the Western mainstream, Chapter 1 develops the three concepts that guide the methodology I employ in this book. Re-narration names a restructuring of the temporal elements (orders, durations, beginnings, endings) that constitute the canonical transition narrative as a 'journey from A to B', a model that trans narrators end up partly reproducing and partly resisting. Trans-inhabitation is a mode of being embodied within, between, and across binary categories that characterises both the way in which gender is understood by trans authors and the ambiguous position of a first-person narrator with respect to the space of their narrative. Renounced reliability defines a tension, faced by trans narrators in fiction and in life, between the need to establish authority over one's own narrative and the refusal to submit to normative notions of what constitutes a coherent and shared truth. Re-narration, trans-inhabitation, and renounced reliability each group together a range of narrative strategies and operations as they are deployed with a specific intention (to combat the particular forms that cis oppression takes) and a specific effect (the simultaneous maintaining and disrupting of forms). Owing to its structuralist origins, narratology often tends toward sorting narrative phenomena into finite categories, sometimes making either/or distinctions. As will become clear, trans texts create disturbances in relation to binary distinctions and negotiate the difficulty of fitting within fixed and bounded spaces: the relationship of trans narrators to systems of classification is accordingly an uneasy belonging.

For each of the concepts developed in Chapter 1, I have chosen three trans narrators from recent prose literature to illustrate their workings. These nine texts are situated, to varying degrees, at the centre of the emerging canon of contemporary trans literature, due to factors such as the popularity of their authors, their success in the literary marketplace, the scholarly work that is beginning to be published about them, or the anthologies and lists that include them. Chapter 2 focuses on how the temporalities of canonical trans autobiography are self-consciously tackled in Juliet Jacques's *Trans: A Memoir* (2015), Travis Alabanza's *None of the Above: Reflections on Life Beyond the Binary* (2022), and Kai Cheng Thom's *Fierce Femmes and Notorious Liars: A Dangerous Trans Girl's Confabulous Memoir* (2016). At a distance of seven years, Jacques and Alabanza testify to the attack on trans rights that has characterised the British (and international) political landscape in the twenty-first century, cumulatively exposing its entanglements with patriarchal oppression, neoliberalism, racism, and new trans normativities. While Jacques struggles against a format that demands a focus on the self, tracing the becoming of a trans public figure as it intersects with the timelines of transition, Alabanza collects an audience's real and imagined questions about their gender and examines why we ask them, showing what is left of the 'self' after everyone has had their narrative about them. Frustrations with the demand to narrate according to a certain pattern of intelligibility are taken up by Thom in a North American context: this author blurs the boundary between the fictional and the autobiographical to reveal the collective extra/ordinary realities of trans communities beyond stories that end in conformity, marriage, or death. Questioning genre boundaries and challenging dominant models for understanding gender identity, these texts negotiate their relationship to the trans narratives that they are not – the more visible narratives and the more invisible ones, the other narratives told about the author and the other narratives that the author could tell about themself. Formal choices such as decelerating pace, centring hypothetical events, and insisting on fictive endings aid these negotiations and help unravel the layers of intersubjective narration that make up a narrator's gender.

Moving from the elusive location of the story's events to the elusive location of the agent who orders them, Chapter 3 discusses the ambivalent presence, multiple identities, and imaginative embodiments of the narrators in Akwaeke Emezi's *Freshwater* (2018), Calvin Gimpelevich's *Invasions* (2018), and Alison Rumfitt's *Tell Me I'm Worthless* (2021). Emezi's articulation of non-binary identity through Igbo metaphysics leads to narrative experimentation with plural narrators who both are and are not 'one', pulling at the seams of Western and Nigerian models for representing identity. Gimpelevich multiplies narrators too: his short stories, in dialogue with one another across their textual boundaries, produce narrators whose bodies are different from each other and from themselves, transforming by way of fantastical leaps, social and medical transitions, and the many possibilities between the two. Taking us back to the UK, Rumfitt includes among the multiple voices that form trans identity that of the very ground from which they issue – Albion, a fictional evil house but also a familiar space of historical violence. The gendered self, in these novels and short stories, is displaced, fragmented, and augmented through alternating narration, ambiguous focalisation, and bodily transfigurations both possible and impossible, revealing the capacity of first-person narrators to traverse spaces and to attain a visibility that is not incompatible with hiding oneself from view. After showing how first-person speaking can diffuse into a fluctuating plurality, I return to what it means to affirm the presence of an authoritative self in Chapter 4, by examining forms of unreliable narration in Jordy Rosenberg's *Confessions of the Fox* (2018), Juno Dawson's *Wonderland* (2020), and Beckett K. Bauer's 'Notes from a Hunter Boy: As Filed by Girtrude the Librarian' (2017). The particular ways in which these narrators refuse to speak, or are impeded from speaking, the truth signal authorial endorsement of their messages rather than a warning to mistrust them. Rosenberg invites us to assess the ethics of different relationships between intra- and extra-textual agents and a trans figure recovered from the archive, producing an aesthetics of equivocation that rejects the dubious opportunities offered to marginalised subjects for making themselves visible. Dawson and Bauer both voice young narrators whose understanding of gender we have good reason to assume might clash with what some readers believe to be real. Dawson shows how voices that wish to deny teenagers the capacity to understand their own gender affect self-worth to the point of compromising one's ability to interpret reality, while she simultaneously empowers a young trans narrator to be as uncertain, externally influenced, and wrong as everyone else is. Bauer, instead, places a narrator who still has a lot to learn into an unfamiliar world about which he knows more than we do, ultimately prompting us to question the reliability of any system of classification that assigns meanings to the body. The presence of multiple authors, audiences, and paratextual participants (cis and trans) that I always understand as vital for reading the formal operations of these texts finally leads to some reflections, in the conclusion, about who and what is beyond the I.

### Notes

[1] An illustrative case is the nomination of a book by Two-Spirit Indigiqueer author Joshua Whitehead for a Lambda Literary Award for Transgender Poetry in 2018. Whitehead withdrew the book from consideration, explaining that 'My gender, sexuality, and my identities supersede Western Categorizations of LGBTQ+' (Whitehead).

2   Magnus Hirschfeld, operating in Germany in the first three decades of the twentieth century, coined the term 'transvestite' in *Die Transvestiten* (1910) to refer to individuals whose well-being was dependent on wearing clothes associated with a sex different from the one they had been assigned at birth. This term encompassed a variety of identities, including some that we would now call trans. The case studies collected by Hirschfeld form an important early canon of (mediated) trans self-representations. Decades later, American sexologist Harry Benjamin published *The Transsexual Phenomenon* (1966), arguing for hormone replacement therapy and surgery as treatment for patients whose gender identity did not match the one associated with the sex that was assigned to them. Benjamin's book contributed to creating norms that still regulate the way in which trans identity is publicly understood – namely, as being born 'in the wrong body', desiring an 'opposite' sex or gender, and conceiving of gender according to a heteronormative framework.

3   For a longer history of trans theorising, see Emily Cousens's *Trans Feminist Epistemologies in the US Second Wave* (2023).

4   As a white cis scholar, I do not enter into debates about what constitutes transness, what trans studies' aims should be, or what concrete steps it is best to take to ensure justice for trans subjects. I map the key concerns of trans authors and scholars in order to investigate what narratives do with transness, what transness does with narrative, and what analytical tools can be developed from the insights of trans studies to analyse narrative.

5   Lena Mattheis's work on non-binary pronouns in literature develops further the connection identified by Young.

6   The attempts to pin down a binary gender in *Written on the Body* by literary critics and in *The Lauras* by Goodreads reviewers make clear how this kind of narrator exposes the enduring presence of gender biases around vulnerability, violence, empathy, and sexuality – when the narrator punches someone or describes an obsession with masturbation, they are seen as a man or a boy; when they are attentive to a lover's menstrual cycle or flee their house with their mother, they are seen as a woman or a girl. Trying to find out the 'true sex' of the narrator is particularly absurd in the case of a fictional character – if this is not in the text, where do readers propose to look for it?

Chapter 1

# Trans Narrators and the Politics of Form: Toward a Trans Narratology

Trans is both a narrative and an anti-narrative operation. Making sense of trans identity, like making sense of identity in general, involves grappling with genre, plot, metaphor, and point of view, and this making sense is valuable in a world that insists that trans people exist at the margins of intelligibility. But almost as soon as they produce narrative forms, trans authors self-consciously disrupt them, creating orders that disorder themselves, embodiments that exceed the body, and reliable narrators who refuse to tell the truth. Real-life trans people have a lot in common with narrators constructing a temporality, with narrators whose bodies inhabit diegetic levels, and with narrators who are on a spectrum of reliability. This is also the case for anyone who lives in time, has a body, and speaks, but the way in which trans subjects have been seen, or have represented themselves, brings these questions of temporality, embodiment, and reliability to the fore. Before attending to these aspects – which are explored in contemporary trans narratives both thematically and formally – it is necessary to clarify how trans identity is understood, across mainstream culture and trans writing, in metaphorical terms. For instance, in *Stone Butch Blues*, Feinberg writes about how being perceived as a binary man is a stopping and trapping, both safe and suffocating:

> The world stopped feeling like a gauntlet I had to run through. But very quickly I discovered that passing didn't just mean slipping below the surface, it meant being buried alive. I was still me on the inside, trapped in there with all my wounds and fears. But I was no longer me on the outside. (173)

As this passage signals, narrating the effects of navigating the gender binary often requires a series of interconnected, and sometimes contradictory, images to help shed light on a number of complex subjects: what gender is; what kind of change or status is represented by transness; how the overall self and its temporary iterations relate to one another; where the I is located with respect to the narrated body; and what kind of environment cis culture creates for the individual.

After exploring the conceptual framework through which transness is understood, I propose three concepts to analyse contemporary trans narrators, which I have called re-narration, trans-inhabitation, and renounced reliability. Each captures a tension between seemingly incompatible moments: a simultaneous construction and disturbance of linear time, an existing both inside and outside a bounded space, and a speaking that at once takes up and refuses the opportunity to participate in truth. These unresolvable tensions resonate with Stryker's description of a trans critical method as *'both and* and *neither nor* and *either this or that'* ('Trans Studies, Trans Feminism' 797). Re-narration, trans-inhabitation, and renounced reliability are hybrid concepts, at once textual and political, sitting at the intersection of trans studies and narrative studies to account for trans narrators both as trans and as narrators. These two fields of inquiry, as I began to show in the introduction, already reach toward each other in significant ways: trans studies is invested in the ways in which narrative form enables and constrains gender-variant identities, and, in turn, many works of narrative studies illuminate how the gender of authors, readers, and/or represented subjects shapes formal elements of narrative. While feminist and queer narrative studies at times considers genders that are other than binary or fixed, a sustained analysis of the relationship between narrative form and trans subjectivity is yet to be conducted. Any such sustained analysis must engage with the field of trans studies, which articulates insights about identity, language, and social relations from the lived experience of gender-variant subjects. At the same time, trans studies can also benefit from a methodological encounter with narratology. The vocabulary developed by this discipline can be used to nuance the analysis of how transness is represented in writing, by naming distinctions such as story and discourse, summary and scene, narrators and characters, reporting and evaluating, and so on. The way in which trans narratives handle these textual elements can then be illuminated as encoding ways of conceptualising gender, the body, transition, and marginalisation.

## Journeys, homes, ghosts

According to the dominant understanding of trans identity, transition is conceptualised metaphorically as a journey, setting off from gender A, traversing the space that separates it from gender B, and arriving at the latter after a series of steps, sometimes interrupted by delays or forked paths and occasionally sped up or reversed. Contributing to a collection titled *Transgender Migrations* (2012), Aren Z. Aizura argues that 'travel narratives are central to understanding trans experience' and explains that they often 'denote a one-way trajectory across a terrain in which the stuff of sex is divided into male and female territories, divided by the border or no man's land in between' ('Travel Narratives' 140). In a linguistic study of trans narratives, Jenny Lederer also concludes that 'transition is primarily understood as a journey through space', as it follows the more general pattern of an 'event structure metaphor' in which 'states are locations, change is motion, progress is forward movement and purposes are destinations' (100). Lederer highlights that this notion of a journey through space relies on 'a dual or binary category model of gender assignment, in which each category is understood as a bounded region in space' (96). Genders as fixed and bounded spaces, and trans(ition) as a linear and unidirectional movement between them, form a conceptual system that is at the basis of a traditional descriptions of trans identity. The idea that transition is a journey constitutes what George Lakoff and Mark Johnson would term a 'metaphorical concept': a systematic metaphor that structures the way in which an experience is understood in terms of another (7).[1] Conceptual metaphors function by downplaying and highlighting different aspects of the concept that is being viewed metaphorically. What 'transition is a journey' highlights is how transition is experienced as forward movement; what it downplays (or even hides) is the possibility that it may not begin, end, or go anywhere specific. This possibility, which many of the authors I discuss attempt to make visible, is difficult to acknowledge precisely because the normative understanding of transition is based on the journey metaphor, and because the transition journey becomes synonymous with being trans.

The metaphorical system of the journey is extended when the body that awaits at the end of it, as well as the gender category into which this body fits, is viewed as an arrival home. Prosser popularised this idea, describing as a home the location of the self both 'in' the right body and 'in' a social intelligible gender: he argues that trans narratives strive 'nostalgically toward home – identity, belonging in the body and in the world' (177). This narrative journey begins from a distressing and alienated situation, an 'unliveable shattered body'; through transition, this body becomes 'a liveable whole' (92). Aizura, among others, has elaborated extensively upon the ideological underpinnings of this journey toward home. In his view, the desire to be culturally locatable at the end of transition, to 'belong without complication to a normative social sphere', conceals the fact that this sphere is a 'fantasy' ('Borders and Homes' 290). The notion of home 'forecloses the possibility that some people never wholly cross that particular border' and it 'precludes the possibility that transpeople may not, for many reasons, blend into normality once sex reassignment is "over"' (296). In this formulation, Aizura points out not only that certain subjects may not be granted a 'home' (legitimation and belonging in an intelligible gender identity) but also that the ability of gender-variant subjects to 'cross borders' may be curtailed. The notion of home as a bounded space of belonging is linked to the bounded space of a nation which welcomes certain citizens and excludes others. When gender is viewed in this way, it is easy to recognise how its borders are equally policed, allowing entry only to those who conform to a certain normative standard – in the case of anti-trans concerns about protecting women's spaces, female gender itself becomes one of these spaces. In trans writing, journeys and homes still recur both as informing conventional expressions (the next step, being at a crossroads, feeling at home, finding the right home) and as objects of self-conscious deconstruction. Trans narrators negotiate the patterns and tempos of this journey, the inhabitation of bodies and gendered spaces, and the compromised credibility that may come from articulating an experience that challenges accepted metaphorical systems.

Extensions and distortions of the journey and home metaphors are often employed by trans writers as a way to expand and critique conventional understandings of gender and identity. As Elena Semino argues, creative metaphors can challenge 'conventional representations of a particular experience' (52) by effecting an 'extension, elaboration and combination' of conventional metaphors (44). These operations can have a political function, highlighting marginalised experiences. For instance, Jennifer Finney Boylan, in her memoir *I'm Looking Through You* (2008), alludes to transition as 'the process that would take me from the world of men and eventually leave me washed up on the shores of womanhood, blinking and half-drowned' (213). The line between conventional and creative metaphor is blurred here. The 'world of men' is a phrase that may not be registered as a metaphor but that rests on the figurative understanding of gender as a bounded territory; 'the shores of womanhood' is compatible with this same understanding of gender while standing out as a novel expression. Being washed up on a shore may not be the kind of journey one had in mind when leaving – 'blinking and half-drowned' further alluding to a lack of control over the process – and there is also no guarantee that this shore will constitute a home. Similarly, Chen reads trans experience in Janet Mock's memoir *Redefining Realness* (2014) not as a journey composed of 'moments of state and medical assisted transition from one sex to the other', but as a voyage 'mirroring her Polynesian ancestors' legacy of navigation' (90). The shift from the journey to the voyage critiques a 'conception of land as raw material for annexation, ownership, and cultivation and ocean as a natural boundary to be crossed and fortified' (90). Challenging the dominant cultural representation of journeys as controlled by the traveller and of territories as bordered and owned, the shipwreck and the voyage represent alternatives to the notion of travelling a charted route and arriving somewhere specific, emphasising that the journey may be unpredictable and without a set destination, and that the home may be unfamiliar and lacking clear boundaries.

The need to imagine the movement of trans 'according to different spatio-temporal metaphors' is stressed by Stryker, Paisley Currah and Lisa Jean Moore in a 2008 special issue of *Women's Studies Quarterly* entitled 'Trans-, Trans, or Transgender?' (13). As opposed to two bounded regions separated by a space that a subject has to cross, these authors see 'genders as potentially porous and permeable spatial territories (arguably numbering more than two)' (12) and 'transing' as something different than 'moving horizontally between two established gendered spaces' (13). Imagining different movements and spaces also entails reflecting on how these metaphors have a material reality. Halberstam warns about the 'danger of transposing an already loaded conceptual frame – place, travel, location, home, borders – onto another contested site' (170). Conceptualising transition as a crossing, and gender as a habitable land, not only precludes alternative imaginings (transition may not be a forward movement, or genders may not be separate territories) but also relies on dominant understandings of travel and location that have political and ideological implications. Referring to Morris's *Conundrum* – which is both trans memoir and travel narrative as it describes the author's journey from England to Casablanca to undergo gender confirmation surgery – Halberstam notes that 'national identity' is understood 'in much the same way' as 'gender identity': as 'stable, legible, and all established through the ruling consciousness of empire' (169). There is a connection between the ability to journey between genders and the liberties of the colonialist subject. Similarly, Snorton argues that the 'freedom to transgress national and somatic borders' that was integral to the media representation of Christine Jorgensen's transition in the 1950s was 'simultaneously counterindexical and intrinsic' to the spatial logics of 'Jim Crow regimes within U.S. borders' and 'antiblack and white-supremacist imperialist policies' (142). Jorgensen's ability to move in and out of the country for her transition, which is mapped on to her perceived movement between genders, contrasted with the segregation of bodies enforced within and beyond the borders of the US, revealing that moving between bounded spaces does not carry the same risks and opportunities for everyone.

Insecure dwellings and the dangers of crossing borders are not only metaphors for the difficulties of transition and gender belonging but are also a material reality for trans subjects. Homelessness disproportionately affects trans people, who may be cast out from their family homes for being trans and are discriminated against in housing markets (Faye 41; Pyne, 'Shelter Services' 132). Trans individuals in general, but especially those who cannot or will not fit neatly into the metaphorical space of a binary gender, also encounter difficulties being accepted in spaces like shelters: shelters are often gender specific, excluding non-binary subjects and generally involving some amount of body policing and the risk of violence for all trans people. Those who cross national borders can also experience threats to their safety linked to both figurative and literal movements, as Martha Balaguera finds in the experiences of trans interviewees who crossed the border between Mexico and the US. She describes the 'cycle of migration and deportation' experienced by Rosario, for example, who flees Guatemala after her family's 'demand that she reverse her gender transition' (650). Rosario sets off from the starting point of a home country in order to resist the demand that she go back to the starting point of the gender assigned to her at birth. Though she is '[s]et into motion by her nonbinary gender', the destination of her journey in the United States does not provide a home, as she faces precarity and state violence (650). The ensuing pattern of crossing, detention, and deportation is described by Balaguera as exemplifying the 'pervasiveness of confinement through permanent displacement', as restriction of geographical movement takes the form of confinement (detention) but also of further movement (deportation) (650). As norms prohibiting the departure of trans people from their assigned gender can be among the reasons for prompting movement across national territories, Rosario's situation highlights that some subjects are prevented from 'crossing' in more ways than one. Similarly, a lack of belonging to the figurative 'worlds' of men and women will result, for many, in restricted access to actual spaces built for safety.

Being barred from entering desired spaces and being confined in undesired spaces characterises many trans people's lives. These realities impede and thwart journeys and arrivals home, both when it comes to gender and more generally. The contributors to *Captive Genders: Trans Embodiment and the Prison Industrial Complex* (2011) show how the spatial operations of policing, detention, surveillance, raiding, and settler colonialism constrain and shape trans lives as much as do metaphorical systems dictating gender boundaries and the possible movements between them. In the foreword to the 2015 edition of the collection, abolitionist activist CeCe McDonald, who was incarcerated after defending herself from a racist and transphobic attack, describes a commitment to 'kicking down the walls' of the carceral system (2). Often, far from providing a way to protect marginalised people from the violence they experience, prisons and the police enact violence against them. Imprisoning trans people who have not had confirmation surgery according to the gender they are assigned at birth, for instance, constitutes another form of spatial enforcement of normativity. Considering metaphors of being 'trapped' in a wrong body or breaching the boundaries of gender cannot fail to take into account trans investments in breaking out of transphobic and racist systems that keep people captive in material ways. Metaphors of space are never neutral: conceptualising transition as a journey raises the question of who can move freely, and thinking of gender categories as spaces entails understandings of who can seek access, or escape confinement, in a space. The spatiotemporal relations that emerge in the lives of trans individuals challenge any simple metaphorical understanding of these experiences. If, as Lakoff and Johnson argue, 'we conceptualize the less clearly delineated in terms of the more clearly delineated' (59), then bodies and genders, on the one hand, and homes and journeys, on the other, are continually in the process of delineating each other, as whenever they seem to become clear they are revealed to be universalisations of privileged experiences. Keeping this metaphorical system, as well as its expansions and critiques, in mind helps us to understand how trans narrators navigate movement and inhabitation across gendered spaces, narrative spaces, and real and fictional settings.

As an additional challenge to the metaphorical system of journeys and homes, haunting and ghostly presences also often appear in trans writing, to signal non-normative embodiments, ambivalent belongings, or relationships with invisible others. Some authors who wish to nuance ideas of having arrived home in a body, in a category, or in a subject position do so by conceiving (explicitly or implicitly) of this home as haunted. C. Jacob Hale describes his position as a trans man as a 'flitting' through 'overlapping border zones constituted by the margins of several gender categories' (55). He points out that flitting 'is a type of movement proper to ghosts', who 'have only partial, limited social existence' (55). Conceptualising trans subjectivity as ghostly existence inevitably complicates the notion of home, which is revealed to be inhospitable to gender-variant subjects: 'ghosts never again expect a social world, structured by discourse, to provide homely comforts; we have already learned that home was an illusion' (55). In line with an understanding of home as a promised space of safety and social acceptance that only some are allowed to inhabit, Hale finds value in speaking as a ghost in these homes. Being a ghost can also signify a multiplicity of embodiments in time. In Boylan's *I'm Looking Through You*, a haunted home is the setting of the story and also a metaphor for the divided self of the narrator. The latter describes repeatedly seeing the ghost of a woman who eventually turns out to be her future post-transition self and, later, the ghost of a boy representing a past self. As she asks, 'From the very beginning, had I only been haunting *myself*?' (249), the trans narrator is not only the ghost but also the haunted home. When categories of male and female cannot fully accommodate some identities, these categories are haunted by what they exclude. In turn, when subjects find themselves assimilating into socially sanctioned homes, they are haunted by what does not fit there, including the very journey that has led to this home, its shifts and movements indicating the possibility of being otherwise.

Rather than wholly disavowing the idea that gender categories and bodies are homes, the language of haunting extends the metaphor in order to expand the way in which these homes can be inhabited, capturing a sense of the self flitting at the borders, partially belonging elsewhere. While trans writing offers a wealth of metaphors that depart more radically from the journey-home system, such as conceiving of gender and the body as spider webs (Hayward, 'Transpositions' 95) or crystals (Sundén 203), the ghost both critiques and remains compatible with this system.[2] Those who are made to haunt the homes of gender are reminders of how the existence of these homes is predicated on an exclusion: a neat division between genders and a separation between subjects who are viewed as legitimate inhabitants of the space and subjects who are haunting it. The authors I discuss in this book more or less explicitly advocate foregoing notions of housable bodies or uncomplicated and singular presence, and highlight instead how the body is opened up beyond its spatial and temporal boundaries by the haunting of what has come before and will come after, by the embodiments of others, and by the norms that regulate these embodiments. The ghost in trans writing conveys the difficulty of affirming that 'there' is separated from 'here', 'now' from 'then', and 'I' from 'not-I'.[3] Against the notion that a post-transition body would be an 'unbroken figure of plenitude', Gayle Salamon defines the body as 'a mixture or amalgam of substance and ideal located somewhere between its objectively quantifiable materiality and its phantasmatic extensions into the world' (41, 64). Rather than investing in a body without history, contradictions, or opacities, Salamon affirms multiple materialities – which exist as pasts, presents, and futures in the body – and ambiguous materialities – the body as mixture of culturally mediated facticity and ghostly extensions. Together with complicating the ways in which spaces are inhabited, as well as normative understandings of what bodies can inhabit these spaces, the movements of ghosts between and across these spaces replace the notion of journeying with a pluri-directional and non-linear mobility.

Despite the invisibility and unintelligibility of ghosts being linked to compromised agency and authority, and to negative affects of loneliness and lack of belonging, many authors in trans studies choose to dwell on these formulations of identity that complicate visibility, wholeness, stability, and progress, and argue that they have phenomenological value in describing their experiences. Disavowing these experiences risks excluding those who cannot or will not conceive of their trans identity as a successfully completed journey toward uncomplicated belonging. For instance, Eva Hayward counters the notion of becoming whole by arguing that she sees 'my trans-sex as a cut-sex that "cripples" an imagined wholeness', and that this position is 'livable' and 'even desirable' ('Starfish' 71). Cameron Awkward-Rich similarly emphasises how 'bad feeling' can be 'an unavoidable fact of being embodied' and suggests we read embodiment with a 'knowledge of the fundamental fleetingness of self-sameness, [...] exemplified in moments of transition' ('Trans, Feminism' 826). These authors describe, respectively, the experiences of surgery and of transition as revealing the fragmentation, disjuncture, and discontinuity inherent in being a self, while at the same time providing for subjects a desired and liveable identity. Being ghostly, split, or flitting does not rule out experiencing joy, comfort, and connection. And even if the safe spaces and the journeys to freedom offered by cisnormativity are rejected as an illusion that is far from the reality of most trans people – who are punished for travelling, who are held captive or cast out of their homes – these metaphors still hold empowering potential. Particularly, finding a home in community and solidarity, embarking on the journey of fighting for justice, and continuing to embody one's gender in the face of attempts to invalidate it are persistent ideas in trans writing. In what follows, I propose a framework for analysing the compromised journeys, haunted homes, and speaking ghosts that appear in trans narratives formally and thematically. Re-narration, trans-inhabitation, and renounced reliability name a tension between, on the one hand, an attachment to narrative strategies for making the narrator's subjectivity intelligible, visible, and whole, and, on the other, a rejection of the pressure to do so.

### Re-narration

Self-consciousness about plotting, duration, beginnings and endings, and narrative sequencing is ubiquitous in writing about trans identity. The legitimation of gender variance in the West has historically depended on a narrative feedback loop, with trans people only being able to obtain treatment for gender dysphoria by giving an account of themselves that conforms to narratives of trans identity from diagnostic manuals, and the latter purportedly aiming to reflect trans people's own narratives about themselves. In the same way, the intelligibility of cultural representations of transness is dependent on their similarity to previous representations. With the term 're-narration', I designate the temporal operations involved in repeating and reworking the narrative that is implicitly or explicitly expected of trans subjects. As I have indicated, a certain metaphorical understanding of trans embodiment as a journey from one bounded space to another is inevitably present whenever considering gender that is other than binary or fixed. Although many authors endeavour to tell a different story, and imagine alternative metaphorical structures, a linear and unidirectional movement of social and corporeal transformation, with a beginning and an end point, is a form that haunts most (if not all) representations of transness. Re-narration consists in modes of uneasily returning to this model, of retelling it with a difference, and/or of turning back to fill the gaps left by it. In the introduction to the first *Transgender Studies Reader*, Stryker uses this word: she explains that trans studies aims to 'renarrate' trans phenomena by telling 'new stories about things many of us thought we already knew' (13). While the meaning I give to re-narration extends beyond this, Stryker's emphasis on returning to an existing narrative of knowledge and revealing it to be misleading, only part of the picture, or even just obscuring other narratives is important to remember. In a sense, considering trans re-narrations will involve telling new stories about things that narrative studies thinks it already knows about gender, temporality, and bodies. Attending to how trans narrators refocus, repeat, and reshape pre-existing ways of narrating transness will then entail refocusing, repeating, and reshaping pre-existing ways of knowing narrative.

Revealing links between the gendered body and narrative unfolding in time is a long-standing aim of feminist narratology, and the ideological implications of linear plots have been central to discussions about gender and form. Page describes a 'binary opposition' set up by early feminist analyses of temporal patterns in narrative:

> these represent the 'male plot' as linear, with a trajectory of rise, peak and fall in narrative tension ending with a defined point of closure. In contrast to this, the 'female plot' is non-linear, repetitive and resistant to narrative closure [...]; contains multiple climaxes or none at all [...]; and is likened to the lyric form which is organized by pre-oedipal timelessness. (22)

An understanding of plot as linear and driving toward closure is found in Peter Brooks's *Reading for the Plot* (1992), which conceives of narrative as a forward thrust occasioned by the 'arousal of an intention', kept in 'tension' through a repetition and ending in 'terminal quiescence' (103). Brooks's connection between plot and sexual desire has prompted feminist narratologists to question the kind of body on to which this model is mapped. Susan Winnett, for instance, views Brooks's configuration as 'vulnerably male in its assumptions about what constitutes pleasure' (506) and she argues that 'another set of experiences might yield another set of generalizations', such as a model based on pregnancy and childbirth (508). Winnett's insight that, when it comes to plot, the 'existence of two models implies [...] the possibility of many more' (508) is now widely accepted in feminist and queer narrative studies: narrative forms, just like genders, are never simply two. As trans writing simultaneously attests to the enduring power of binaries and imagines possibilities beyond them, this writing reveals that narrative form is often a question of both and/or neither. Accordingly, re-narration names a tension between seemingly contradictory temporal operations: adhering to and disrupting causal or climactic sequencing; granting and refusing narrated events their 'appropriate' duration; providing and eschewing an ending that resolves contradictions; and foregrounding and obscuring the author's/narrator's active role in making these choices.

Trans texts, singularly or as a whole, are characterised by the coexistence of different and sometimes opposing temporalities that are specifically linked to trans embodied experiences and relationalities. One of these temporalities is what Laura Horak calls 'hormone time', which is 'linear and teleological' and 'directed toward the end of living full time in the desired gender' (580). Horak considers

YouTube videos documenting the progressive changes made by hormones on the bodies of the trans video creators, who usually present photographs of themselves in chronological order through a time lapse. This technique speeds up the pace of the process, allowing for the effect of hormones to be shown as a gradual and continuous shift toward a desired appearance. Horak notes that, despite the more complex temporalities that might be experienced in reality, hormone time is an 'insistently affirmative structure' which is 'powerfully enabling to trans youth trying to imagine a future' (580). Privileging this progressive teleology as the paradigm for representing transness, however, risks producing an experience of temporal discordance for those who are not able to embody it. Hormone time becomes a chrononormativity, to use Elizabeth Freeman's term for 'forms of temporal experience that seem natural to those whom they privilege' (3). Hil Malatino argues that the pervasiveness of narratives of hormone time occludes 'exploration of the more difficult affective experiences of trans becoming – becomings that are often shaped by a dwelling in lag time' (643). Lag time emerges when hormone time fails to manifest, due to factors such as compromised access to 'transition-related technologies', the 'experience of waiting' constitutive of medicolegal transition, 'dogged misrecognition' of one's gender by cis society, and 'transphobic hostility' more broadly (641). Representing experiences of lag time, Malatino argues, can foster empathy and connection between subjects who are similarly excluded by the affirmative temporality of hormone time. Re-narration, in the texts I examine, experiments with weaving together hormone time and lag time, promising and stalling progression, going forward and backward – attempting to control time and invent the future (whether this be a changed body or a world in which one's body can exist) in the face of forces that take away the power to do so.

The way in which Malatino characterises lag time, as a 'space of looseness and possibility, not yet overcoded and fixed in meaning, signification, or representative economy' (644), recalls the possibilities that Judith Roof's queer narratology sees in the narrative middle. Roof conceives of the narrative middle as a 'set of imbalances and mismatches (bad timing, misinformation, inappropriate pairings)' on the way to resolution (111). The middle, for Roof, has the potential to call into question the supposed fixity of the gender binary – which narrative always promises to return – through chaotic shifts, exchanges, and multiplicities.

But by confining subversive possibilities to the middle, narrative enacts a 'covert closing down of gender complexity' (111). In this queer formulation, the threat that the middle could jeopardise (heteronormative) closure is welcomed, and narrative solutions act as a limitation of gender's radical potential. It is certainly important for trans authors to challenge the normative impulse to overcome the middle, especially when a cis gaze views some gender-variant identities as unfinished, or as an intermediate stop on the way toward a final gender, rather than as a possible destination in themselves. However, dwelling in in-between spaces, as with Malatino's lag, can be accompanied by negative affects: lag can be a gift or a compromise, a necessity one learns to work with, a realistic but not necessarily aspirational description of experience. A temporary and unstable middle is sometimes the way in which cis epistemology reads a trans person's intentionally embodied gender – in this case, overcoming the middle feels like a disciplining of gender brought about by external forces. On the other hand, a perception (internal or external) of mismatch or imbalance leads to instabilities and misrecognitions that can be painful and dangerous. Overcoming the uncertainties of the middle will then take on a positive connotation. Both a lack of closure and a definitive ending can represent what one wants, what one can get, or what one learns to accept. These multiple narratives coexist in the texts I discuss, meaning that trans narrators remain ambivalent about (neither quite desiring nor rejecting) the possibility that narrative progression will fix fluctuation and stabilise looseness.

Some of the negotiations involved in re-narration look like what Hilary P. Dannenberg calls a 'dialectic between convergent and divergent tendencies' (2). For Dannenberg, convergence involves 'closing and unifying' the narrative world, while divergence 'creates an open pattern of diversification and multiplicity' (2). The conventional transition plot (the journey home) is a plot of convergence in its tendency toward reconciliation, achievement of goals, coherence, and the 'meeting' of differently gendered selves. Re-narration, then, makes space for divergence: lack of coincidence of gender with itself, mismatch between the gendered reality of the narrator and that of others, open endings, uncertain beginnings, and alternative possibilities. Daniel Punday's discussion of the relationship between body and plot, though it does not specifically consider gender in this way, can also be enlisted in understanding trans temporalities that oscillate between disordering and resolving. Punday argues that plot can be conceived of as the relationship between an 'overarching bodily image', as the culturally intelligible and normative body, and an 'unruly body that resists that overarching body' and endeavours to be reconciled with it over the course of the narrative (99). In canonical trans narratives, the unruly body deviates from a status quo (the gender assigned at birth) and is in tension with the socially sanctioned body that it strives to become (the overarching body, or the gender of 'destination'). While the two bodies are at odds, narrative (the movement of transition) occurs. This model is linked to the chrononormative understanding of the transitioning body as necessary but temporary. As Aizura notes, detaching oneself from the gender assigned at birth is only admissible if this 'transgression' is a 'momentary lapse on the way to a proper embodied belonging, a proper home and full social inclusion' ('Borders and Homes' 293). The transitioning body is the 'unruly' body, a deviation needed for there to be anything to narrate in the first place, but the demand is that it converge with the 'overarching body' and reassimilate into social normality. Re-narration can introduce divergence by foregoing this destination, by highlighting its costs, by haunting, or even by converging too much.

What converging too much might look like can be envisioned through Bettcher's description of the 'two versions' of the 'wrong-body model' ('Wrong Theory' 383). In the first version, the individual, 'through genital reconstruction surgery, *becomes* a man or a woman'; in the other, 'one affirms that one has always really been the woman or man that one claims to be' (383). I see, for instance, a shift from a narrative of 'becoming' to one of 'being' captured in the recent widespread adoption of the term 'gender confirmation' over 'gender reassignment'. Both ostensibly describe the same process, but the latter as a narrative of movement and relocation and the former as one of recognition of what is already there. The model of 'always having been' can yield a certain narrative staticness. Against the idea that transness consists in an extraordinary transformation – the sensationalist premise which has traditionally guaranteed the success of trans memoirs among cis audiences – re-narration can show that bodies and minds before, during, and after transition are not really that different from each other, or at least not in the way one would think. Scrambling chronological order and juxtaposing distant moments in time can reveal a discontinuous self, but also a self that is always discontinuous in the same way. Of course, even if one 'has always been', there can be narrative developments: a struggle to make others understand gender in the same way as the protagonist does from the start, for instance, or seeking acceptance as the gender one has always known oneself to be. This movement, however, may be less defined (slower, meandering, diffuse) relative to the 'becoming' model. Relative staticness can then be employed to show that perhaps a journey is only necessary if genders are seen as separate spaces positioned at a distance from one another, and only inhabitable one at a time. An extreme version of this re-narration would be to affirm that there is no narrative at all, because there is no difference between the starting point and the destination – therefore, one way to re-narrate would be to not narrate. Not narrating gender change is of course an option that many trans authors choose to take.

By negotiating hormone time and lag time, the middle and the overarching body, convergences and divergences, being and becoming, trans texts re-narrate existing timelines and patterns for conveying gender and identity. Sometimes, they re-narrate not only shared cultural models but also specific texts. For instance, J. R. Latham's article '(Re)making Sex: A Praxiography of the Gender Clinic' (2017) presents a narrative of the author's own experience of transition reconstructed from clinicians' reports and his own personal records. The psychiatrist's report, reproduced in the article with emphasis added by the author, indicates that a second opinion has been sought on whether Latham should be allowed to undergo a double mastectomy because 'his transgender treatments are likely to fall outside the *usual trajectory* for most trans-men i.e. testosterone therapy preceding chest reconstruction' (190). This document attests to the perception that there are typical consecutive stages of transition, with hormone replacement therapy coming before surgery. Latham's deviation from this trajectory ends up stalling the progress he wishes to make, as considerable delays follow in referring him to a surgeon. When this finally happens, although the surgeon ultimately agrees to perform the mastectomy, he states in his report, 'she seems rather reluctant to consider [testosterone] and I really wonder what her final aims are' (198). Tellingly, the uncertainty of the ending (the unknowability of the subject's so-called final aims) leads the surgeon to misgender Latham, implying that male pronouns can only be earned at the end of the (correct) journey. The difficulties encountered by

Latham are evidence of chrononormative effects: only those who experience the temporal dimension of their gender in a specific way are allowed access to ways to embody, and be recognised as, their actual identity. Otherwise they remain unruly, uncertain, and stuck in the middle of the narrative. Latham's re-narration consists in recontextualising the specific texts that enforce this chrononormativity, affirming the experience of gender that exists in their gaps. Citing and assessing medical reports, which refer to Latham in the third person, as an authoritative 'I' also reverses the circumstances in which gender 'experts' would cite and assess (and most often silence) their patients, thereby taking discursive control back from medical authorities.

Another particularly explicit way of clarifying what is being re-narrated is what Jacob Tobia does in their memoir *Sissy: A Coming-of-Gender Story* (2019): in order to show the script that they are about to deviate from, they craft a template for a conventional trans narrative as a game of Mad Libs. The template starts with, 'I was born in the wrong body. The doctors told my parents that I was a _____ [boy or girl], but I always knew that I was the opposite of that' (12; brackets in original). As the story continues, most of it is already written, leaving blanks to fill in with '[More trauma]' (13; brackets in original). Finally, the template's ending reiterates the key expectations of a binary gender, a neat conclusion, and a cis audience: 'I reintegrated into the gender binary and "fixed the problem," so now I'm a _____ [man/woman] just like you!' (13; brackets in original). While not all trans narrators are as specific as this when alluding to the narrative pattern from which they intend to depart, an element of disnarration is often integral to re-narration. As Gerald Prince defines it, the disnarrated refers to 'all the events that *do not* happen but, nonetheless, are referred to (in a negative or hypothetical mode) by the narrative text' (2). The disnarrated elements in trans narratives often take the form of reflections about genre expectations: narrators will state, for an audience understood to be familiar with these narratives, that the narrator did not, in fact, feel different from other boys or girls, or did not, in fact, encounter rejection from their family when they transitioned, before actually describing what they did feel and experience. For instance, Grace Lavery's highly self-conscious experimental memoir *Please Miss* (2022) handles in this way the description of how she did and did not always know something about her gender: 'So, although

I can't say, "I always knew *x*," I can say, "I never knew not-*x*," and perhaps even, "I always knew not-*y*"' (25). Here, re-narration starts by disnarrating and then proceeds through explaining how one's experience approximates to, but does not quite coincide with, the disnarrated.

The less self-reflexive a narrator is, and the less the text constitutes or resembles an autobiographical narrative, the less this kind of disnarration is likely to take place. Many narrators regularly tell stories without acknowledging a narratee and what their expectations might be. But even if re-narration does not take place as disnarration or as a specific mention of other texts, structures and patterns that variously uphold and disrupt popular understandings of transness can be identified in the texts that trans authors produce. Prosser notes that the narrative through which trans subjects make sense of themselves for clinicians and (sometimes) audiences needs to present events 'clearly and coherently', with conclusions 'carefully supported by appropriate episodes presented in an orderly manner, sufficiently but not overwhelmingly detailed' (108). In essence, 'the subject must be a skilled narrator of his or her own life', who does not 'falter, repeat, disorder, omit, digress' (108). A narrator who does falter, omit, and digress, with a narrative that is disordered or repetitive, is then implicitly re-narrating the story that would have been uttered if the demands of cisnormative audiences had been met. In particular, topics that could be seen to constitute a digression from narratives of trans identity are instead foregrounded by some re-narrations, to show that stories of transness are as much about gender as they are about race and white violence, work and class struggle, art and writing, love and friendship, culturally specific histories, and the future of the Earth. Re-narration can involve shifts in structure, topic, and style: as Lavery puts it, there are 'as many genres of transness as there are genres' (82). And, as I argue in 'Temporalities Beyond Transition' (2023), shifts in genre often entail an exploration of new temporalities. While it is mostly in Chapter 2 – about texts that explicitly write against canonical trans autobiography – that I focus on re-narration and what it attempts to discard, reshape, and reveal about trans subjectivity, this narrative strategy is also relevant in the other chapters, as it is apt for representing a mode of embodiment that is powerfully multiple and anti-coherent and voices that are deliberately omitting and faltering.

## Trans-inhabitation

Trans narrators negotiate a number of interconnected spatialities: the way in which the gendered self exists within/on/as the body; the extent to which trans embodiments can be housed in linguistic categories, material spaces, and narrative settings; and the dwelling and movement of the I in and across narrative levels. This network of relations is navigated through what I call trans-inhabitation. Trans studies understands the body as radically changeable but also as being 'pliant to a point, flexible within limits, constrained by language, articulation, flesh, history, and bone' (Hayward, 'Starfish', 74). Trans-inhabitation aims to capture this tension between transformability, flux, and multiplicity, on the one hand, and wholeness, rootedness, and locatability on the other. While 'inhabitation' designates the experience or desire to find a sort of home (and with it, sometimes the undertaking of a journey that does go somewhere), 'trans' signals that this inhabitation is taking place often in multiple and divided places by multiple and divided selves. Stryker, Currah and Moore define the movement of 'transing' as 'a practice that takes place within, as well as across or between, gendered spaces' (13). These three positions (within, across and between) are facets of trans-inhabitation, and often co-occur in a text. These simultaneous and contradicting ways of being located also characterise first-person narrators, who are inside and outside their own story, are ambiguously embodied, and speak as an I that can refer to multiple versions of the self. If re-narration is a reworking of a canonical narrative to show that transness does not always coincide with a steady, progressive and finite transition from one fixed gender to 'the' other, the goal of re-narration is then to re-narrate the body as a trans-inhabiting body. Trans-inhabitation refers to trans narrators' embodiment as a journey (across), a home (within) and a haunting (between, both without and within), as well as a dwelling in multiple bodies or social locations. The I of trans-inhabitation is multiple and mutable, but always embodied – both seeking some place from which to speak and partially resisting it, both fleshing itself out as character and flitting at the borders of the narrative as narrator.

Trans-inhabitation is connected to David Getsy's definition of 'trans capacity' as 'the ability or the potential for making visible, bringing into experience, or knowing genders as mutable, successive, and multiple' (47). Intersecting with the three sets of relations designated by across, within, and between, Getsy's three characteristics of trans genders are all named together by my notion of trans-inhabitation. If the term 'inhabitation' implies that both bodies and gender categories are spaces, the term 'trans' shows the movements and dwellings that occur in and around these spaces. There can be movements from one inhabitation (as body or gender of origin) to another (as body or gender of destination), in the sense of the successive and as the result of moving across. There can be ways of existing between bounded spaces or at the borders of them, and ways of being mutable in potential or actuality. There is also the sense of multiplicity, of inhabiting a plurality of spaces at once, or being at the same time inside and outside the boundaries of a specific area. Finally, these operations can happen singularly or together, or in the way in which Stryker defines the 'trans critical method': '*both and* and *neither nor* and *either this or that*' ('Trans Studies, Trans Feminism' 797). As I anticipated at the beginning of this chapter, spatial metaphors are not neutral: they are grounded in a world in which crossing, housing, moving, and settling are politicised realities. These realities inform our understanding of figurative inhabitation, but are also themselves shaped by abstract spatialisations (as in how viewing genders as separate 'territories' leads to actual gender segregations), meaning that how we conceive of identity metaphorically has material implications. In texts, trans narrators trans-inhabit not only gender, but also their status as narrators. If we take 'narrator' and 'character' as being different territories (akin to how 'man' and 'woman' are conventionally viewed), then first-person voices inhabit, move across, and flit at the borders of these territories. They inhabit these spaces mutably, successively, or multiply. They ultimately reveal that, like genders, 'narrator' and 'character' are not quite as simple as separate territories, but they are distinctions that still hold value for understanding where one stands.

The I, in narrative studies, is often in some way more than one, difficult to locate, or in a state of crossing. The distinction between the diegetic level in which the character experiences events and the level external to that, in which the narrator tells the story of that experience, becomes blurred when both this character and this narrator are designated by the same 'I'. As Monika Fludernik puts it, even if the narrator may not explicitly cross over into the world they are telling us about, 'the barrier between the diegetic and extradiegetic levels is already porous' ('Category of

"Person"' 122). When a narrator and a character are both called 'I', this implies an identity between them – in the sentence 'I tell you I was there', both instances of 'I' are understood to designate a unified body and consciousness. The more these two instances, then, are differently embodied or understand their genders in different ways, the more this 'I' will name a contradictory, ambiguous, and shifting self. Franz Stanzel posits that the experiencing self and the narrating self are separated by a 'narrative distance' which measures 'the degree of alienation and tension between these two manifestations of the self'; the experiencing self 'undergoes a development, a maturing process, a change of interest' in order to transform into the narrating self (66). This narrative distance keeps the two separated by a space that needs to be crossed. At the same time, 'the illusion of the identity of the narrator and a figure from the fictional world is continually renewed by the use of the pronoun "I"' (60). There may then be something inherently trans about a first-person narrator, whose identity hovers between supposedly separate places, undergoes a becoming and/or reveals itself to be the same despite these changes. The experiencing-I and the narrating-I, to go back to Getsy's three characteristics of trans gender, are successive (one turns into the other through a development journey), multiple (one 'I' is both), and mutable (the stability of these positions can be called into question).

A challenge to the stability of the narrator and character positions in the first person occurs for instance through focalisation (or articulation of 'point of view') across both. When Genette conceives of homodiegetic narrators as 'present' in the story they tell (245), thereby straddling two diegetic levels, he also notes that the 'oneness of person of the narrator and the hero' does not mean that 'the narrative is focalized through the hero' (198). This means that a first-person narrator can see and perceive objects and events through the eyes and bodies of others. But does it not also do so from the body of that other who is a different version of themselves? Marking the distinction between different versions of the I may not always be easy, depending on how vast the distance that alienates the narrating-I from the experiencing-I. In fact, attempts to assess this distance give rise to some of the temporalities discussed above, such as the plots of being and becoming, or the tension between the unruly body and the overarching body. Re-narration can work to increase or reduce this distance, for instance by choosing or declining to create a vivid narrating-I that will contrast for readers with the description and actions of the experiencing-I. But even when a distinction between the two is clear, shifting focalisation can blur them back together. When Feinberg's narrator, in *Stone Butch Blues*, reports that they have stopped injecting testosterone, they ask, "Who was I now – woman or man? That question could never be answered as long as those were the only choices' (223). Is the self who perceives the question as impossible to answer through a binary framework the character who experiences this moment or the narrator who looks back on it? Both interpretations are possible. The experiencing-I has, at this point, understood that certain ways of being a man or a woman have not worked, but the clarity that the narrating-I has reached is perhaps needed to articulate the possibility that there could be an additional option. As the I trans-inhabits both positions, like it does both genders, it both is and is not the same, reaching across distinctions without fully erasing them.

A more explicit trans-inhabitation of narrative spaces can occur as metalepsis. Metalepsis can consist, for instance, in the 'projection of the narrator into the story world [which] may be expanded into literal presence of the narrator on the scene' (Fludernik, 'Metalepsis', 385). In *None of the Above*, Alabanza's narrator physically moves closer to a childhood memory, inviting an audience to do the same: 'If you put your ear up to the wall, you could have a listen ...' (22). This scene, in which the experiencing-I is performing a song while wearing heels, is one that the narrator finds themself repeatedly holding under 'the magnifying glass of perspective' to look for the 'signs that this is when we all knew the kid would be "different"' (24). In this case, metalepsis allows for a re-narration of this moment, as the narrator can 'look close enough into my eyes' and 'see the joy so vividly on my face' (25) to rediscover an experience of gender-nonconformity not yet retrospectively fitted into a cohesive story of gender identity. For an example of what Fludernik would call 'postmodernist transgressive' metalepsis, creating 'anti-illusionistic effects' ('Metalepsis' 385), we can look at Lavery's *Please Miss*. In this book, the experiencing-I receives anonymous letters that may be sent by a version of herself, 'through a crack between worlds' (203), as the letters seem 'capable of speaking from every position I could ever see myself having occupied' (202). As in Alabanza's case, this self interacting with another (future, past, possible) self accentuates the discontinuities of experience, revealing both the desire to smooth them out and the costs of doing so. The ordinary situation of the narrator and their former self in the story being designated by the same I may be too generic to constitute metalepsis, being more of an identification across narrative levels than a violation of the boundaries between them; but it is not always easy to make this distinction. Trans-inhabitation occurs everywhere on the continuum between regular first-person narration and metalepsis, which I have called elsewhere 'a spectrum of narrative transing' ('When Narrative Studies Meets Trans Studies'): trans narrators dwell both in and outside the storyworld, rooted and detachable, embodied and transcending the body.

Trans narrators show that inhabitation of narrative worlds is inflected by experiences of marginalised embodiment. The notions of 'presence' and 'location' in cognitive narratology take on particular meanings in relation to trans narrators. As Marco Caracciolo and Karin Kukkonen explain,

> The 'location' of the narrator, or his/her deictic indications, can extend from almost 'nowhere' to highly detailed spatial descriptions. The 'presence' of the narrator, or the degree to which embodied language is foregrounded, can extend from no mentions of embodied states [...] to highly complex integrations of exteroceptive and interoceptive experiences for the narrator herself. (46)[4]

Presence and location can be particularly uncertain negotiations for trans narrative agents: being nowhere, moving through a space, registering embodied states, and being perceived by others are highly affective and political experiences for trans people. As Malatino explains, being trans means engaging in 'a carefully considered curation of where and how one appears, among whom, in what kinds of built spaces', meaning that 'occupying space with a degree of un-self-consciousness, lack of anxiety, and without projections about what forms of violence might occur', in other words, 'being present', is 'a form of privilege that the majority of trans subjects lack' (646). In examining trans narrative, this meaning of presence can be used in tandem with that of narrative presence. For instance, when Alabanza relates a transphobic incident that they experienced, and that later became national news, they switch from homo- to heterodiegetic narration, and from largely interoceptive to exclusively exteroceptive language (156). The narrating-I ceases to signal identity with its body in the storyworld and retreats part of its narrative presence; importantly, the 'presence' that is left is the one of their person as an object of narrative to be viewed from the outside, mirroring the objectification they experience. As trans narrators gain location and presence to different degrees, speaking from unclear or multiple places and revealing an elusive embodied wholeness, they show that these shifts can correlate with, or be motivated by, experiences of safety, isolation, connection, fragmentation, and more.

As it trans-inhabits bodies, narrative spaces, and gendered categories, the trans narrator is both anchored in and detachable from a textual corporeality. Being embodied and locatable carries risks that can be avoided in narrative, as even a narrator who exists as a fleshed-out character can tend toward becoming invisible, non-gendered, easily mobile, and disembodied. The risks associated with visibility and with relating to other bodies in space are made manifest in the trope of the reveal, a visual unveiling of a character's trans status. As Danielle Seid explains, this narrative climax centres on the display of anatomy as 'previously "hidden" or unknown information to the audience', and is 'often highly sensationalized, dramatized, or eroticized, though it is also sometimes depicted as comic' (176). As well as being constructed to elicit feelings in the audience, thereby decentring the feelings of the person being looked at, the reveal strips trans subjects of their right to self-determine by suggesting that 'living a transgender life involves concealing "the truth" of sexed bodies' (176). This making visible consists in enforcing a supposedly objective truth that runs counter to the truth that gender-variant individuals are expressing about themselves when they are not forcibly exposed. In order to avoid this kind of coercive visibility that invites a violent reading of the body according to cisnormativity, a hiding of the body might instead provide greater agency and safety. On the other hand, being seen and taking up space are empowering gestures when they are initiated by the subject who makes themself visible. Trans-inhabitation in narrative allows narrators to alternately offer and withhold presence, to exist in multiple locations (and therefore have multiple bodies) at once. This is a way to resist an objectifying reveal, elude a cis gaze, and exert control over when and how one is seen. The fact that Seid's examples of corporeal reveals are from film is telling, as visual media have the capacity to give rise to spectacularly unambiguous images (though by no means always do). Writing can permit a particularly veiled representation of materiality through contradictions and omissions, which are at the disposal of trans narrators who wish to significantly reduce a reader's capacity to visualise or locate the body.

Declining to present the body as an object of observation may also open up opportunities for a more equal relationship with readers, whose otherwise unfettered access to the bodies of narrative agents is never fully reciprocated as they are never gazed at in turn. Because they represent contested embodiments, trans narrators expand the scope of questions asked in narrative studies about the link between textual corporeality and narrative authority. Punday discusses the relationship of *'differential embodiment'* between a relatively disembodied narrator/author and the 'characters' who 'are to be known by their physical marks', a strategy adopted by eighteenth-century novels for producing 'authority for the representations presented to the reader' (156). Gendered and racialised narrators in contemporary literature still contend with the cost of 'being known by their physical marks', risking a shift away from the active position of narrating agent toward the passive position of narrated object. Since revealing a situated subjectivity can compromise textual authority, Punday argues that 'the most common way in which to imply that a narrator is not to be entirely trusted is to attribute to him or her strong physical dispositions' (176). Certain genders can become such a form of 'physical disposition'. Lanser suggests that in cultures where 'women's access to public discourse has been curtailed', women have sometimes been able to access '"male" authority by separating the narrating "I" from the female body' (*Authority* 18). In a context in which cis epistemology is the dominant paradigm for understanding identity, genders that are other than binary or fixed similarly constitute embodied positions that carry reduced authority. Despite this, trans narratives do not give up the body: against the idea that 'any disjuncture at the level of the body or the psyche [...] must be disavowed or repudiated to secure subjectivity' (Salamon 41), these narratives re-signify the body, multiply the body, and write the body in all its pluri-directional complexity and ambivalent presence. If the risk of representing embodiment, with all its contradictions and limitations, is that authority, reliability, and social locatability will be compromised in the eyes of some cis readers, many trans authors gladly run this risk in order to affectively resonate with other readers.

Trans narrators trans-inhabit genders and texts, anchored and crossing, ambiguous and substantial, multiple and speaking with one voice. Ultimately, trans-inhabitation aims toward securing authority in elusive and mobile places. In a reflection on writing entitled 'Notes on Craft', trans author K. Patrick explains that to 'operate within a language that often serves to exclude, or even destroy you' means having 'to reinvent, find new associations, dodge logic'. One way to do so is 'to stay agile, to offer something tumbling and nonstop'. In this formulation, I see the distortions and escapes of trans-inhabiting narrators, who highlight the capacity to 'stay agile' inherent in both transness and narrator-ness. Patrick's piece is describing poetry here, and it may be the case that lyrical writing is one that better allows this freedom. Despite the need for movement, however, Patrick also describes wanting to centre the body: 'This body of mine that isn't always mine, I have to bring it back over and over again.' Renouncing the body, the inhabitation of flesh, narrative, and social belonging, is not possible or desirable. However, trans movements across, between, beyond, and variously within these homes can provide some resistance against being pinned down by the visual and linguistic epistemologies of power. These movements lead to a deliberate opacity when it comes to textual embodiment: for many voices in trans studies, rendering legible is a contested operation. As Bey explains in *Black Trans Feminism*,

> Opacity refuses reduction and perfunctory transparency and preserves the singularity of those who are so often coerced into making themselves digestible. Opacity also allows for a kind of quiet (or loud) claim to something unable and unwilling to be given to others. [...] Opacity is more robustly a tactical evasion that eludes medicalized, biometric, and regulatory frameworks of 'knowing' a subject. (10)

Making oneself digestible, being able or willing to give everything, and submitting oneself to being understood according to accepted ways of knowing are the demands imposed upon trans narrators by cis audiences. Trans narrators re-narrate against this demand, and they trans-inhabit against this demand. They also act against this demand when they engage in what I call renounced reliability.

## Renounced reliability

The act of telling the truth, for trans narrators, has historically involved nothing less than undoing dominant understandings of what counts as real, gaining the trust of a hostile audience, and clearing oneself of the accusation of being a liar before the story can even begin. In her memoir *Redefining Realness*, Janet Mock describes the suspicion of those asking her why she did not publicly come out as trans sooner: 'What people are really asking is "Why didn't you correct people when they perceived you as a *real* woman?" Frankly, I'm not responsible for other people's perceptions and what they consider real or fake' (257). With this refusal to be dragged on to a terrain of cis logic that would invalidate her gender, Mock shows that trans people are continually (and often violently) confronted with a version of truth and reality that contrasts with what they know to be the case. As Bettcher argues, trans people have to navigate multiple systems of meaning: for instance, while mainstream cultures will attribute gender based on 'a particular sort of genitally based anatomy [...] some trans subcultures simply don't center genital reconstruction surgery at all' ('Wrong Theory' 401). Statements like 'I am a woman' or 'I am a man' will yield different realities depending on the framework that is being used to assess the meaning of these sentences – not to mention the risk of unintelligibility incurred by statements about gender that depart from these two. It is only in particular (culturally contingent and historically changing) ways that trans people's statements about their gender will be deemed acceptable by dominant discourses. When this is the context in which trans people speak, how can we talk about (un)reliability in trans narratives? The dialogue I want to foster here between narrative studies and trans studies responds to Vera Nünning's call to open literary analysis to 'the insights that other disciplines have achieved in their studies of unreliability' (3). Trans studies, as an interdisciplinary field itself, can offer notions of unreliability and trustworthiness that are political, ethical, philosophical, and historical as well as textual.

With renounced reliability, I name a set of strategies employed by trans narrators to reject the binary choice between submitting to cis culture's epistemologies and not speaking at all. The sense of defiance that accompanies this rejection is the one with which Stryker takes leave from the dehumanising rhetoric of anti-trans groups: 'I do not fall from the grace of their company – I roar gleefully away from it' ('Frankenstein' 239). Stryker's statement, in an article adapted from a performance piece delivered at a conference in 1993, is a refusal delivered in the first person: it announces a departure while staying firmly in view. Among the accusations that she stands present against is the one that trans people are 'a fraud' and 'alienated from their true being' (239). The imputation that one is not able or willing to recognise their real self, and is drawing others into their distorted world, profoundly compromises a person's well-being and ability to live fully – taking leave from it is a gesture of self-preservation. Renounced reliability is a refusal to participate in the game that establishes what counts as truth when this game is stacked against trans subjects, while also simultaneously communicating something about trans reality. This can take various forms, most of which can be encountered in the texts I discuss in this book: constructing a naïve narrator, such as one who does not know how gender is supposed to work in cis culture; a self-conscious avowal of unreliability, like that of a memoirist who admits that a continual demand to search for signs of transness in their past has irreparably warped their memories; a deliberate confusion between fact and fiction to critique modes of 'objective' knowledge that erase trans existence; exaggerated compliance with the narrative hostile audiences have about trans subjects to signal a disinterest in explaining oneself to others. While narrative studies provides a framework for analysing some of the formal strategies employed to do this, an engagement with trans studies is vital to elucidate the specific mechanisms of oppression that regulate the attribution of trust and the validation of reality when it comes to the utterances of trans narrators, mechanisms that inevitably factor into any interpretation of these utterances.

While in Chapter 4 I mostly discuss renounced reliability in the case of fictional narratives, which employ particular ways to signal what may or may not be true in an invented world, considering trans autobiographical writing is necessary to understand the relationship between trans narratives and questions of reliability and authenticity. In tracing the historical links between autobiography and gender, Linda Anderson notes that definitions of autobiographical writing traditionally insist on an '"honest" intention' that 'guarantees the truth of the writing' (2). However, because we have not 'necessarily believed all subjects in the same way', autobiographical writing becomes the prerogative of those whose honesty and ability to tell the truth about themselves is not questioned (3). If we read the truth of autobiography by honouring the author's 'signature', Anderson asks whether all signatures have in fact 'the same legal status' (3). If the power of the signature is compromised for women, this is also particularly the case when considering trans authors, as trans people's very names are routinely dismissed as false names. Trust in the signature can be undermined, for instance, through transphobic practices of 'deadnaming', which operates on the basis that a trans person's name, just like their gender, is less valid than the one assigned at birth. Even when writing in a genre that does not signal that they are telling their own story, trans authors encounter the imperative to be honest, and the risk of not being believed, whenever they include trans characters. In discussing her debut novel *Bellies* (2023), Nicola Dinan explains that, as a trans author 'representing characters historically excluded from mainstream literature' (trans and of colour), she feels a 'duty not to misinform' ('Trans Art'). Faced with this duty, she describes a keen awareness that the novel 'doesn't fully represent trans experience'. The sense of responsibility to represent accurately is heightened by the hostility trans people encounter especially in the UK, the place of publication of Dinan's book. Not only will the authenticity of a trans character's experiences be questioned by readers who are invested in maintaining their misinformed assumptions about transness; this authenticity will also be demanded by readers who wish to learn how to redress these assumptions.

While hostile readers may not question every single assertion by a trans narrator, they will believe them to be unreliable (either intentionally or not) about particular things. Even if no one would doubt a narrator's assertion that they took the bus or ate a sandwich, widespread and pernicious suspicion about trans narrators' statements about their gender forms the context in which they perform any narratorial act. There may be variations in whether a transphobic audience would believe avowals of gender to constitute – to follow the model of axes of unreliability developed by James Phelan and Mary Patricia Martin – cases of misreporting, misreading or misregarding. According to this model, misreporting takes place on the axis of 'characters, facts, and events', misreading on the axis of 'understanding and perception' and misregarding on the axis of 'ethics and evaluation' (Phelan, *Living*, 52). When trans people are not believed to be the gender they say they are, they are often simultaneously viewed as reporting wrong facts, understanding the situation incorrectly, and subscribing to an ideological model that leads to wrong judgements. But, when encountered in texts, narrators are also reporting, reading and evaluating a number of other objects in addition to their own gender. And sometimes trans narrators will be as unreliable as all first-person narrators are, be influenced by feelings and struggles with mental health, be unaware of something they later learn, or engage in ordinary reality-altering activities like taking recreational drugs (all of these happen for instance in Dawson's *Wonderland*). Renounced reliability can in fact take the form of creating trans narrators who, like all humans, do not have to be reliable about everything even if they are to be reliable about their gender. However, if an audience believes trans narrators, in fiction or otherwise, to be unreliable about the latter, would they then become more generally untrustworthy? And, conversely, would detecting that a trans narrator is unreliable about some aspect of their telling lead to suspecting their statements about their gender too, considering that this in an area in which reliability is historically hard-fought and still precarious in mainstream culture?

This kind of contagious unreliability is one that, to use Halpern's words, would be 'in the eye of the beholder' (48) more than in the text. However, it is also to be found in the text when, having some idea of what the beholder might think, texts actively renounce reliability. Even in the presence of a narrator whom the author has intended to be reliable, the existence of multiple audiences complicates the situation, as attributions of unreliability are highly dependent on which audiences are taken into consideration. The statement that one does not have a gender, for instance, may be read as misreporting and/or underreporting[5] by readers who base their understanding of gender on an anatomy that cannot but be present: these readers might construe the narrator as having a gender and concealing what it is, withholding important information, or as uttering something that is patently impossible (and most likely extend this unreliability to the author or to the trans people that the narrator resembles). Trans readers or generally sympathetic readers, on the other hand, may know that this is all that needs to be said, and will fill in the gaps by imagining that the narrator may have been assigned a legal gender, and has a body that may have been read by others as signifying a gender, but has themself rejected these classifications. These details are then irrelevant information, and their omission has no effect on the overall impression of the narrator's honesty and ability to tell the truth. As is mostly the case for contemporary trans narratives in mainstream culture, the audience will probably be formed by some combination of both kinds of reader (and everyone else in between): authorial intent will then be influenced by not knowing which particular reader one is going to get and by not having control over whether one will be read as reliable by everyone. This can result in rhetorical passing, the intentional encoding of texts with two 'mutually exclusive ways of reading', one for 'gullible readers' and one for 'discerning readers' (Halpern 58). Increasingly, though, contemporary trans authors are openly speaking to discerning readers, refusing to compromise for those who cannot or will not discern.

Historically, however, the most visible audience of mainstream trans narratives has been one that needs to be won over. As Prosser argues, trans subjects have been 'an intrinsically unreliable text in the eyes of the reading other' (112). This reading practice is first found in clinical encounters in which '[t]he patient's position is to confess, the professional's – half priest holding the key to the patient's salvation, half detective decoding this clinical narrative – to listen, to take note – and precisely to police the subject's access to technology' (111). The clinician as gatekeeper and guarantor of trans reality makes an explicit appearance in twentieth-century trans memoirs too: the preface to Jorgensen's *A Personal Autobiography* is written by sexologist Harry Benjamin, who '"grants" the autobiographer a narrative voice, vouching both for its representationality (authenticity) and its representativeness (exemplarity)' (Prosser 126). Given this context, trans movements have been centred on claiming the right to self-authorise. Increasingly, trans texts show a rejection of the audience's authorising powers too, their right to assess and confirm the truth by textual or paratextual means. To position the audience as a jury to whom the validity, dignity, and good intentions of trans subjects must be proven is to render admissible versions of reality that would justify thinking otherwise. These versions of reality are invoked in the transphobic act that Bettcher calls 'reality enforcement': the act of revealing a body in a situation in which 'public gender presentation and private genitalia are construed as misaligned', resulting in 'the erasure of a trans person's gender identity through an opposing categorization (e.g., trans person sees herself as a woman, but she is categorized as a man)' ('Wrong Theory' 392). The climax of corporeal reveal that I mentioned earlier, which trans narrators may avoid by trans-inhabiting narrative spaces, constitutes such a gesture. Reading a trans narrator as unreliable where the author has intended reliability would be a form of reality enforcement; when they renounce reliability, trans narrators take the question of reality off the table first.

Renounced reliability is then a reaction to an environment in which one's ability to speak reliably is heavily compromised. While many readers honour the intentions of authors in constructing trustworthy, authoritative, and sympathetic trans narrators, invitations to be suspicious of trans people are issued daily by powerful groups in the media and from governments across the world. It is necessary to acknowledge this context when using narratological categories for unreliability to describe trans narrators. As Bettcher argues, for instance, invalidating the reality of trans people can take the form of viewing them as 'deceivers' – as if intentionally 'disguised as a woman or man' – or 'pretenders' – as if delusionally engaged in 'a kind of pretence' of gender ('Wrong Theory' 391). Not disclosing that one is trans is equated with lying, and being out as trans is equated with creating a fake reality. This distinction bears a remarkable resemblance to the two types of untrustworthy narrators identified by Nünning: the liars (those who 'set out to deceive others and try to profit from their misconceptions') and the fools (those who 'want to tell the truth but are unable to do so') (11). These two kinds of unreliability characterise quite accurately how trans subjects are represented by others. What comes close to some examples of what I call renounced reliability in trans narratives is Uri Margolin's added category of the 'playful' (53), a type of unreliable narrator who, like the liar, intentionally misleads but does so for less nefarious purposes. In the case of a playful unreliable narrator, Margolin argues, 'the misrepresentation is employed not to deceive, but rather to be identified and deciphered for its reliable direct message', and detection is 'often hoped for' (53). Misrepresenting oneself as a liar or a fool can in fact be one of the ways in which reliability can be renounced in this playful way. But because the association of trans subjects with liars and fools is part of a system of oppression that has dangerous material consequences, playfulness is often mixed with pain, anger, and exhaustion; the hope that the 'reliable direct message' about the realities of trans life will be deciphered has particularly high stakes.

The first reliable direct message that trans narratives hope will be understood is that trans subjects are playing a losing game when trying to speak the truth and assert their reality. In her memoir *A Queer and Pleasant Danger*, Bornstein reveals that this message is what is behind her renounced reliability. First, she declares, 'I promise you I'll be telling lies in this book – little lies, to make the story more fun' (7). Then, she explains, 'I got real good at lying because of the great big lie I told day and night for nearly twenty years – that I was a boy' (7). Bornstein's relationship with the act of lying subverts the notion of trans individuals as deceivers and pretenders by noting that it is precisely in order not to be seen as a deceiver or a pretender that one has to lie: because her being a woman is considered a lie in cis environments, she has to lie by agreeing that she is a boy. Signalling that her book contains lies calls attention to the impossibility of adhering to clear notions of truthfulness and deception in this situation. The second reliable direct message being communicated by trans narrators is that there is value in recognising that truth is generally ambiguous, that reality is in flux, and that the self will never be fully knowable. Alabanza elucidates this when writing about the consequences of a world 'that has told you who you are from birth and then given you daily reminders of that non-consensual choice, forcing you to become extremely articulate and strong in your denial of it' (185). As a result of having to firmly consolidate their own reality when others attempt to undermine it, trans people construct an unshakeable narrative of themselves that is not 'untrue' but that has to be characterised by 'rigidity': 'I cannot show any doubt, because if I do, it will prove all those against me right' (186). By taking away 'the possibility to be unsure' (186), cis culture limits trans people's 'full humanity and honesty' (187). Given this context, trans narrators claim the right to be unreliable, unknowing, in progress, discovering.

Speaking for oneself, however unreliably or equivocally or contradictorily, is still vital for trans subjects. When reliability is renounced, the right to be reliable is still invoked: it is a choosing to be unreliable about yourself rather than having someone else be unreliable about you. When Hale traces the silencing of trans voices across both medical studies and gender studies in the 1990s, which take trans people as their object of observation but do not seem concerned with their perspectives, he asks, 'With so much invested in and contested on our bodies, on our tongues, how can we speak in and on our own terms?' (53). Hale's suggestion to speak as ghosts, from 'dislocated locations' (56), is aimed at recognising that trans subjects construct their realities from the gaps and overlaps between normative categories,[6] from a position of invisibility coupled with exaggerated scrutiny, and in a context in which the possibility to have a discourse about one's own reality has been severely curtailed. Re-narrating and trans-inhabiting are operations that convey the instability, while still claiming ownership, of one's own body and narrative. With renounced reliability, trans authors ultimately aim the effects of any resulting unreliability toward undermining transphobic societies rather than their own trans narrators. Renounced reliability can then be classed as a bonding unreliability. In bonding unreliability, discrepancies in the telling 'have the paradoxical result of reducing the interpretive, affective, or ethical distance between the narrator and the authorial audience', meaning that the narrator still communicates something that the author 'endorses' (Phelan, 'Bonding Unreliability' 225). In this way, the agency of the narrator is not denied and their capacity and right to speak is fostered. In Chapter 4, I explore the forms of 'literally unreliable but metaphorically reliable' narration (228), 'naïve defamiliarization' (229), being unsure, and playful and defiant equivocation of truth that bonding renounced reliability can take. Through these choices, authors establish a relationship of care with the narrator, even, and perhaps especially, if the narrator is an autobiographical version of themselves.

## A framework for reading

The conceptual metaphors of the journey and the home can have an enabling effect, providing a language that allows trans experiences to be understood through comparison with something that appears more universal. But they can also constrain, by downplaying and hiding marginalised ways of moving and dwelling both when it comes to gender and when it comes to material spaces. The ghost emerges as a rem(a)inder of this exclusion, allowing the articulation of negative affects, ambiguous modes of presence, disavowed connections, reduced intelligibility but also empowering escapes. As these metaphors inform plot structures, tropes and motifs, patterns of narration and focalisation, the production of further metaphors, and other aspects of contemporary trans narratives, they are returned to, distorted, expanded, and unravelled through re-narrating their orders and durations, trans-inhabiting the positions from which they are told and experienced, and renouncing the reliability that comes with using conventional narratemes. In discussing re-narration, I have noted that temporal operations of beginning, ending, stalling, moving forward or backwards, lagging and coinciding have complex and sometimes contradictory ideological effects: each can come to signify both safety and disciplination, freeing and trapping, obstacles and opportunities. As a result of this, re-narration weaves disparate temporalities, oscillating between adopting and critiquing them. The concept of trans-inhabitation proceeds from the starting point that existing narratological descriptions of first-person narrators, characters' bodies, and textual inhabitations of worlds have significant capacity for describing how trans people exist in narrative, and resonate with how trans authors discuss presence, corporeality, fragmentation, taking substance, hiding and being seen. Trans narratives show a desire for both the mobility of trans and the fleshing out of inhabitation, and the opacity of writing when describing the visible can help achieve this balance. When noting that trans narrators renounce reliability, I have considered reliability in its political and ethical dimensions. Attributing textual unreliability involves imputing actions and intents that gain particular significance in connection with the systemic oppression of trans individuals: deceiving, being deluded, not saying enough, or demonstrating compliance with the truth of others. Renounced reliability can be adopted out of necessity as the impossibility of telling the truth, at the same time as it can be a deliberate gesture of defiance against the demand to be clear and certain; it can be playful, obstructive and/or sincere in its effects.

In a context characterised by both an excess and a lack of narratives about trans people, the narrative operations I have grouped under re-narration, trans-inhabitation and renounced reliability reiterate and challenge what is already known. A simultaneous attachment to and suspicion toward taxonomies and categorisations grounds the methodology of trans narratology that I have described here. Each of the chapters that follow presents readings that are guided, respectively, by a particular emphasis on re-narration, trans-inhabitation, and renounced reliability. However, all can be found to occur across the chapter segregations that

I am imposing, as temporality, embodiment, and reliability are interlinked aspects of narrative: embodiment occurs in time, and reliability is supported or undermined by certain kinds of temporalities and embodiments. These three categorisations do not name ways of doing narrative that are necessarily unique to trans texts either. They each encompass a number of possible strategies and operations (such as disnarration, metalepsis, or bonding unreliability) often already identified by narrative studies. These strategies and operations are grouped into these categories according to their overall effects and/or intentions; in other words, re-narrating, trans-inhabiting, and renouncing reliability are achieved through a number of possible narrative means. Temporality, embodiment, and reliability are areas of narratorial activity at the same time as they are matters of (political) significance in trans studies: re-narration, trans-inhabitation, and renounced reliability are then terrains of encounter, in which concepts of narrative acquire the significance of trans studies and vice versa. Trans studies, grounded in the lived experience of trans people, provides ways for rethinking bodies, individual and collective identities, spatialities, justice, and history that are taken for granted in many disciplines, including narrative studies. Re-narration, trans-inhabitation, and renounced reliability describe not one way but multiple and sometimes irreconcilable ways of doing this rethinking, because trans writing attests to disparate and sometimes contrasting desires, experiences, investments, and epistemologies that coexist in a community or even for a single subject. A trans narratology allows us to recognise that, when it comes to both gender and narrative, it is not always easy to make the distinctions one thought could be made, and that it is not always easy to discard the distinctions one thought could be discarded.

## Notes

[1] The way in which spatiotemporal linearity governs understandings of more general concepts, such as life and narrative, is a topic that narrative studies has extensively covered, as discussed for instance in Hilary P. Dannenberg's *Coincidence and Counterfactuality: Plotting Time and Space in Narrative Fiction* (2008). Here, I am interested specifically in how orientations in space, metaphors for time, links, paths, and multiple worlds take on significance through trans studies and trans experiences in relation to culturally mediated bodies.

2   For an analysis of plant and animal metaphors in trans writing, see Van den Bossche.
3   Notions of haunting in trans writing have an affinity with Jacques Derrida's hauntology, a mode of existence of the past that calls into question 'the border between the present, the actual or present reality of the present, and everything that can be opposed to it: absence, non-presence, non-effectivity' (39). What is important to acknowledge in the wake of Derrida is that ghostliness can characterise not only the dead but those who have material existence in the world. In a book that discusses ghost metaphors in contemporary culture, Esther Peeren addresses 'living ghosts': 'those people who, already in their lifetime, resemble dispossessed ghosts in that they are ignored and considered expendable, or [...] become objects of intense fear and violent attempts at extermination' (14). While Peeren does not specifically examine trans people as part of this category, her appeal to '[r]ecogniz[e] and tak[e] responsibility for the way these ghosts *of* the present are created, perceived and treated' (14) resonates with my own aims, as I examine how ghosts can gain agency in a world that makes them ghosts. Peeren also notes that, for Derrida, ghosts are always othered: 'we' are 'the haunted ones', looking at ghosts who are external to us and disavowing the possibility that 'one may be the ghost one moment and ghosted or haunted the next – or both at the same time' (27). Since trans narrators appear in literature as both ghosts and haunted, the flitting between the two positions suggests that even those who are seen as 'properly' inhabiting abstract or concrete spaces always have the potential to become ghosts.
4   Interoceptive experiences are 'perceptions of inner bodily states and feelings' and exteroceptive ones are 'perceptions from the outside' (Caracciolo and Kukkonen 46). The kind of first-person narrators I discuss normally report both.
5   So far, I have mentioned misreporting, misreading, and misregarding, but according to the same model narrators can also underreport, underread, and underregard. Trans-hostile audiences may attribute all these kinds of unreliability to trans subjects too, in the forms of not saying enough about one's gender or body, missing the big picture, and underestimating. In my readings, I am especially interested in the first of these, as trans narrators often renounce reliability by using omissions in order to obfuscate textual corporeality.
6   Speaking from dislocated locations is a condition that has been richly articulated by queer and decolonial perspectives. Gloria Anzaldúa's *mestiza*, for instance, is a figure who is '[c]radled in one culture,

sandwiched between two cultures, straddling all three cultures', who 'undergoes a struggle of flesh, a struggle of borders, an inner war' (78) and develops 'a tolerance for ambiguity' (79). This resonates clearly with trans movements and inhabitations within, across and between worlds.

Chapter 2

# Trans Narrators and Temporality: Time Beyond Transition, Truth Beyond Memoir

Autobiographical writing always involves some form of re-narration: returning to a story that already 'exists', shaping it retroactively from a present moment of reflection, negotiating which steps of the author's experience and growth may be expected by audiences, and doing all of this self-consciously in the first person.[1] The context in which trans narratives are being produced, however, renders re-narration particularly explicit. For a long time, memoirs and personal accounts focusing on social and medical transition (themselves modelled on clinical case histories) were the only widely available texts authored by trans people. This resulted both in the codification of highly recognisable conventions and in the frustrated desire to write and read something else, a desire that is given voice most forcefully from the beginning of the 1990s. As Salah succinctly puts it, 'Since the beginning of the queer moment (c. 1991), we hate our autobiography' (186). However, three decades later, autobiographical texts about trans experience show no signs of disappearing: the majority of titles listed under Amazon's category of 'Transgender People Biographies' (which encompasses mostly trans memoirs) have been published in the last five years. Contemporary autobiographical narratives often have a fraught relationship with their predecessors: they continue a tradition of writing about transness from the first-person voice of the author, but are critical of stereotypes and clichés to which decades of explaining trans lives to cis audiences have given rise. The examples I discuss in this chapter – Juliet Jacques's *Trans*, Travis Alabanza's *None of the Above* and Kai Cheng Thom's *Fierce Femmes and Notorious Liars* – all engage in explicit re-narrations as they measure the distance between their narrative and other (previous, possible, more visible) narratives. Trans memoirs, and more broadly narratives that involve 'telling one's own story', exist ambiguously between old narratives that are reworked and new ones that are produced: they harness the potential of textual forms to order experience while being alert to what these forms obscure. They shape notions of transness from within, outside, and/or the margins of canonical narratives by adopting and transforming their temporal operations.

As I anticipated in Chapter 1, engaging in trans re-narration involves negotiating hormone time and lag time, the middle and the overarching body, convergences and divergences, being and becoming, disnarration and intertextuality, centring and decentring expected topics and genres. By mixing these temporalities, structures, and operations, trans writing often displays a suspicion toward the very act of narrating a recognisable story about gender identity, in its function of conferring intelligibility to the subject and in its chrononormative effect of denying validity to experiences that deviate from it. Given the fraught relationship to truth that haunts trans people's discourses about themselves, which I have outlined in my discussion of renounced reliability, autobiographical texts are characterised by an uneasy promise of authenticity, as well as an equally uneasy adherence to conventional linear structures of transformation and growth that would make one's 'truth' knowable. This involves a re-narration of not only trans autobiographical forms, but also related patterns of maturation and change, such as the *Bildungsroman*. Especially when transition is viewed as a 'second puberty' (Jacques, *Trans*, 223), it is perhaps unsurprising that trans memoir forms would partly overlap with the structure of the *Bildungsroman*. In the *Bildungsroman* as well as in the transition narrative, a process is depicted by which a younger protagonist gains progressive knowledge of themselves and the world as their body and mind transform, learning to recognise and follow their desires as well as to fit them within social norms for adult identity. When this is told in the first person, the moment in which the experiencing-I becomes a narrator is both the culmination of the narrative, as the completion of the 'maturation' process, and its precondition, as this 'final' and current version of the self is the one that has retrospectively been revisiting and ordering the events leading up to this becoming. Trans autobiographical narratives usually re-narrate (meaning that they both reproduce and disrupt) this general structure, by questioning whether change has taken place or ought to take place, or by showing that change may not proceed gradually, have a particular direction, or be over in the narrator's present.

While re-narration can occur in many fictional genres and with any type of narrator, the kind of explicit re-narration I focus on here is one that involves a first-person narrator self-consciously shaping what they tell about a person who is in some way understood to coincide with the author. Beyond the long-form narratives I explore in this chapter, collections of short autobiographical stories by different authors also deserve a brief mention, as they are key sites for seeing re-narration at work. Volumes from Tracie O'Keefe and Katrina Fox's *Finding the Real Me: True Tales of Sex and Gender Diversity* (2003) to Laura Kate Dale's *Gender Euphoria: Stories of Joy from Trans, Non-Binary and Intersex Writers* (2021) simultaneously codify and contest the conventional temporalities of trans autobiographical narratives. In *True Tales*, the journey metaphor is explicitly invoked in the editors' preface and in the titles of four of the twenty-six stories, prefiguring how it serves as an unquestioned structuring principle for some narratives and as a trope to be challenged by others. All stories are divided into titled sections; the titles at times explicitly outline narrative steps – 'Realization' (254), 'An Epiphany' (21), 'Crisis Point' (249), 'The Big Decision' (121), 'Resolution' (100) – and at others either give no clue toward or explicitly stall these steps – 'Paradox' (5), 'A Third Gender' (206), 'Thoughts' (177), 'United We Stand' (74). In *Gender Euphoria*, while some narratives present a linear account from childhood to gender affirmation, the overall focus is on moments rather than timelines: most stories centre a particular episode and hinge on the intersection between transness and a specific context (such as a Pride event) or aspect of identity (such as nationality). The editor herself authors eleven of these stories, exploring a range of themes and topics relating to her life that do not add up to a progressive narrative of gendered transformation. The individual narrative of transness is therefore multiplied in two different ways: through presenting multiple stories by one person, and through interweaving them with stories by others. As exercises in collective re-narration, collections provide an opportunity to enact a multiplicity of repetitions and differences, as stories overlap and contrast with each other. But individual narratives, while not necessarily placed side by side with others, can still invoke similar intertextual effects.

## Juliet Jacques: Politicising pace

Juliet Jacques's career as a writer bears witness to the shifting relationship between trans people and the British media over the course of the 2010s, and Jacques herself played a prominent role in shaping this relationship.[2] Between 2010 and 2012, she authored a column in *The Guardian* entitled *A Transgender Journey*, documenting her transition, and became a sought-after public commentator on trans issues. Her book *Trans: A Memoir*, which is partly based on this column, also discusses the experience of writing it and the public's reaction to its publication. While there were many positive and encouraging responses by both trans and cis readers, demonstrating an interest at least in trans stories if not in supporting trans justice, Jacques reports no shortage of antagonistic comments, nor of contemporary articles dismissing and belittling trans people in most national media outlets, including the one in which the column appears. Toward the end of *Trans*, Jacques explains that she has resolved to stay out of the 'trans culture wars' amplified by platforms like Twitter, but up until the last pages she is still posting and writing pieces denouncing transphobic media (286). Since the book's publication in 2015, and partly as a backlash to the proposed 2017 reform of the UK Gender Recognition Act (GRA), anti-trans groups that view the dignity and freedom of trans people as incompatible with the protection of cis women have gained further prominence. Despite being a minority, these voices are disproportionately represented in the media, and vocally support policies aimed at restricting the rights of trans people championed by a Conservative government that has been in power for a decade.[3] At a public lecture in 2023, Jacques herself was asked by an audience member what she thought about the fact that trans rights may be encroaching on women's rights (the reaction of the rest of the audience, in which I was sitting, was to loudly protest the premise of the question). In this context, what are the functions and political implications of 'telling one's own story'? As will become clear, Jacques shares with other trans authors a frustration with autobiographical forms, while also understanding the enduring need for narratives that affirm and illustrate the realities of trans lives with the aim of building community and articulating resistance.

Jacques is explicitly critical of the view that memoir should be the privileged form to explore trans identity. In *Trans*, she describes the adjustments she is required to make to her first drafts for the *Guardian* column, as an editor asks: 'Can you make it less theoretical and more personal?' (181). Even after her profile is raised with the articles' popularity, Jacques explains, 'I still struggled to persuade editors to commission anything other than pieces about being transsexual' (229). The last of these 'pieces' is in fact the memoir itself. In an interview that concludes the book, she clarifies that 'having written my life story once already, I found it incredibly frustrating [...] [to] cannibalise myself a second time before I could do anything else' (299). As Jacques authors her own story over and over again, in various forms and in relation to various topics, this repetition ends up creating its own critical effects, as her work becomes a testament to the autobiographical expectations imposed on trans writers. An opportunity to challenge these expectations comes with Jacques's *Variations* (2021), a volume of short stories that explores the boundaries between fictional and non-fictional genres. At the start of each story, an authorial voice contextualises the piece that is about to follow (a film script, a series of letters, an excerpt from a diary, a scholarly article, a collection of blog entries, and more) in the manner of a historian or editor introducing a found document. As they explore gender-variant life across the UK in the last two centuries, these fictional documents re-narrate history by imagining the voices that may have been lost and reflecting on the kind of textual artefacts that preserve and shape trans identity. Through fictionalised means, the collection attests to the existence of gender-nonconforming people in a country that continually rewrites its history to erase them. While this represents a clear expansion of scope with respect to narrating individual experience, it is still possible for the latter to take place in a collective context by foregrounding its relationship with a multiplicity of other stories. This is what *Trans* does, showing how the demand to write an autobiographical account of transition can be resisted from within even while appearing to conform.

*Trans* is first of all a re-narration in a very literal sense, being partly based on the *Transgender Journey* column. The book therefore explicitly repeats and reflects on a transition that not only has already been experienced but also has been narrated before. As a challenge to the journey metaphor chosen by the newspaper and to the linear trajectory that the metaphor is usually understood to entail, *Trans* rearranges the sequence of the original articles and presents an increasingly self-conscious narrative that at times delivers dizzying temporal effects. For instance, Jacques reports in the memoir that transitioning while writing about it in *The Guardian* 'added a layer of complexity to every social exchange' (226). But as the 'writing about it' is now written about in turn, the complexity is redoubled. This complexity has to do not only with a heightened self-reflexivity, but also with the paradoxes of trans visibility. On the occasion of one of Juliet's appointments at the gender clinic,[4] when the doctor recognises her as the author of the column, she realises that writing publicly about her transition carries a risk: '*If you write* anything *they don't like, they might throw you off the pathway*, I thought. *Yes, but if they do, you'll document it in the* Guardian, *so it wouldn't reflect well on them*' (218). The ability to present her own narrative in a national publication, a situation that contrasts with the historical silencing of trans voices in encounters with medical professionals, gives Juliet an unusual amount of agency while also entailing increased vulnerability. On the one hand, the articles provide gatekeepers in the healthcare system with additional information about her thoughts and feelings that may contradict whatever 'correct' narrative she may need to present in order to access technologies of transition, thereby 'throwing her off' the path toward hormones and surgery. On the other, her public platform can be used to express criticism of this very dynamic. While Jacques often cites trying to avoid 'perpetuating a stereotype of trans people as concerned mainly with themselves rather than their communities' (205) as the reason for being reluctant to write about her own transition, I see this scene as illuminating further reasons for her ambivalence toward publishing personal accounts of trans experience.

In one sense, *Trans: A Memoir* belongs quite straightforwardly to the genre that its title announces. The book covers Juliet's life in a mostly linear manner from her youth in the early 2000s to April 2013, shortly after her gender confirmation surgery. However, the text's structure goes some way toward complicating this. A first gesture of defiance is to place the account of the gender confirmation surgery at the beginning of the book. While this choice may not too dramatically unsettle the expected temporal order of transition, and may even seem familiar as a sort of 'cold open', it acquires particular significance as a re-narration. In fact, this first chapter is an exact reprinting of an article from the *Transgender Journey* column, which originally occurred in its 'proper' place in the chronological sequence of medical transition. Through this anticipation, Jacques defuses the climactic potential previously held by the surgery and signals a refusal to let it propel the narrative as the 'be-all and end-all' of her life (252). Frustrations of forward movement characterise the text at the level of both story (Juliet's experiences) and discourse (Jacques's narration of these experiences as a narrator). In a review of the book, Chu argues that *Trans* replaces a notion of transition as 'going places' with a 'going nowhere, slow', resulting both in 'making transition *boring*' and in developing an 'ethics of getting by' ('Wrong Body' 143). Jacques re-narrates a forward trajectory not by deviating, stopping or reversing its course (as other texts do), but by revealing its circularities and stagnations. Finding meaning beyond chrononormative demands for a strictly entertaining life story, the text testifies to the bureaucratic quagmire of medicolegal transition against the promise of a triumphant plot. The chronological unfolding of *Trans* ends with an uneventful last visit to the gender clinic designed to deny readers a satisfying closure, an anti-climax that Jacques explains she had to 'argue for', against an editor who felt like this should be 'a moment of triumph' ('Interview' 111). The interview that concludes the book, finally, most explicitly allows Jacques to expresses her ambivalence toward writing the narrative that has just finished.

A critique of two conventional trans temporalities – hormone time as linear and progressive change, and the 'becoming' narrative of sudden transformation into a woman through surgery – shapes the text implicitly and explicitly. The memoir shows uneasiness with both patterns by refusing to represent change as an abrupt shift or, alternatively, as a singular smooth path. In *Trans*, progressive steps toward increasing happiness and comfort are not a wrong description of the experience of transitioning, but they are a simplistic one. Juliet realises early on that the 'journey [will not] be as simple as moving from A to B' (Jacques, *Trans*, 175). After deciding to transition, she waits to come out at work until the end of her current contract, but she explains: 'going to work in my old shirt and trousers after coming out as transsexual proved to be one of the most dysphoric experiences of my life' (163). These contradictions are heightened when, now living full-time as a woman, she agrees to wear 'male clothes' at her brother's wedding (208). Looking into a mirror produces an effect of temporal discontinuity:

I thought back to 2004, when I'd worn these clothes and revelled in what I thought was androgyny. Looking back, I saw that time as a step towards transition, but returning to it felt like regression, even though I knew it was just for a day. (208)

An active moment of re-narration is shown here: while a certain appearance had in the past been placed in relation to a certain narrative of gender identity (androgyny), it is now retroactively fitted into a different narrative, that of a transition begun even before it was consciously embarked upon. This re-narration is itself occasioned by the repetition of this appearance in the present (a reappearance) now signifying not a 'step' but a 'regression' – all of this, in turn, is told in the past tense by a retrospective narrator. By showing that operations of re-narration (in the sense of challenging past narratives of the self) characterise the experience of transition and disturb a sense of linear progress, the text engages in a broader re-narration, in the sense of challenging shared narratives of transness that would hide how much re-narration it involves.

While the temporality of hormone time is challenged by thematic and formal displays of 'lag' – 'being out of temporal sync, left behind' and the 'negative affects associated with it' (Malatino 639) – the idea of a sudden becoming is critiqued in *Trans* by showing continuity. When the gender confirmation surgery, which is supposed to be the ultimate site of gender metamorphosis, is moved to the beginning of the book and isolated from the rest of the narrative, what is left is the account of a long transition process during which it is not always easy to register change. In the place that surgery would have occupied if the story was told chronologically, Jacques inserts a short reflection, entitled 'Before and After', on sensationalistic media coverage of 'sex change' as a quasi-magical transformation. The narrator recalls magazine articles with titles such as 'Now I'm a Beautiful Woman', dramatising trans people's changed appearance through juxtaposition of pre- and post-transition photos, and suggests that 'Before & After photographs have the effect of masking processes of change even as they ostensibly reveal them' (266). In wanting to expose 'the potentially limitless terrain' of smaller transformations that lie in the gaps between these extremes (for instance, the slow effect of oestrogen), Jacques critiques instant becoming by appealing to hormone time, a form of linear progression that is itself critiqued elsewhere in the text. The somewhat contradictory patterns of gradual change and sudden transformation can both become transnormative ways of imagining the body in relation to a future ideal, and they are therefore both questioned by Jacques at different points in the text. Following the 'Before and After' section, a new chapter begins in which Juliet returns to her childhood home to recover from surgery, viewing her life as 'a huge, traumatic circle' (272) which eventually becomes 'a newfound sense of peace with my past' (276). Transition is then also revealed to be going in the right direction not because it moves away from the past, however progressively or abruptly, but because it is a way to reconnect with it.

As the 'Before and After' reflection indicates, Jacques mixes personal experiences with commentary on trans history, politics and media. Every few chapters, short interludes organised around a specific topic – such as 'The History of Sex Change' (65) or 'Conundrum: The Politics of Life Writing' (203) – interrupt the chronological unfolding of the life narrative, placing Juliet's own story in a broader historical context. These sections are self-sufficient and detached from the primary timeline of the text; they are still in the voice of the autobiographical narrator, but they are not always filtered through personal experiences, and they gesture beyond the world of the experiencing-I with expressions like 'I hadn't known about it at the time' (31) and 'unknown to me as a teenager' (103). The presence of these sections has the effect of pausing and denaturalising the otherwise smoothly running account of Juliet's transition, by referring to events 'out of order', repeating material that occurs in the main chapters, or momentarily veering away from the self as the proper subject of the memoir. Like the interview that concludes the book, these sections also help contextualise and achieve a critical distance from the narrative, opening it up at various points to provide a longer history of the particular problems that Juliet is experiencing. For instance, chapter 4 ends with her sitting in a therapist's office just before she begins to speak, and chapter 5 resumes the scene there, with Juliet beginning to utter what will later become 'the well-rehearsed narrative of my gender variant youth' (218). In between the two chapters, however, the scene is interrupted by the interlude entitled 'The Birth of Transgender Theory', which introduces readers to authors like Stone, Bornstein, and Feinberg and to their efforts to nuance popular and medical cisnormative understandings of trans identity. It is with the knowledge that trans is a contested and multiply signifying label that we then begin to read Juliet's conversation with the therapist, a conversation in which she articulates a relationship to her gender that is itself subject to change over the course of the text.

A similar self-reflexive distance is achieved by references to how the experiences depicted in the memoir already have a textual presence. Of the medical appointment in which surgery is discussed for the first time, we read: 'Oddly, given how significant this was, I can't find any correspondence about the appointment or even remember it, and the words quoted here are the ones I published in the *Guardian*' (233). The more the milestones of transition are re-narrated, the more their 'significance' is displaced. The documentation of medicolegal transition in a range of public and private records is only part of what contributes to the denaturalisation of reality that comes to characterise it. An awareness of the precarious and intersubjective nature of reality can in fact result from the demand to embark upon the Real Life Experience (RLE), which is what gender identity clinics call the requirement to live full-time as one's avowed gender for a certain period of time (usually one year) before a surgery referral can be obtained. As Faye explains when discussing the practices of UK clinics, the RLE requirement means that

> trans people wishing to access surgery are tasked with demonstrating to doctors that they are actively seeking (and receiving) acceptance (or at least tolerance) from cisgender people within cisgender-dominated environments. This sense that you need the social consent of others to access surgery can be further intensified for trans people of colour and neurodivergent trans people. (94)

In *Trans*, Juliet is often able and willing to perform the correct steps that will speed up the process as much as possible. At her second appointment at the gender clinic, she explains that she has come out at work and to her friends and family, has changed her name on her documents, and is taking measurable steps to pass, such as starting hair-removal treatment and speech therapy. This is met with approval, and she is told, 'You're rare in sorting all of these things so early' (218). However, there is still a clear gap between the validation she receives and the depression, frustration, and fear that characterise her real experience – without capitals.

The re-narration of medicolegal milestones, as they are recounted in the column and then in the book, offers an opportunity to convey to readers the temporal experience of transition through formal manipulations of sequence and duration. On two different occasions, scenes in which Juliet is visiting a therapist or a doctor start with her being late, rushing around in fear of missing the appointment (Jacques, *Trans* 102, 235). As the surgery approaches, the narrator describes alternating feelings of 'just want[ing] it over so I can get on with my life' (252) and of the date seeming 'terrifyingly soon', since she does not feel 'at all ready' (237). At the same time, the monotony of waiting for appointments to be scheduled or take place is palpable in *Trans*, which stalls the narrative through diversions and repetitions to convey this. Juliet's experience reveals the link between the pace of transition and the economic status of the transitioning subject, as she is forced to conform to an externally imposed timeline because of her reliance on the UK National Health Service (NHS). As she cannot afford private healthcare, she is warned early on by her doctor that the process 'will be slow', showing that limited financial resources correlate with reduced agency in shaping the temporality of one's transition (150). Together with the discrepancy between Real Life Experience and real life experience, with the representation of change as sometimes gradual instead of sudden and sometimes sudden instead of gradual, and with the paradoxes of a process that can feel both too fast and too slow, the tempos of precarious employment and financial instability contribute to the temporal effects of the narrative, and Jacques describes her book as ultimately 'about being stuck in boring jobs' ('Interview', 112). The day-to-day routine of 'boring jobs' acts as deliberate re-narration of sensationalistic or exotic accounts of 'sex change'. In this way, the text continues its self-conscious comparison with other stories of transition by showing that its own plot progression is uniquely determined by the overlapping temporalities of neoliberal structures such as precarious short-term employment, the waiting lists of an underfunded NHS, and the unpredictable rhythms of freelance writing.

Jacques's life as writer and public figure begins to displace the traditional topics of the transition memoir in the final chapters of *Trans*, mirroring the same shift of focus in the life of the experiencing-I: 'I let myself wonder if, even before my surgery, the transition might cease to be the dominant aspect of my life' (245).

(Re)narrating the transition, rather than the transition itself, emerges here most clearly as the real subject of the narrative. Juliet's acts of self-narration accumulate throughout the text, from the childhood stories repeated to doctors and therapists, to articles she writes about queer and trans politics, to letters and emails to explain her transition to friends and co-workers, to the *Guardian* column and, finally, the memoir itself. This multiplication of narratives can be read as leading up to the moment of the text that is in many ways its actual climax: the realisation that the memoir is less a narrative of gender becoming and more a narrative of becoming a writer. In the interview that closes the book, Jacques gives this interpretation:

> When I think about who I dreamed of being [...] it wasn't that I had a certain conception of my body, because I was still figuring that out, but I had an idea of what sort of person I wanted to be—a writer. [...] and in a weird way I have become exactly that person. [...] I ended up taking such a circuitous route that I barely recognized my destination once I arrived. (308)

This statement re-narrates the beginning (desire for becoming, for transformation), the middle (a circuitous route), and the end (the 'barely recognised' destination) of the memoir as being about something other than, though not unrelated to, gender identity. If there is a process of maturation, a *Bildungsroman*, its resolution is brought about after a significant amount of misdirection. In this way, Jacques's re-narration maintains a relationship with what it deviates from: transition is still central to the memoir, but this is in part due to it being what allows Juliet to launch her writing career.

Even if *Trans*, with its chronological account of the author's transition, maintains a linear movement that is easier to track compared to the other texts I am about to discuss, this movement is in fact the result of a complex negotiation of progression that includes repetitions, stalling, disjunctures, and short-circuiting. Multiple and sometimes contradictory temporalities characterise both Juliet's experiences in the story and the construction of sequence and duration at the level of discourse. This is also self-consciously discussed in the text, as the I takes on an essayistic voice to offer commentary and context. Through the foregrounding of processes of writing, the text does not outright refuse to report the kind of personal experiences that the public wants to read, but it invites readers to consider how, why, and for whom these experiences are shared. Rather than an unfiltered personal truth that is known in isolation, transness is revealed to be made up of layers of textuality, shaped through interactions with others and bound up in representational traditions that offer ready-made forms such as the 'before and after', the triumphant ending, and the medicolegal 'pathway' – forms with which individual subjects may find themselves at odds. At the same time, the reality of transness, which the media discourses that Jacques continually struggles against would want to invalidate and erase, is affirmed in the plain account of the ordinary life of the experiencing-I. Alongside its richness of autobiographical detail, *Trans* achieves a critical distance from the act of telling one's story, which is partly rendered possible through the avenue of publication: the memoir is published by Verso, valued by Jacques in its being 'an explicitly left-wing publisher' ('Interview' 108). In this context, the re-narrating gestures of the text constitute not only the positioning of one's narrative as different from other possible alternatives, but, more specifically, as a political critique of neoliberal structures that shape transness as a relation to the medical establishment and the state, revealing how narrative can be complicit in these realities but also open up avenues for resistance.

## Travis Alabanza: Dinsnarrating the binary

While *Trans* shows the processes of re-narration resulting from writing autobiographically about a medicolegal process of transition, a transition narrative exists in Travis Alabanza's *None of the Above: Reflections on Life Beyond the Binary* only spectrally, at its margins. In a sense, this book is precisely about what it means to not transition, revealing how cisgender society punishes those who not only transgress the borders of the gender they are assigned at birth but neither do they take socially sanctioned steps toward another binary gender. A narrative of transition, for Alabanza, is something that has not happened, that may happen beyond the ending of this book, and that may not happen at all. Even as it centres autobiographically on its author, *None of the Above* eschews easy categorisation as a memoir: its subtitle announces its status as a collection of observations and theorisations about gender that draws on personal experiences in a non-chronological manner, to produce an accumulation of understanding for readers rather than a *Bildungsroman*-style journey of change for the narrator/author. Yet, throughout this process, the linear journey of transition still informs the text in some way – evoked as an external imposition, a narrative blueprint, or a suppressed possibility. Alabanza's award-winning book was published at the height of their career as playwright, performer, speaker, and activist honoured in the Forbes 30 Under 30 list and the Dazed100 list. What *None of the Above* makes clear, however, is that Alabanza's visibility as a public figure and generally as a Black, mixed-race, and gender-nonconforming person in Britain has made them the target of constant transphobic attacks. Alabanza's plays, published before this book, tellingly centre on fraught locations for trans subjects experiencing harassment: *Overflow* (2020) is the monologue of a trans woman delivered from a public toilet cubicle, and *Burgerz* (2018) is based on the author's experience of having a hamburger thrown at them on a London street. Persistent violence and gender policing also shape *None of the Above*, which is a re-narration not only in the sense that the text expresses an ambivalent relationship with the clichés and misunderstandings of canonical trans stories, but also in the sense that it articulates, in the negative and the hypothetical, a different life narrative: one that is not always already tainted and warped by cis norms.

This book is constructed explicitly as a response to the narratives of others. Each chapter is titled with a phrase that has been said to the narrator in a specific context – such as 'But I mean, *proper* trans' (35) or 'This ain't a thing we do round here, son' (94) – while also more generally illustrating the expectations and demands that are continually projected on to them. One of these phrases, 'Children sacrificed to appease the trans lobby' (153), is also the title of a 2017 article from *The Times* that most clearly exemplifies the need for re-narration as counter-narration. This article responded to the introduction of gender-neutral changing rooms by the retail chain Topshop by personally attacking Alabanza, who is considered to have prompted this policy after tweeting about their experience in one of the chain's branches. The policing of the presence of trans, non-binary, and gender-nonconforming individuals in gender-segregated spaces is a routine form of transphobia embedded in white heteronormative logics. Pearce, Erikainen, and Vincent have pointed out that cries to protect women-only spaces from trans people often 'have racist undertones, as the implicit whiteness of the women who are the subject of protection means that racialised and especially Black women and non-binary people are more likely to be considered dangerously masculine' (680). As with other phrases that inform the chapter titles of *None of the Above*, the alarmist title of the *Times* article reveals that Alabanza is viewed as posing a threat to white cisgender standards. Misguided narratives constructed by others prompt a desire to explain the truth, which is a clear impetus behind the book. However, the author shows ambivalence toward the act of explaining. In the prologue, they write, 'I start to write long sentences about how *None of the Above* will bring you an understanding of [long list of items follows]' (Alabanza 3). However, they eventually discard 'the desire to make things neat' (4), and state, 'I delete four paragraphs of efforts to aid you in understanding' (7). This gesture of renounced reliability announces the kind of re-narration we will be given: one that is less 'neat' than the simplistic and harmful paradigms of intelligibility that it wants to challenge.

As is anticipated by the reference to deleting paragraphs, re-narration in *None of the Above* often takes the form of discussing the material processes of writing, reading, and accessing paratextual information. When the narrator mentions performer David Hoyle, whose phrase 'Ladies, gentlemen and those lucky enough to transcend gender' is the title of chapter 3 (68), readers are instructed to take advantage of typographical space to do some research: 'I give you the next paragraph break to google him, so that we can all be up to speed on who he is' (69). The space of the page is referred to again later, this time to translate the narrator's experience into that of a reader: 'Harassment could be the only word written on this page and it still would not resemble how much it consumes your day when you present as we did' (149). The shapes that the text takes are used to illustrate, metaphorically or metonymically, the shapes of trans living. The same is the case with the explicit discussion of decisions made about event selection and sequencing, such as when Alabanza juxtaposes two temporally distant scenes: 'There is something in placing the 16-year-old in their room directly next to their hero on stage years later, that reminds me of the magic of transition and change' (71). References to the editing process – 'if you have read the last sentence, it means that I have chosen not to edit out my instincts' (135), or '[w]hen I first wrote this chapter, I had to delete most of it after giving it to a friend' (155) – serve a similar illustrative function by conveying a hesitation about speaking that is the result of being simultaneously silenced, misunderstood, spoken about, and compelled to speak as a trans person. The agency that Alabanza displays in shaping their own text contrasts with their powerlessness in the face of the words of others, a powerlessness they attempt to defy through acts such as printing out and cutting up the *Times* article that attacks them (161). Reflections on editing call attention to processes not only of narration, but specifically of re-narration: replacing, reworking, and reshaping previously existing narratives.

Through narrative gestures such as indicating that other versions of the story have been deleted, disnarration recurs in *None of the Above*. Disnarration, as I discussed in Chapter 1, names the acknowledging of narratives that the text is not. For Prince, the disnarrated serves a 'rhetorical/interpretive' function: at the level of discourse, it signals that '[t]his narrative is valuable because it follows a different and more interesting narrational strategy', and at the level of story, it communicates that 'this narrative is worth narrating because *it* could have been otherwise, because *it* usually is otherwise, because *it* was *not* otherwise' (Prince 5). *None of the Above* aims to convey both messages: the 'narrational strategies' that are not pursued are indicated as less 'interesting' only insofar as they are less apt for capturing the truth of trans experience, and this truth is valuable because certain genre conventions have given the impression that it 'usually is otherwise'. In chapter 4, when Travis is shamed in their neighbourhood for presenting as gender-nonconforming, the narrator makes sure to clarify that, at this point in their life, they were not struggling to accept their non-binary identity: 'That is not the theme of this chapter [...] the problem I had when I was 15 [...] is not self-acceptance, but others' doubt' (Alabanza 95). Because young Travis does not have a problem with 'self-acceptance', the usual forms that this story might take will not work: 'I am not going to give you the inspirational pathway to freedom from this moment of attempted shaming' (99). The expectations of cis audiences are the target of the disnarrated: it is only necessary to clarify what the experiencing-I did not feel and what the chapter is not going to be about because an existing body of narratives would lead one to believe otherwise. The narrator in fact goes on to explain that a 'neoliberal hijacking of gender politics' has created a culture in which 'often, the fixation with gender-non-conforming stories is whether or not we believe in ourselves' (95). The prejudices and privileges of cis people, rather than the trans person's struggles to accept themself, are instead reframed by disnarration as the focus of the text.

While the narrator often tells us that the book we are reading could have taken other directions, disnarration also extends to reflecting on how their life and sense of self could have been different, implying that the narrative of *None of the Above* might not have existed at all. These kinds of counterfactual statements relate to Alabanza's relationship with gender norms, imagining a version of events in which these norms had less of a hold on them: they are upward counterfactuals, situations 'in which a character constructs an improved version of reality' (Dannenberg 120).[5] Reflecting on how their way of embodying trans identity is policed by white cis and trans people alike, Alabanza envisions a life with more Black gender-nonconforming role models:

> It makes me wonder if my dysphoria is only here because I have spent too long looking at certain examples and markers of transition; that if I surrounded myself with more versions of those paving their own ways of being, I would not feel so trapped. (59)

Crucially, disnarrating this reality is a way to bring it about in the present. While it might be too late to erase the harm of being continually punished for falling short of white standards of womanhood, this text becomes a place in which Alabanza can share their research about trans historical figures like Marsha P. Johnson and Sylvia Rivera, who used 'so many words [...] to describe themselves' beside 'woman', and wonder '[i]f being understood by the gender binary is actually just trying to be understood by whiteness' (64). Normativities in relation to non-binary identity, Alabanza notes, have also begun to emerge, centring the 'white, skinny, masculine-of-centre person' (103). As with desires for 'reinstating only womanhood in figures like Marsha and Sylvia' (63), this normativity is itself counterfactual to 'history and present realities holding multiple ways to be non-binary' (102). What is expressed through acts of disnarration is therefore the pain of not having known more, sooner, about the historical realness of one's identity. A re-narration of white models of womanhood, transness, and non-binary-ness is effected in the text through an affective relation to suppressed realities.

But re-narration, for Alabanza, is not only an opportunity gained when writing their own story: it is also a demand, as trans subjects are continually required to repeat, explain, construct causal links. Pressure to re-narrate is particularly evident in chapter 1, titled with the phrase 'So, when did you know?' (15). The chapter opens with a brief scene in a doctor's office, in which Travis answers '*Always*' when asked this question, '*because I've heard simplicity gets results*' (15). As the chapter moves on to list a number of other situations in which the question has appeared, the narrator explains the difficulties of answering it. In addition to the fact that the 'simplicity' required by those who ask may be incompatible with the messiness of the truth, Alabanza points out that strangers appear bafflingly comfortable in displaying curiosity about something so private. This curiosity can only be met with equivocation: 'Sometimes, I need a punchier line to diffuse the affront, something along the lines of being raised by a pack of wolves who only spoke to me in quotes from Judith Butler books' (19). The instinct to reply with humour or defiance is an example of what I call renounced reliability, a way of signalling that the question should not be asked or cannot be answered in the terms in which it is posed. What becomes clear is that the asking already prescribes a narrow range of possible answers: 'People want to know [...] when you first tried on the red lipstick and dress from your mother's closet (even if you, in fact, never did)' (17). One of the text's many hypothetical or negative assertions, this 'never did' is perhaps a less clear example of disnarration than the ones I have mentioned so far, but it similarly confronts a counterfactual reality imposed by others. Alabanza is not confirming that the lipstick and dress did not happen, but is suggesting that others would expect it even if it was not the case. Being compelled to narrate something regardless of whether it has taken place, the chapter shows, ends up affecting the status of events that did/did not happen in one's memory, precluding the possibility to narrate even when one wishes to do so.

After outlining the simplifications and refusals they have given to others, the narrator does set out to consider in earnest the matter of when they 'knew'. However, they quickly discover that 'I can't find a memory untainted by the heavy lens of this questioning' (20). The memories that the narrator offers of dressing up, performing, and wearing heels are immediately framed by the reactions they have received from others when telling these stories in the past – a casting director once 'nodded, as if that was an answer that made sense to him, so he could move on' (27) – or that they imagine they would receive – 'If I were telling this story at a dinner party, in response to another person asking me the question yet again, I would receive full marks for this one' (25). There is also a lack of clarity in the text (and presumably in at least some of the situations in which Alabanza has received this question) about what exactly one is supposed to know – that they are trans? That they are not a boy? That they want to style their appearance in a certain way? This means that uncertainty pervades both the quest for signs and the truths they are supposed to signal. What Alabanza clarifies is not that these childhood stories did not happen, but that their status as 'signs' of something is not inherent in them but retrospectively imposed:

> In fact, *knowing* feels like the exact opposite of what encompassed that memory, because I was too busy *doing*. There was not a surrounding consciousness about my choices, my gender non-conformity or my early signs of anything – because I was allowed to be present: present in action, without speculation. (25)

In expressing the wish to experience being 'present in action, without speculation', the re-narration of this moment (and of moments in which this moment has been narrated) reveals the desire to not narrate. This is a way of both answering and not answering the question 'So, when did you know?', one which conventionally may be expected to guide the first chapter of a trans memoir.

As the text expresses the difficulty of accessing feelings and events that exist outside of a narrative of transness produced for others, Alabanza suggests that – while it unquestionably holds that they are not a man – the meanings and truths of their transness are constructed intersubjectively. The narrator calls upon the narratee as complicit in this situation: 'I am trans because of you, not because of me. I did not always know, because I once imagined a world where I would not have to know' (29). That identity is produced dialogically is already suggested by organising the chapters as responses to phrases spoken by others, and the use of the second-person pronoun in the text reinforces this. At times, as in the passage I have just quoted, the 'you' stands for a cisnormative reader, and one who has already 'read' Travis's identity before this book was written. At others, it is a generic 'you' that ends up referring to people in the narrator's situation, as when we are told, 'You often become a place to hold other people's confusion' (10). In this case, the 'you' is tantamount to an 'I'. In one instance, 'you' addresses a specific person, the one who has uttered the phrase that gives chapter 2 its title: 'But if at this point you are reading and have remembered this fleeting moment: I want you to know that I don't repeat it in scorn' (45). The you and the I are shifting identifiers, with respect to which the narrator negotiates their positon. Being addressed as a 'you' by other 'yous', with 'phrases that can only be said to the *you* that I am' (11), means that Alabanza's identity has to unfold within the parameters set by the cis structures in which we all participate. These structures interpellate us through making 'gender two unmoveable posts to define myself within' (31). Shifting the referents of 'I' and 'you' can then be read as a way to unsettle positions, to fluctuate between them, to chip at 'unmoveable posts'.

Creating a record of moveability and flux becomes an important goal of *None of the Above*. As much as narrative can signify coercion in this book, a demand to explain and disclose, it simultaneously provides a place for articulating what will otherwise be erased. The middle space between binary genders is seen by Alabanza as particularly at risk:

> despite an ever-growing fear of what it means to put unfinished thoughts, possibly wrong sentences, and opinions, on paper [...] I want to archive this version of myself as I sit in a liminal space. [...] I'm tired of the liminal space of gender non-conformity continually being seen just as something we pass through to get to something else. (197)

Asserting this becomes important even (and especially) when the narrator begins to wonder if a narrative of joyous liminality has ceased to define their life: they find themselves wanting to transition, be it for survival in a world that crushes those who do not pass in conformity with the binary or because the way they wish to embody their gender has simply changed. But because re-narration, for Alabanza, has been centred (in and before this book) on painstakingly affirming the validity of non-binary identity against a dominant narrative of transness as a journey from one point to its 'opposite', there is ambivalence about changing course. The book could in fact be seen as capturing a moment of 'transition' between a narrative of non-transition and a narrative of transition.

This is illustrated when Travis attends an appointment to have laser hair removal on their face: 'I tell the lady who is burning my hair off that I've always dreamed of not having this stubble [...] Yet this is not particularly true' (92). Catching themself in crafting this version of the past that covers over the pride they've previously taken in their beard, the narrator wonders when 'me with a beard and wearing a dress went from feeling like a lucky gift I had unlocked [...] to a damnation' (92). What is committed to the page here is an active and unfinished re-narration, rather than a complete and overarching counter-narrative. The narrator's liminal position as a non-binary person is amplified further by an ongoing remaking of the self – as soon as narratives are presented, they are questioned, edited, and revealed as provisional.

If uncertainty, as a space for doubt that does not invalidate the reality of transness, is necessary for a full and nuanced exploration of gender, re-narration is then not only a filling of the gaps left by other narratives, but an active creation of gaps. The question of gaps comes most prominently to the fore in the chapter titled 'So, what do you want me to call it?' (122), in which all the words for the narrator's genitals are replaced with '_____'. In a reported conversation with a lover, this open space renders all possible names equally provisional and re-signifiable, from the avowed preference – 'Just call it my _____ and be done with it' (124) – to humorous hypotheticals – 'but imagine if I called it _____' (124) – to options offered earnestly – 'If you want to call it _____ or _____ or even _____, just know that I asked' (125). Alabanza explains that being asked this question 'sits within a timeline of experiencing gender as something you are told about, instructed upon, and corrected if you fail at' (133). Just as they learn to claim the agency to choose words to name their body, they also exercise this agency by not disclosing them to readers of this book. To clarify how precious this agency is, the text turns once again to dis-narration and reflection on the process of writing: 'I laid out a plan to start this chapter with a phrase like, "I liked you better without/with the skirt"' (126). But, realising that by doing this they would be centring the desires of the men who have often harmed them, the narrator decides that '[c]isgender men have rid me of so much of my agency in the bedroom, I refuse to let them also be the beginning of this chapter, or its dominant theme' (127). With the blank spaces breathing gaps into cisnormative ways of understanding the body, memories of harm are pushed to the margins, even though 'it will be impossible for their smell not to linger on these pages and my life' (126). Like the ghost, a smell is an apt way to describe the status of the narratives that are being repeated, contested, and discarded through re-narration: an echo of presence, ambiguously substantial.

In *None of the Above*, gender is expressed through re-placing, re-moving, and re-formatting existing narratemes. This work is done by a narrator/author who self-consciously discusses acts of writing and claims the authority to refuse and delay definitive answers. If there are any answers, they lie in revealing the always incomplete process of understanding oneself in a world in which the expectations and misrecognitions of others can be deafening. At the beginning of the book, we are offered a series of spatiotemporal conceptualisations that go beyond gender as a journey:

> *Cis people ask me what my gender feels like and that never allows me to say what my gender really is.*
> *My gender is something stopped halfway through.*
> *A badly formatted tape-to-CD conversion, missing full potential.*
> *The second character on a video game, without levels, no up or down.*
> *It is an unfinished–* (13)

These images convey experiences that are inscribed in the materiality of different media, imperfect renditions of something that might have existed elsewhere in its wholeness. Throughout the list, it remains unclear whether these metaphors are presented for or against a cis gaze, which still 'never allows' one to say what 'gender really is'. Alabanza's re-narration is a record of disentangling themself from the stories they are not telling. This re-narration can be understood in different forms: a spectral relationship with a transition narrative that the text is not; a wish to tell a different story than the one they are telling, not weighed down by white cis norms and violence; a provisional counter-narrative contesting transphobic views, which sometimes can only happen through leaving gaps; a testimony of the impossibility of narrating truth once one has been asked to narrate so many times. All these facets of re-narration appear at the same time, in an active and unfinished process that continues up to the last stages of editing and is only – for now – frozen in time by publication.

## Kai Cheng Thom: Confabulous layering

So far, I have focused on non-fictional re-narrations: real-life accounts in which highly self-conscious narrators reflect on how their own story exists in relation to other – previous, dominant, sometimes misleading – narratives. To some extent, this is also the case with Kai Cheng Thom's *Fierce Femmes and Notorious Liars: A Dangerous Trans Girl's Confabulous Memoir*. But what this book also reveals is that the mixing of genres (fictional and non-fictional) can become a crucial avenue to explore factual and counterfactual truths and histories, the creation of the self in time, and the relationship between trans identity and narrative forms. Thom's career as a writer spans several genres, from poetry to journalism to children's picture books. Her advice column for *Xtra Magazine* – 'Ask Kai: Advice for the Apocalypse' – also embeds a nod to fictional imaginings in its title as it figures the difficult world experienced by her and her readers as an 'apocalypse', and often references famous poems, novels, and plays as a springboard for answering readers' letters about real-life situations. An emphasis on surviving and flourishing in a dangerous environment, with stories and imagination as tools to become strong together, also characterises *Fierce Femmes*. While this book takes place in a fictional setting, there are indications that it takes some of its material from Thom's experience as a young person growing up in a Chinese community in Vancouver and then encountering love and protection among other trans women of colour in a new city. As an important voice in Canadian queer and trans culture alongside figures like Casey Plett and Trish Salah, Thom is involved in shaping transnational discourses of gender. But specifically Canadian realities, such as the legacies of settler colonialism, become part of Thom's reimagined world, in the same way in which the persistence of transphobic views in the liberal press and the status of NHS services in the UK characterise the context to which Jacques and Alabanza (in different decades) are responding.[6] Ultimately, Thom's re-narration is a layering of stories that confound the boundaries between fact and fiction, to tell truths that eschew the parameters for understanding trans identity that have been set in dominant (white and middle-class) Western cultures.

Re-narration in the form of announcing what this narrative is not (a dynamic I have noted at work in other texts too) appears in

*Fierce Femmes* from the first page. In a prologue called 'Dangerous stories' (1), the narrator offers an account of the genesis of the book we are reading, which begins with describing a programme about a trans woman on television and ends with the television exploding into a swarm of butterflies. The programme prompts reflections on the 'archetype that trans girl stories get put into':

> if you're good and brave and patient (and white and rich) enough, then you get the big reward... which is that you get to be just like everybody else who is white and rich and boring. And then you marry the prince or the football player and live boringly ever after. We're like Cinderella, waiting to go to the ball. [...]
> Those are the stories we get, these days.
> Or, you know, the ones where we're dead.
> Where are all the stories about little swarthy-skinned robber trans girls waving tiny knives made of bone? (3)

Simplistic fairy-tale plots, behaviours authorised by cis audiences, and the endings that exist for trans women in popular culture are all invoked here as narrative elements in need of transformation. Instead, this book offers the stories of a diverse community of trans women, girls, and femmes who are friends, enemies, lovers, and eventually members of a gang that terrorises local predators and transphobes. As Malatino points out when arguing that this text embodies the affects of lag time, the difference between 'princess narratives and accounts of brutal homicide [...] hinges on questions of racial and economic status' (650). Rather than investing in the hope that following the correct steps will lead to rewards afforded in reality only to those who are most privileged, Thom shifts the focus on to the 'scrappy inventiveness, creativity, and intimacy cultivated by trans folks to survive in radically imperfect, irreparably broken worlds' (Malatino 647). In proposing to craft 'a transgender memoir, but not like most of the 11,378 transgender memoirs out there, which are just regurgitations of the same old story that makes us boring and dead and *safe* to read about' (Thom 3), *Fierce Femmes* refuses to blunt the sharp edges and jolting euphorias of trans living.

The emphasis of Thom's re-narration is danger: stories – like trans femmes – can fight back, by taking on material existence and spilling out into the world. Stories with the agency to disturb and transform are both an inspiration for creating the text we are reading – as the narrator wishes to tell '[t]he kind of story that doesn't wait for you to invite it to enter' (1) – and a recurring presence in the text itself. The City of Smoke and Lights, the main setting of the book, is a space of reinvention, where the fairy-tale fantasy of 'anything can happen if you dream it' (20) is reappropriated to illustrate the miraculous resourcefulness of those who are most harmed by white patriarchal powers. The narrator explains, 'As soon as a tall tale leaves your wicked mouth, it falls to the ground, moist and warm, wriggling with thick possibility. It sinks in deep, puts down roots' (20). Narratives are embodied, take on flesh: they can poison the world and they can enact justice. Community storytelling is presented as the main way in which the lives of trans femmes are not only preserved – as objective recording of truth – but invented, engendering their own possibilities. As the text progresses, the individual narratives of various characters are introduced gradually, often in stand-alone analeptic chapters with titles such as 'The legendary romance of Kimaya and Rapunzelle' (44) or 'The legend of Valaria the Goddess of War' (91). Sometimes, these stories are conveyed through dialogue, with the narrator reporting both the story she is told and the circumstances of this telling. When she asks for 'Valaria's story', for instance, we are given a description of how each friend contributes to it: 'the other femmes jump in, taking over and adding to the narrative so that Valaria's past is handed to me in a tapestry woven with femmes' voices' (92). The book explicitly defies a distinction between fact, hearsay, and imagination – to which a further layer is added if we consider the text as being in some way autobiographical and connected to 'real' people – and figures stories variously as intruders, weapons, wriggling creatures, inherited objects, and building blocks of identity.

A refusal to pinpoint clear distinctions between historical detail, exaggeration, metaphor, and invention characterises the 'confabulous' style of the text: the use of this word in the book's subtitle evokes joyful and defiant acts of gossiping, conspiring, misleading, and dazzling. The first chapter situates the narrator historically and geographically by way of a myth-like re-narration of Canadian colonialism in her native city of Gloom: 'Gloom was built on the edge of the sea, on land that was once inhabited solely by several Indigenous nations to whose peoples the land and the water were sacred' (7). The bleak weather of Gloom is explained to be a consequence of the settlers' violence: 'because they had won in so corrupt a fashion, the sky and the ocean have been sad ever since' (7). While confabulation, in psychology, is tied to misremembering and the fabrications that arise from memory gaps, the confabulous in *Fierce Femmes* signals an alchemic transformation of truth into something greater than itself, in tension with 'fables' (both to be contested and to be created) and in reverence to the 'fabulous' beauty and strength of trans women. The confabulous is an instance of what Salah calls 'trans genre', which 'associates cross genre writing with writing that interferes with or intervenes in the classification of gender' (182). The genre of Thom's book escapes definition in the same way in which its characters resist the narratives that have been prescribed for them. Rather than providing a careful immersion into an unfamiliar counterfactual storyworld, *Fierce Femmes* makes quick and indiscriminate use of realistic and fantastical settings and elements. For example, the presence of mermaids in Gloom is casually alluded to in the second chapter, when we are told that they are dying: 'To this day, not a single scientist has come up with an explanation for this – except, of course, that we had poisoned the seas with our oil and trash, and that it was the end of the world, which everyone knew already' (Thom 11). The mermaids are never mentioned again in the text, remaining an ambiguous symbol that is used once but has the potential to resonate thematically in multiple ways, especially considering popular associations of mermaids with transness.

Alongside elements like mermaids and cursed weather, the characters' stories that variously make up and interrupt the plot of the text have the style of folk tales, featuring witches, warriors, and royals, often to metaphorically connote strengths and feats that may appear superhuman. The language of myth is used to soothe pain by deflecting from the ordinary horrors experienced by marginalised subjects, and magic represents a way to escape realities in which the agency of trans women of colour is severely compromised and to symbolise lifelines that feel nothing short of miraculous. When the narrator hears and reports Valaria's story, in which she is called 'the Duchess' because this was once her drag name, we learn that Valaria's past lover was killed in a homophobic attack. The femmes equivocate about what happened next:

> they're sure that some kind of terrible magic was made that night, that the Duchess sold her soul or some other precious part of herself in return for the chance to speak with her lover's ghost, or perhaps

for invincibility in battle, or maybe just for relief from the pain of her sorrow. (95)

Magic here is figured as the only way to explain Valaria's extraordinary resilience. At the same time, the failure of magical solutions is revealed elsewhere in the stories from the City of Smoke and Lights, especially if these solutions are the ones offered by cis narratives. In the story of Alzena the Witch, we learn that Alzena used to wish 'for a handsome, rich man to take her away from the poverty and desperation that she lived in' (134). But when this man finally arrived, 'the only catch was, he was already married to a nice white lady in the suburbs' (135). While fantastical elements are embraced in order to celebrate and make sense of the miraculous survival of trans femmes, reminders not to rely on patriarchal myths of happiness are offered to affirm the existence of those that cannot participate in dominant narratives of hope: re-narration operates in multiple directions, to show that the reality of these characters is both more and less 'fabulous' than what other texts have led us to expect.

While the stories of these characters realise the intention announced in the text's prologue to depart from stories 'where we're dead' (3), affirming the existence of trans femmes of colour against erasure does sometimes take the form of registering lost lives. For instance, a chapter titled 'The story of Soraya' (65) does not feature this character's story in a straightforward sense, but begins with detailing the narrator's regret of not learning it before Soraya was murdered:

> Soraya's story. Why didn't I ask her before it was too late? [...]
> How many stories of trans girls have been lost here?
> Soraya's story. I invent the details to the sound of the moth's wingbeats: She was born in a city far from here, to immigrant parents a little like mine. (68)

Acts of re-narration like correcting, disputing, and embellishing are shown here to give way to acts of invention when this is the only way to deal with absent stories. Along with her imagined story, Soraya's name is also added in this chapter to a list of others. This recalls the way in which trans murder victims are enumerated around the world in observance of the Transgender Day of Remembrance, forming what a poem by Awkward-Rich calls a 'flock of names' ('Anti-Elegy'). In Awkward-Rich's poem, the stories of the dead appear as fleeting syntactical fragments that refuse to fully reanimate them, expressing an ambivalence toward 'the insistence that someone ought to be alive in a world that did little to support that life' (Awkward-Rich, 'Craft Capsule'). In Thom's version of this listing, the focus subtly shifts from mourning lives ended to affirming lives lived: 'I can hear some of their names filtering through the murmur of the crowd: *Marilene. Lotte. Ilsa*' (65). The lives of lost femmes take substance through the shared voice of the 'crowd', the community that endures, in a practice of storytelling that, like Awkward-Rich's poetry, 'takes death as its impetus, but not its object, that mourns but also (and because of this) hopes' (Awkward-Rich, 'Craft Capsule'). As important as the enumeration of the dead, in *Fierce Femmes*, is the enumeration of the living.

Around twenty different trans women and femmes are named in the text, some only once, some twice, some with an accompanying 'story', some as fully fleshed-out recurring characters. Many unnamed others are alluded to as being present with the narrator in certain scenes, as living and working in the neighbourhood, and as having witnessed the legendary moments retold. Together with the episodic nature of the narrative, the proliferation of these characters orients the I of the text in multiple directions within a constellation of other trans subjects, with whom she compares herself and creates bonds that produce her identity in a relational manner. The listing of third-person characters sometimes has the effect of establishing the narrator as the perceptual centre of the text, as in this very literal example: 'I look around and I see Noor, Morena, Laurentine to my left. Ivana, Ying, and Alzena to my right' (139). But the presence of so many others in the story of the I also has the effect of diffusing the focus from the latter. Even if undergoing a linear and individual journey – which still does in some way occur as the protagonist grows, transitions, learns, increasingly accepts herself, and travels toward and away from cities – the text shows a self entangled, and at times disappearing, in a collective story. In the City of Smoke and Lights, the narrator is first welcomed by Kimaya, who runs the health centre for trans women and sex workers at the heart of the community, and who represents the opening up of a new world: 'Kimaya's smile is a key: it opens doors to places that I desperately want and am afraid to go. It is a map, guiding the way. [...] It feels like sisterhood. It feels like open arms. It feels like home' (41). A destination (home) and a departure (map) are offered to the narrator by Kimaya. As we are gradually introduced to the other women – a cast of friends, lovers, enemies, and allies – this world expands to encompass a network of intersecting departures and destinations.

The way in which the focus on individual identity is dispersed through the proliferation of other characters mirrors the stylistic diversity of this trans genre text. In between chapters of the main narrative, which I have already described as episodic and pluri-directional, poems frequently appear in sections entitled 'from my notebook–', and letters to the narrator's sister conclude each of the five 'parts' of the book. Both the poems and the letters re-narrate elements of the main narrative in various ways. The poems revolve around the object of a pocket knife, 'someone I keep with me / always' (30), insisting on a part of the narrator's interiority, her guardedness, that serves to clarify some of her motivations. Toward the end of the book, the boundary between the poems and the narrative is breached: a chapter about a 'storytelling night', in which the narrator is about to take the stage, ends with the sentence 'I open my mouth and begin to speak' (141) and is immediately followed by a section 'from my notebook–' presenting the poem that she performs. The letters, instead, construct a sanitised version of the events that have unfolded in the main narrative; after attacking a strange man who harasses her on her way to the City of Smoke and Lights, the narrator writes to her sister, 'I slept on the bus the whole way here, and I didn't even talk to anyone or get into any fights or anything' (31). The poems and the letters contribute to forming the narrator as an elusive figure, offering us glimpses into her half-disavowed feelings and instincts as well as into the narratives of herself that she produces for others. The narrator is never named, forging an undecideable relation between this ambiguous I and its author. This is the already slippery identity of the individual that blends into the collective narrative of the community. Sometimes, her function is simply that of a witness, fleeing classification as an 'auto'-diegetic narrator: two chapters, 'Overheard: Lucretia and Valaria' (97) and 'Overheard: Kimaya and Rapunzelle' (148), adopt the style of a playscript to which the I is positioned as hidden audience. The narrator's description of herself as an 'escape artist' (7) seems apt for describing this movement at the boundaries of first person(s).

The question of escape is also focused thematically through a rejection of middle-class respectability. In a re-narration of dominant academic values, the text centres the diffidence of the femmes toward the interests of a group of researchers who 'call themselves the Social Justice Warriors of the Ivory Tower, and they want to write a book about us or something' (102). When they visit the university, the femmes are surprised at being asked their 'preferred pronouns': 'Ivana snorts, as though she can't believe that university people have the time to worry about things like that' (104). At this meeting, the narrator meets a trans boy called Josh, a university student who takes an interest in her writing and who seems to promise a future hitherto unimaginable: 'And then I'll get published and become a super-famous Transgender Writer, and we'll get married and be a Transgender Power Couple, and have Transgender Children and raise them on a cloud of Transgender Happiness™' (178). Through the romance with Josh, the genre of the text seems to get away from the narrator:

> What is even happening to me? I'm not this girl, in a dress, in a car owned by a boy with blue eyes who goes to university.
> This is someone else's story, someone else's teen romance. Where's my weirdo punk transgender novel life gone? (167)

Despite the relationship proceeding smoothly, the narrator remains suspicious, as it feels 'like somebody cast a magic spell' (177). Even if the 'magic' seems to be working for this particular character, whose Prince Charming does not fail her like the already married lover of Alzena the Witch, the end of the relationship is presented as inevitable, as the narrator explains, 'I ran away to find myself, and so that I would never, ever be stuck in a story that someone else wrote for me' (185). The novel promises and refuses the climax of class mobility, which it equates with fairy-tale transformation: it regains agency against the 'spell' of a normative ending and celebrates the 'confabulous' present of the narrator's current life, with its disappointments and pains, rather than whisking her away from it.

The re-narration of this ending, which is anticipated in its familiarity and then disrupted, is accompanied by a direct address: 'Oh, please. Don't look so surprised, now. You knew this was coming' (185). Readers are lured to engage their genre expectations and explicitly confronted with their failure (or rewarded for not taking the bait), the narrator metaleptically returning their gaze by reading their potential surprise. The relationship with a 'you' is engaged from the start, as the narrator asks in the prologue, 'Where are those kinds of stories about trans girls like you and me?' (1). While the 'you' who might have anticipated the ending is less clearly defined, this one is explicitly imagined as another trans girl. Not unlike the narrator's own identity, the you is a shifting and elusive position, multiply gendered, variously cis or trans, bringing to the text normative expectations or a desire to hear a new story. Direct address elsewhere in the book appears to accompany moments of re-narration in action, often serving to displace the importance of factuality. At one point, the narrator describes being trapped in a swarm of bees without being stung. Then, she interrupts herself: 'Wait. Sorry. That's not what happened. Here is what happened' (17). In this second version of the story, some of the bees become trapped in the protagonist and become a recurring symbol of dysphoria, disconnection from the body, and fear. Later, a similar backtracking occurs. When the narrator kills a policeman who was beating up another femme, the situation seems hopeless as the characters hear approaching sirens and contemplate the horrors of incarceration. But the narrator intervenes again: 'No, wait. That's not what happened' (113). After a sort of cinematic rewind, we are offered a changed ending: vines sprout to cover the dead body and hide it in the ground. The injunction to 'wait' draws in the reader/narratee as a co-conspirator, a participant in a collective storytelling and reimagining of realities through miraculous and metaphorical solutions. While Alabanza's references to editing and rewriting centred on how to disentangle their reality from the narratives that have become superimposed on to it, Thom does the work of re-entangling, confounding any notion of what the original story might have looked like 'before' re-narration.

*Fierce Femmes* ends with one last letter to the narrator's sister, which offers a metafictional reflection:

> Someday, I'm going to gather up all of the stories in my head. All the things that happened to me and all the things I wish had happened. I'm going to write them all down one after the other, and I'll publish a famous best-selling book and let history decide what's real and what's not. Because maybe what really matters isn't whether something is true or false, maybe what matters is the story itself: what kind of doors it opens, what kind of dreams it brings. (187)

Summing up the text's investment in the agency of stories and the power of truths remembered or imagined, this passage invokes the authorial figure perhaps most explicitly out of all the self-reflexive gestures of the narrating-I. While claiming the authority to tell one's version of events, concerns with giving a reliable account of facts are firmly displaced here in favour of conveying layered realities. I take up this issue again in Chapter 4, in which I explore the political and formal dimensions of reliability. Thom's transformed and transformative reality takes shape through many more ambiguous symbolic elements beyond the ones I have mentioned, including the sexual touch of a Ghost Friend and a doctor called Mr Crocodile to whom the narrator pays a mysterious price for accessing transition care. Most importantly, the text's truth is created through the texture of collective storytelling. The invocation of shared folk narratives serves different functions: criticising 'fairy-tales', delighting in the community's own 'myths' and 'legends', recording and sharing trans stories, conveying what confabulously exceeds the narratives assigned to marginalised subjects, and dispersing the self beyond a clearly delineated individual identity. The network of relations around the narrator is not a utopia free of pain and conflict: the femmes fight, hurt each other, and sometimes hate each other, but maintain a foundational solidarity against the outside forces that wish to harm them. In this complex context, the distance of other existing and potential narratives from the reality of the characters is both an injustice to be denounced and a resource to be exploited.

### Time will tell

The temporalities that emerge from the texts I have discussed retain more or less explicit traces of the transition journey as a unidirectional, teleological, and individualised movement from one gender to another, but this long-established metaphorical understanding of transness becomes a model to be expanded, negotiated, or rejected.[7] At the same time as trans narrators' textual operations challenge canonical narratives of change that are specific to a trans normativity, they also re-narrate a *Bildungsroman* structure of 'maturation' from the experiencing-I to the narrating-I. Through intersecting, interrupting, and layering different narratives, the meanings that 'being trans' takes are produced discursively, through re-narration of other texts and through intersubjective negotiations of identity. As autobiographical I, the narrator in these texts self-consciously shapes pre-existing material from the past, simultaneously reflecting on the extent to which it is possible or valuable to make visible certain truths about trans life: while it seems necessary to represent erased experiences, this visibility can result in increased scrutiny, invasive curiosity, and even threats to one's safety. In the first person, Jacques, Alabanza, and Thom authoritatively shape a past, present, and future for the self while creating a connection between the person speaking and the author, re-narrating the latter's memories, experiences, and projections for others. In this outward-facing gesture, trans narrators exercise the agency to articulate identity on their own terms. But because this must be done in a manner that is intelligible to an audience, the demand to speak by re-narrating (narrating yet again) is also resisted, in the form of distorting or deviating from what is expected. In order to gauge these expectations, various audiences are imagined in turn – trans, cis, hostile, sympathetic, familiar, or unfamiliar – and occasionally addressed through a 'you'. The gaze of a heterogeneous group of potential readers shapes these re-narrations, meaning that some gaps are filled, other gaps are created, old understandings are discussed, new logics are explained. In the process, the sequences, tempos, durations, and rhythms that these different readers might anticipate are reorganised, sometimes (almost) beyond recognition.

What Jacques, Alabanza, and Thom re-narrate – to different extents – is their life, but also other available narratives of gender identity, as well as the possible stories they could have told and the possible ways in which they could have told this story. Re-narrating means reworking the temporalities of these 'other' narratives by variously reproducing them, repurposing them, departing from them, or contrasting them head on. While Jacques's narrative in *Trans* features some identifiable steps, starting points and destinations of a canonical transition narrative, its narrator self-consciously crafts a story that insists on acts of writing and foregrounds the disorienting effects of transitioning while writing about it, as well as of becoming a writer while transitioning. The pacing of the transition experience, and of its narrative, is shaped by a multiplicity of external forces, producing temporalities that are in tension and sometimes even in contradiction with one another. A political critique of normative (trans) gendering as shaped by white patriarchal and capitalist structures also characterises *None of the Above*. Alabanza shows that renarration is both a demand to resist (when being asked to probe into the past to make sense of a current gender) and a prerogative to claim (when editing the story to refocus truths against the grain). Confronted with the past misrecognitions of others and with the possible future freedom of discovering oneself beyond them, the text dwells in the present, showing an identity in active formation as reflection on, and remixing of, existing ways of ordering and fixing transness. Thom similarly conveys a present in the process of being shaped, evoking and refusing normative endings and celebrating instead the precarious but enduring day-to-day resourcefulness of marginalised communities. The narrator's elusive identity (an I that moves between styles, genres, and versions of the self) is woven into a tapestry of other stories – overheard, remembered, and imagined – which ambiguously overlap with existing realities, are rooted in diverse pasts, and orient characters toward multiple futures. Particular temporalities (as well as traditions for representing the body and mechanisms for attributing reliability) are encoded in different genres: my reading of *Fierce Femmes* has begun to indicate how trans narrators can make use of generic conventions to write beyond autobiographical constraints, a question that continues to emerge in the chapters to follow.

The 'truth' of trans narrators – and, with it, the autobiographical pact according to which readers would view the experiences of these narrators as being the ones of their authors – does not always function according to the criteria of externally verifiable objectivity. The latter, as the authors I discuss often make explicit, is precisely the tool employed by cis authorities that police the borders of gender identities. Telling the truth is instead a matter of first-person authority: the expertise that trans people have about themselves. I have noted Bettcher's argument that first-person authority – a 'superior epistemic position' ('First Person Authority' 98) – should be ethically attributed to trans individuals when they make statements about their gender, as they have been historically dispossessed of their 'capacity to avow' (114). Exercising the capacity to avow the truth of one's gender can take the form of emphasising the discrepancies between different accounts of the same transition experience (in *Trans*); of leaving a blank space to designate parts of the body that are in a continuous process of being re-signified (in *None of the Above*); and of offering magical/metaphorical explanations for pain and for healing (in *Fierce Femmes*).

These ways of affirming a complex reality sidestep the demand to construct a simple, plausible, coherent, and finite story of transness that would be judged as acceptable by an external observer. As I move on to focus more explicitly on the truths about gender that are conveyed by trans authors through textual embodiments, I take up notions of the multiplication of the I that have already been raised in this chapter: in Jacques's repetitions of her own first-person narrative across print media, in Alabanza's suggestion that their I is made of the multiple 'yous' projected on to them by others, or in Thom's creation of a relational and collective identity by which the narrator is formed alongside and through the stories of others. More broadly, trans-inhabitation already starts with the ordinary situation of the I designating different versions of itself as narrator and character (and as 'author'), sometimes successively, sometimes simultaneously, and sometimes ambiguously.

## Notes

1. I have chosen not to mark or theorise distinctions between memoir, autobiography, and other forms of life writing. Some of the texts I discuss are classed as memoirs, some are not – when I refer to autobiographical writing by trans people, I often designate a broad range of acts of 'telling one's own story'. This can take the form of a traditional memoir, of essayistic writing encompassing reflections on personal experience, of hybrid semi-autobiographical and semi-fictional forms, and more.
2. An early version of this analysis appears in Pellegrini, 'Posttranssexual Temporalities'.
3. A British Social Attitudes Survey conducted in 2020 indicates that the majority of British people feel positively or neutrally toward trans people (Morgan et al.). Despite this, transphobic views are almost ubiquitously represented in major UK media outlets in the name of providing a 'balance' of perspectives whenever trans issues are reported. For an example of both anti-trans policy and the uncritical reporting of anti-trans views, see the BBC's 'Trans Women May Be Banned from Women's NHS Wards'. See also Jacques's *Front Lines: Trans Journalism 2007–2021* (2022), which reprints many articles discussing, among other topics, the pervasive attacks by governments and the media on trans rights.
4. When discussing autobiographical texts, I often mark a distinction between the author, designated by their surname, and the character,

designated by their first name as would be the case with a character in a fictional narrative. The narrator, of course, remains an ambiguous entity that exists in between the two.

5 Occasionally, alternative realities are imagined in which gender norms have more, not less, of a hold on the narrator, as in the assertion that '[t]here is a version of my life where I continued to look like and accept that I was what they told me I was: a man' (87). This is a downward counterfactual, a situation 'in which a character imagines how his or her life might have been worse' (Dannenberg 120), and Alabanza employs it rarely, focusing on present harms rather than hypothetical ones. The widespread use of 'his or her' as in the definition I just quoted coincidentally provides an example of the binary reality that Alabanza has to confront.

6 With this shift from a British context (itself mostly limited to Southern England) to a Canadian one, I cannot hope to meaningfully account for the ways in which geographical variations affect acts of re-narration in mainstream anglophone trans literature. The nature of case studies is to make generalisations difficult. But what I can do, in this chapter and in the ones that follow, is show some forms that re-narration can take, which should make it easier to spot this dynamic at work in other texts.

7 The chapter has ended up focusing mostly on trans women and transfeminine narrators. There could be a number of reasons why these narratives have presented themselves to me as particularly illustrative examples of re-narration; a possible answer could lie in the greater cultural visibility of narratives about trans women, creating a more widely recognisable canon for a new author to acknowledge and challenge. But narratives of transmasculinities also contain re-narrations, as I show at other points in this book, for instance as they distance themselves from narrative identities such as that of the butch woman or that of the man who seamlessly benefits from patriarchal privilege after transitioning.

Chapter 3

# Trans Narrators and Embodiment: Textual Corporeality and Gender Multiplicity

When constructing corporeality, trans narratives engage, multiply and elude classificatory principles. In the three texts that I discuss in this chapter – Akwaeke Emezi's *Freshwater*, Calvin Gimpelevich's *Invasions*, and Alison Rumfitt's *Tell Me I'm Worthless* – innovative strategies for representing trans narrators' bodies are rooted in the traditions of the different genres to which the books belong as well as in specific cultural contexts. While similarly negotiating dominant understandings of gender that circulate in Western anglophone culture, these narratives inflect embodiment according to different paradigms: Emezi articulates an Igbo metaphysics that challenges African and American corporeal orderings; Gimpelevich's relationship with non-hegemonic masculinities and queer cultures in the US influences the fluidity of embodied gender in his stories; and Britain's imperial history and its legacies of racist and gendered violence are explicitly weaved into Rumfitt's Gothic imaginings. In what I call trans-inhabitation, the body, gender, and the narrator are simultaneously one, less than one, and more than one: they are singular, plural, and under erasure. Pluri-directional crossings, ambiguous hauntings, and a fleeting selfsameness characterise these texts; however, the solidity of community belonging, of personal agency, and of safe dwelling places is still an object of positive investment, highlighting desires for the stability of 'inhabitation' alongside the fluctuations of 'trans'. The goal of finding some sort of 'home' in the body (and undertaking a journey that takes one there) persists despite, and sometimes precisely because of, an awareness that homes and bodies are metaphorical and material sites of political conflict. The destination of the journey may then be not an entirely new and perfect home but a multiplied, fragmented, or expanded home, as Hayward suggests when she writes, 'We create embodiment by not jumping out of our bodies, but by taking up a fold in our bodies, by folding (or cutting) ourselves, and creating a transformative scar of ourselves' ('Starfish' 73). Regardless of the presence or prominence of medical interventions that might come to constitute such a 'cutting', trans narrators fold and proliferate their textual bodies and the gender categories that these bodies occupy and exceed.

If the borders of the embodied self and its semantic designations are porous, so are the boundaries between narrative worlds. I have already noted some ways in which a reaching across diegetic levels can occur – to start with, by referring to the 'external' voice telling the story and the 'internal' protagonist of this story with the same 'I'. With this link, the possibility of contact and exchange between distinct entities, and thus a relaxing of narrative borders, is already established. As Fludernik reminds us when discussing metaphorical extensions of the crossing of diegetic boundaries that occurs with metalepsis, 'the ontology of narratological levels exists only in the mind of readers and critics' ('Metalepsis' 396). In this chapter, I focus on texts that call into question a number of ontological separations: the one between this narrator and other narrators, between this character and other characters, this setting and other settings, this storyworld and other storyworlds. This is not to say that these distinctions prove themselves to be unnecessary; they do, however, prove themselves to be trans-inhabitable. Emezi, Gimpelevich, and Rumfitt create textual indeterminacies and contradictions that amplify the ways in which trans narrators (and perhaps all narrators) routinely engage in trans-inhabitation. In Chapter 1, I indicated some forms that this takes: presence and location that are ambiguous or in flux; fluctuations in detail and precision when representing the body (sometimes differentially in relation to other bodies); movements within, across, and between identity categories and corporeal presentations; and foregrounding the way in which the narrator shares an identity with a multiplicity of experiencing selves. When Bey argues for 'gender-self-determination' as a 'movement toward dissolving given gender ontologies', we are reminded that the use of taxonomies is inextricable from a history of racialised and gendered violence (24). In this chapter, I often focus on the extent to which it is possible to textually encode what Bey calls 'illegible genders, genders that abolish the bestowal of gender, genders that allow us all to be and become expansively outside the very desire to have to bestow onto ourselves gender' (24). I am interested, however, in how this occurs in narratives that, while being often lyrical, anti-mimetic, or experimental, on the whole confer to their narrators recognisable character developments, retaining textual distinctions between narrative agents and spaces even as they play with them.

Through fragmentations, redoublings, and escapes, trans-inhabiting narrators still claim a unified wholeness from which it is possible to speak. An ambivalent relationship with two concepts that I have invoked before – visibility and haunting – is useful to recall in this respect. Metaphors of haunting in trans writing emerge both as representing the pain of erasure and exclusion and as signalling a liberation from fixity and from cis desires for an objectifying corporeal reveal. Making ghosts visible can effect a critique of the notion that transness consists in a quest for an unambiguous belonging, showing the difficulty of fitting neatly into one body and one category. This status can be seen as both an affect to be resolved, produced by the boundaries of 'man' and 'woman' being delineated by others in exclusion of gender-variant subjects, and an empowering position from which the I can partly resist the demand to shape itself to fit conventional moulds. The texts I discuss in this chapter articulate trans-inhabitation as both imposed and liveable, as they conceive of the space of the body (and the homes inhabited by the body) as shared with (ghostly) others. This situation can complicate what is visible: when looking at the body, do we see the ghost, the haunted 'container', a past self, a future self, an indivisible mix of the two, one version out of many, or something else entirely? In literature, a narrator's disembodiedness and invisibility can increase agency – by refusing readers the entitlement to read the bodies of others – but also diminish agency – by confining characters to the margins of a visualisable world. The opportunities and risks associated with visibility (representation and unwanted exposure, intelligibility and misunderstanding, legitimisation and singling out) depend on who is making what visible for whom. Being a ghost, being represented, being seen, being haunted, or being absent are not inherently positive or negative states, but become so according to whether they are enforced, chosen, embraced, or rejected. The trans narrators I now turn to materialise in different ways – through form and content – an idea that cuts across these affective and political concerns: that one inhabits other bodies and that one's body is inhabited by others.

## Akwaeke Emezi: Spatialising the 'we'

After its publication in 2018, the challenge to binary categorisations at the heart of Emezi's *Freshwater* rapidly spilled over into the extra-textual world. The judges were reportedly unaware of the author's non-binary gender when the novel was longlisted for the Women's Prize for Fiction, but celebrated their inclusion when this was discovered (Flood). However, when Emezi's book *The Death of Vivek Oji* (2020) was considered for the award the following year, news spread that the Prize had requested information about the author's 'sex as defined by law' (Flood). The difficulty of fitting this author into the systems of classification that structure Western cultural industries recurs more broadly throughout their prolific production of prose, poetry, music, and visual art. In *Dear Senthuran: A Black Spirit Memoir* (2021), Emezi recalls being hesitant about marketing *Freshwater* in relation to their 'national and racial identity': 'My main character's life and experiences weren't centered on her being African, or Black, or an immigrant. [...] Her core conflict was that she was embodied: that she existed, that she had selves, that she was several' (50). The life of the novel's protagonist, Ada, overlaps with Emezi's in many respects, including in the way in which they are neither a man nor a woman and eventually come to identify as ọgbanje, spirits from Igbo cosmology.[1] Through an autobiographical process that the author has described as 'excavating myself', *Freshwater* turns away from adhering to culturally recognisable locations and instead aims to create new space: a space for 'those of us living in shifting realities, worlds framed by madness, bordered by unknowns', and a space 'for writers of color working in the experimental' (*Dear Senthuran* 52). The ọgbanje, Emezi's (and Ada's) 'metaphysical identity' (50), is a figure that has trans-inhabitation as its essence, as it straddles different worlds and flits at the borders of human categories. In Igbo traditions, ọgbanje names spirits who are repeatedly incarnated in children from the same mother and drive each child to die prematurely. In literature, they have often been seen to represent 'metaphysical and political discomfort with life, aggravated by the instability of coming from the otherworld to frequent this world' (Ogunyemi 664). Many of the ọgbanje's characteristics are highlighted in *Freshwater*: their role as tormentors of families, striving to return to death by killing their human incarnations, is invoked, for instance, to explain the protagonist's actions toward their mother and their desire to end their life. The ọgbanje's centrality in the text's negotiation with gendered embodiment is particularly relevant for my reading. In this novel and in scholarship about this concept, ọgbanje is both singular and plural: it is the name for spirits that become incarnated in a body but it is also the name for their temporary human vessel, troubling – like the text as a whole does – the boundary between inhabitant and inhabited, and between plural and singular 'they'.

The ọgbanje's trans-inhabitations cannot be solely reduced to a metaphorical representation of non-binary and diasporic identities, but they decisively inform how the latter are explored by Emezi. The author explains that, in reading their embodiment as both ọgbanje and trans, they 'inhabit simultaneous realities that are usually considered mutually exclusive':

> The possibility that I was an *ogbanje* occurred to me around the same time I realized I was trans, but it took me a while to collide the two worlds. I suppressed the former for a few years because most of my education had been in the sciences and all of it was Westernized — it was difficult for me to consider an Igbo spiritual world equally, if not more valid. ('Transition')

*Freshwater* is spatialised across worlds: it takes place between Nigeria and the United States, mixes Igbo and Christian references, and features Igbo phrases untranslated for its English-speaking readers. Ada, being ọgbanje, is described as having 'one foot on the other side', hinting at a multivalent dislocation (*Freshwater* 27). As Chikwenye Okonjo Ogunyemi argues, the ọgbanje often 'emerges as a trope for the writer writing in a European, instead of a Nigerian, language', the ọgbanje's displacement from their home mirroring the alienation of the Nigerian writer from their 'emotional language' (69). Misty Bastian further highlights the connotations of this in-between-ness in regard to gender: 'to be *ogbaanje* is to be categorized as other and to bring alterity home in a way that transcends the more ordinary bifurcated "otherness" of gender' (59). She argues that the incarnated ọgbanje can be considered as inhabiting a 'third gender category, that of the human-looking spirit': the appearance of the spirit as a sexed child 'may, indeed, be seen as a sham – yet another promise that the *ogbaanje* is likely to break in its refusal to act according to human norms' (59). In addition to signalling broader dispersals of identity, this figure defies the legibility of the human body through conventional paradigms, and their otherness disrupts societal norms. In particular, as the ọgbanje are incarnated in a body whose reading by others does not immediately make clear who they are (they seem human, but they are more), their mode of existence is resonant with experiences of gender-variant identity, such as the one that Emezi often describes of seeming a woman but not being one.

The pluri-directional movements of the ọgbnje impact not only characters' identities but also narrative form. Emezi explains that Ada, in *Freshwater*, 'is not possessed by spirits; people think in binaries a lot, so that one thing has to be possessed by another. But with ọgbanje, these things are collapsed' ('I'd Read Everything'). The dissolving of a hierarchical relationship between the possessed self and the possessing other results, in the text, in a struggle between narrating voices. The 'we' of the spirits, the 'I' of an individuated spirit, and the 'I' of their human incarnation take turns narrating the latter's life, explaining changes in behaviour through internal shifts in how the protagonist's multiple identities relate to one another. While it is difficult to neatly separate a primary 'one' and secondary 'others', this does not mean that the one and its others coincide: there is always a 'stretch of emptiness between us' (*Freshwater* 36). The 'We' (designated as such at the start of chapters narrated in this grammatical person) is distinct from the individual voice of the protagonist (speaking in chapters marked as 'Ada'), from another narrator (speaking in chapters marked as 'Asụghara'), and from other named individual spirits who do not narrate; but 'we' also contains all of these identities. The spirits then cross not only physical and metaphysical worlds, but also narrative spaces. If the 'I', in homodiegetic narration, designates a narrator and a character at the same time, the multiplication into a 'we' introduces more crossings that we can count. Naming some of the spirits and signalling shifts in narrating voice through chapter breaks and titles goes some way toward giving narrative shape to these crossings, but the partitioning is always incomplete and asymmetrical, resulting in a narrative that hovers between fragmentation and unity, collective and singular. The ọgbanje's movement as the 'running back and forth' of 'unstable, "unsettled" spirits who can never be at home in this world', with a 'mobile, boundary-transgressing quality' (Bastian 61), produces a trans-inhabitation of gendered identities and of the positions, locations, and boundaries of narrative agents.

The We is the first narrator of *Freshwater*: their entanglement with Ada, the human they speak of/in/through, begins at birth. 'We' initially 'flit', like ghosts, through the walls of a uterus (1) – partly within and partly outside the body – but after Ada is born and is 'no longer flesh within a house but a house itself', they are 'locked into' and 'trapped' in this house-like body (4). Resonating with other trans imaginings I have discussed, this novel views the body both as a house and as housed, conceiving of the self as divided to allow for metaphors such as being 'trapped' in a body. If the relationship between Ada and the spirits is meant to invoke this popular metaphor for transness, however, it is re-signified almost beyond recognition. The situation is in fact substantially complicated by the multiple subjectivities involved: the narrators insist throughout the novel that they both are Ada and 'yet not' (5). While the ọgbanje call Ada their 'vessel' or 'she (our body)' (27), any attempt to understand this as a distinction between a true self in the mind and a false self of the body is frustrated as the text works precisely to destabilise and question the location of Ada's self, collapsing the distinction between inner and outer. As Ada grows up, we are told that the ọgbanje exist 'inside the marble room of her mind' and we see them interact there (41). At the same time, the first person plural can expand to contain Ada as well, in passages such as 'We (the Ada and us) do not remember our mouth's sounds' (23). Here, the mouth is 'ours', and 'we' refers to 'the Ada and us'.[2] Owing to the shifting referent of the deictic 'we', it can never be said with certainty if Ada is included in the We. Because she sometimes is contained in this 'we' and sometimes contains them, the text invokes distinctions between container and contained but continually disrupts them, finding and losing footing in separating its 'characters'. It is with this We, and not against it, that the I of Ada will ultimately be able to find agency and a voice.

The first I of the novel is not Ada, but Asụghara, who becomes a narrator in chapter 6 and remains the dominating voice until chapter 16, a few chapters short of the conclusion. Asụghara is a spirit that becomes individuated, separated from the 'larger we' (69), when Ada is sexually assaulted at university. Her function is to protect Ada: she inhabits and animates Ada's body so that the latter can become absent when confronted with traumatising circumstances. This narrator describes Ada as an external vessel: Asụghara is 'locked into her flesh, moving her muscles' (75). She animates Ada from the inside, 'running Ada's fingernails' on her lover's skin, using 'Ada's face and practiced smiles on it' (74). Asụghara gradually attempts to erase all spaces within Ada so that she can gain as much agency as possible: 'I expanded against the walls, filling it up and blocking her out completely. She was gone. [...] I was here. I was everything. I was everywhere' (64). The text implies that remaining multiple, allowing for space within the We, cannot provide Ada with a clear position from which to act, and therefore Asụghara taking over as 'one' becomes necessary. But the very existence of multiple others is what protects Ada in the first place, as it is the precondition of them being able to take over, allowing her to be absent. Whether this protection is ultimately beneficial is ambiguous, given Asụghara's selfish and self-destructive nature, which prevents Ada from intervening even when she perhaps no longer desires this absence. Speaking as a narrator, Asụghara acknowledges that Ada is trying to speak too: 'she was saying something but her voice was small and tiny, and I was pressed up against the walls of her mind, growing and growing until she was a dot in a corner and I couldn't hear her voice anymore' (145). By taking up space, Asụghara becomes the main self, so that Ada is no longer (only) a vessel containing the spirits but somehow a 'small and tiny' voice 'inside' Asụghara. To add to this confusion about where and what Ada is, her own voice, by this point, has not been formally established as distinct from the We and Asụghara, who have narrated the entirety of the text so far.

Although Asụghara endeavours to take up all available room, the We still exist and occasionally narrate, leaving open a space beyond the boundary of her 'I' that allows 'something else' to stand 'beside' her (121). This other is named Saint Vincent, and his location is ambiguously 'beside' Asụghara, even though she is seemingly everywhere, and even though she fills Ada up – Ada continuing to be both the containing body and 'a dot in a corner' of her own mind. This other spirit, this time from a Christian tradition, represents a masculinity that is part of Ada, but it becomes clear that the trans identity that Ada eventually comes to embody is neither a trajectory from female to male nor a perfect symmetry of the two. In fact, Saint Vincent never speaks in his own voice in the novel and remains in Ada's mind 'because he couldn't survive her body' (121). There is a jumbled coexistence and simultaneous inhabitation of different spaces by different characters here. Describing Saint Vincent, the We explain that he moves 'inside the Ada's dreams, when she was floating in our realm, untethered and malleable' (122). While most of the text describes a human world in which the spirits are visitors, Ada is now the one who visits another realm – although these are 'her' dreams, the We claim the space as 'our'. Adding to this ambivalent inhabitation, there is an ambiguous mode of embodiment: in Ada's dreams, Saint Vincent has 'molded her into a new body [...], a dreambody with reorganized flesh and a penis', and he 'used the dreambody as his' (122). The spirit has made the body for Ada, but then uses it as 'his'. This overlapping of the two conveys a movement between identities that is akin to other gendered hauntings I have discussed: this is reinforced by Saint Vincent's description as 'soft as a ghost' (122). This haunting, however, occurs across multiple worlds and runs in multiple directions, with each 'character' as a haunted/haunting I/we: trans-inhabitation occurs without necessarily settling who is inhabiting whom, what, or where.

Even as Ada contains and is contained by a plurality of others, her isolation cannot be breached: she is 'pursued by space, gray and malignant, cold as chalk' (36). However, it becomes increasingly clear that getting rid of spaces, and thus achieving a situation where Ada can be one, and fully in one world, is impossible, and a form of co-embodiment that does not do away with multiple subjectivity must be found. The ọgbanje, speaking as We, clarify that the dislocation of the I from the spirits, the reason why they are not 'synched', is due to a failure to separate incompatible spaces: 'When transition is made from spirit to flesh, the gates are meant to be closed. [...] Perhaps the gods forgot' (5). An accidental opening – notably occurring during a transition – creates 'a distinct *we*' where there should be a 'fully and just *her*' (5). The empty space between these positions marks their multiplicity, makes them not one: the gates 'infect with space, gaps, widenings' that cannot be closed (36). But while there is certainly distance between narrators and other textual entities (materialised formally through choices and necessities like distinct proper names and typographical spaces), there is also always overlap. The We admit as much, clarifying that it would be 'hard' to take 'a piece of chalk and draw where she stops and where we start' (43). If trans studies already urges us to consider genders as 'porous and permeable spatial territories [...] numbering more than two' (Stryker et al. 12), permeability in *Freshwater* is more like a gaping wound, a bleeding of one world into another – and the numbers are not adding up. Viewing non-binary gender through Emezi's portrayal of spiritual alienation can help rethink trans spatialities as entanglements and distances. In articulating that 'I was born, and no one's come to take me home. Embodiment is the stranding. I am marooned in flesh' (*Dear Senthuran* 215), Emezi describes a separation that is both undeniable and made home for now.

As it is impossible to categorically distance the I from the We, gender-affirming medical interventions in the novel do not constitute a progressive emergence and materialisation of a singular true self, but a discontinuous coming to the fore of a multiplicity. In the novel, after Asụghara has dominated Ada's body for a long time, she lets 'Saint Vincent step to the front a little more' (164), and this leads Ada to date women and start wearing a chest binder. The emergence of the male spirit, however, is never complete. The ọgbanje explain that '[p]erhaps in another world, where the Ada was not split and segmented, she and Saint Vincent might have been one thing together' (122). Like Alabanza's disnarrations that I discussed in Chapter 2, this upward counterfactual measures the distance between this reality and one in which the self could be whole. As Ada does inhabit other worlds, and is inhabited by them, this never results in a full and neat locatability, and this trans-inhabitation struggles to make itself legible in the realm of the visible. Reflecting on Ada's pre-mastectomy body, the We explains,

> That form had worked for Asụghara [...] but we were more than her and we were more than the saint. We were a fine balance, bigger than whatever the namings had made, and we wanted to reflect that, to change the Ada into us. (187)

While the surgery is motivated by the need to change a body that is 'too feminine, too reproductive' (187), this change is not subsumed to a journey from one gender to another singular (and opposite) gender. Emezi's own transition, they explain in *Dear Senthuran*, resisted normative models of trans identity, to the extent that even a '"trans-friendly" surgeon made me jump through hoops to prove I was sane enough to get surgery' (161). Emezi also reports the protests of cis women when faced with someone who is removing their own uterus and 'healthy' breast tissue, signalling a 'territorial' attitude about these body parts (163). The territory of the body, expected by others to be a canvas for the projection of a cohesive gender, is in the hands of *Freshwater*'s narrator(s) the material for carving a multiplicity.

It is unsurprising, then, that Ada continues to speak as a 'we' when narrating as an 'I'.[3] The first time that the I of Ada intervenes, almost halfway through the novel, they doubt that they 'even had the mouth to tell this story', and relinquish authority to the We: 'whatever they will say will be the truest version of it, since they are the truest version of me' (93). By the end of the book, in a final chapter that names Ada as its narrator, this fragmentation of self is embraced as an identity, by both a singular and a plural first person: 'I am here and not here, real and not real [...] I am my others; we are one and we are many' (226). In order to find this liveable position (multiple but acting and speaking as one) there is a return to the metaphor of the journey toward 'wholeness', but one that has to go through further splitting: 'when a thing has been created with deformations and mismatched edges, sometimes you have to break it some more before you can start putting it back together' (210). By allowing the We to show on the body, Ada can be whole because they can be multiple. An investment in a resolution, not beyond but in reconciliation with contradictory embodiment and dislocated identity, is evidenced when Ada explains that 'this thing of being an ọgbanje' is 'the only path that brought me any peace' (218). Directionality and a sense of unity are regained by the author, who similarly comments elsewhere that their own well-being has only become possible once 'I began to look at my life through the lens of Igbo ontology and craft it as a story' ('I'd Read Everything'). Trans-inhabitation, in the sense of dwelling in multiple spaces at once (the human and the spirit worlds, Igbo and Western conceptions of identity, male and female genders, narrator and character), never neatly belonging in any of them, is in *Freshwater* a mode of being that can unify the self in its own way and be embraced as one's chosen embodied and narratable identity.

To signal this unity in multiplicity, the novel makes use of narration in the first person plural in ways that resist existing accounts of 'we-narration' in narrative studies. Since these discussions largely assume the 'we' in we-narration to refer to distinctly embodied subjectivities, *Freshwater*'s ambiguous voice can enrich and transform existing categorisations. For instance, when Lanser identifies forms of 'communal narration' (a mode in which authority is shared by more than one narrator), these include both 'a simultaneous form in which a plural "we" narrates' and 'a sequential form in which individual members of a group narrate in turn' (*Authority* 21). In a sense, both modes could describe Emezi's novel: the We narrate collectively but also alternate with more than one I. A situation in which a co-embodied collective narrates remains to be described. Similarly, Natalya Bekhta's definition of we-narration as being 'unlike first-person singular narration in that it is based on the collective experience and agency of a collective body', and as 'transcend[ing] the individual subject in the scope of its knowledge, temporal, and spatial limitations' (172), could be seen as both characterising and excluding *Freshwater*. The notion of a 'collective body' takes on a special significance in the case of a text in which the body, a singular human body, is host to multiple agencies. Additionally, the spatiotemporal 'limitations' of the 'individual subject' are here both maintained (Ada is one character, with one perspective) and transcended (Ada is constituted by others who have existence and wisdom beyond this world). Ultimately, the I (in the case of Asụghara and in the case of Ada) both is and is not the We, as they mutually constitute and escape each other. In the same way as it challenges conceptions of gender already theorised by trans studies, this novel raises questions for narrative studies to consider, such as: what happens to categories and distinctions used to describe we-narration in the presence of a 'we' that is (in) one body, which should conventionally express itself as an I? Once again, the way in which trans narrators make sense of their identities, with and against norms that would want to fit them within the boundaries of binary and fixed categories, can generate linguistic strategies that are yet to be accounted for in existing models.

When asked, in an interview for *The Guardian*, if 'the voices' are 'different sides' of Ada, Emezi replied: 'Yes, the way I describe Ada is as a singular collective and plural individual. Ada is described as a "girl" but is not, actually. "She" has gender-affirming surgery and it is not said but she is trans' ('I'd Read Everything'). This explanation helps categorise the novel as having a trans narrator, but it also calls into question what this categorisation means: pronouns, gender categories, the boundaries of the self, and the identity of a narrating 'character' are trans-inhabited. To convey this trans-inhabitation, Ada's corporeality in the text is constructed through lyrical and elusive descriptions of dizzying movements and fragmentations, creating a complex and sometimes contradictory space (which blurs distinctions between internal and external) in which the I and We meet. In this process, hierarchies are subverted between the one who speaks and the one who is spoken about. If the narrator can be understood as the subject (who has agency and control over the story, who speaks and allows others to speak), and everything in their narrative can be seen as the object (viewed from the outside, spoken about, at the mercy of the narrator's decisions), the double existence of the first person as narrating-I and experiencing-I folds these two positions into one. Emezi's novel introduces a particular nebulousness to this common circumstance, as it is not always clear to what extent Ada is the We, Ada is Asụghara, Ada is Saint Vincent, or Ada is the author. Therefore, they are both narrating and narrated, a host for other voices and an incarnation of those voices into a distinct subjectivity that allows them to be heard, a body that hides its multiplicity and a surface on to which to inscribe it. As I move on to narratives that take us to other bodies and other spaces, this chapter continues to return to these questions: the play between subject and object, the presence of others in the self, and a polyphonic narrative of gender.

### Calvin Gimpelevich: Collecting invasions

If a semi-autobiographical narrative like *Freshwater* can give voice to the multiplicities that are already present in the author's body, fiction can further allow one to 'take on' different bodies, an idea that is often taken literally in Gimpelevich's short-story collection *Invasions*. The author's only book to date, *Invasions* exists alongside Gimpelevich's essays and other stories, which refract and expand his reflection on bodies that are transformable in specific cultural ways. In an essay that discusses his own transition, Gimpelevich writes: 'I used to be a butch woman; passing changed me into a small Jewish man' ('Among Men' 57). As the movement of passing from 'woman' to 'man' affects the extent to which the author is perceived as butch or Jewish, his behaviours and abilities are translated according to a new gendered reading: 'Clumsiness is, if not impressive, acceptable in weedy bookish neurotic American Jewish men. There is a basic assumption of intelligence (deserved or not) lacking before' (50). These reflections on relational identity can be applied beyond processes of passing and transition, to inform how we read the inhabitation of bodies that occurs both figuratively and literally in *Invasions*. In this book, Gimpelevich speaks through embodied characters distinct from himself, and some of these characters inhabit worlds in which it is possible to insert their consciousness into the bodies of others. Instead of (only) an appropriation or violation, the taking on of other bodies is figured in this collection as enmeshing and reciprocity, an encounter between subjects who navigate their commonalities and differences and locate each other relationally through desire and care. This also resonates with the ethics of 't4t'. Most often translated as 'trans for trans', this term evolved beyond its initial use in online personal advertisements to denote a 'contingent separatism' that allows for 'greater complexity, in excess of reductive cis- and transnormative interpellations of trans subjects' (Malatino 657). Transferring this meaning to literature, Gimpelevich's Boston-based reading series featuring trans authors, 'T4T – Trans4Texts', affirms a space for the relations that arise between (trans) authors and readers, (trans) texts and authors, (trans) readers and texts, away from a cis gaze that would pin identity to one body and to one possible reading of that body.

In a Trans4Texts space, identities are formed reciprocally within and across textual boundaries. Gimpelevich's collection of short stories accordingly gives rise to complex textual renderings of corporeal presence and location. This is perhaps most evident in the two stories that feature an explicit crossing of one subject into the body of another that they inhabit as theirs, 'The Sweetness' and 'Rent, Don't Sell'. Before going into detail about these narratives, a glimpse of the prose will be sufficient to signal what linguistic choices accompany trans-inhabitation: 'I tried forcing us to look at their terrified faces [...] But I couldn't make our head move; he was ignoring me' (Gimpelevich, *Invasions* 75). In this passage from 'The Sweetness', the 'I' of the inhabiting consciousness and narrator, the 'he' of the body being inhabited, and the 'us' that designates the ambiguous fusion of the two are alternated to convey competing agencies. Similarly, in 'Rent, Don't Sell', an invading person, Nok, and an invaded body, Carol, uneasily mix into one: 'She knew this body. She rolled her head. Carol's neck always hurt, stiffness here and in the mid-back. As Nok took over, that tightness released into the latticework of her own tension' (34). Here, the situation is somewhat redoubled as the heterodiegetic narrator also in some sense 'inhabits' the 'she' that is Nok through focalisation. A certain separability of body and mind, which is what allows such fictional invasions, is expressed by Gimpelevich in what he calls 'two contradictory theories':

> The first, that appearance has no relation to the abstract sense of myself—to that voice, without gender or possibly even culture, that speaks in my head; the *I* transcending temporal corporeal worlds—and the second, that I am made of my body and context; that these create the substance of me. ('Among Men' 63)

While the transcending 'I' may be one, the body, shaped through transition or other corporeal transformations and refracted intersubjectively, is multiple. This tension between a unified identity and the worlds that it traverses, which in turn create the 'substance' of it, takes shape fictionally through the idea of taking on different bodies, which multiply within and across the individual stories.

If we take the collection as an ambiguously 'whole' text, then the first story, 'Velcro', can be read as a sort of prologue that anticipates key themes, concerns, and narrative operations. This story has an unnamed first-person narrator, which functions both to establish the authority that pertains to narrating personal experience and to open up the possible selves that this 'I' could designate. I reproduce 'Velcro' here in its entirety:

> When the doctors told me that I would lose all sensation, that the procedure required unhooking my nerves and repasting the flesh, and I wouldn't have breasts but a flat, what they call masculine, chest with a little red line to mark out my pecs, the subtraction, and I'd be able to walk on the beach with my shirt off, to go to the gym, to show my senseless dead nipples in public, I decided against the basic needle and thread, for them, the doctors, that is the surgeon and his assistant, to use velcro instead.
>
> It's given me so many options. I can wear one on my forehead, a triclops, or cover my ears. I can put them over my ribs. I can leave them at home. It's strange how disturbing that looks, no nipples, how alien—though I don't feel it about my nude body, sans penis

and breasts. Maybe it brings me back to childhood, having the same layout, more hair. When I was a teenager and my friends had just discovered transsexuals, we thought trans women were best because they had the most of all worlds. With men, it seemed like subtraction. I know better now. (*Invasions* 9)

As I move on to discuss 'Velcro' and the stories that follow it, I am interested in the extent to which this narrator sets up a thematic and formal concern with trans-inhabitation, which is explored through the taking on of multiple and multiply-signifying bodies and voices. The experience of being trans, which is addressed explicitly across Gimpelevich's work, constitutes a starting point for broader reflections on how our culturally mediated bodies function to create a narrative of who we are for ourselves and for others.

The first paragraph of 'Velcro' is one long sentence describing a hypothetical future – glimpsed from a past conversation with doctors – in a body with the 'masculine' chest that is the standard outcome of mastectomies performed on trans men. The introduction of the choice of 'velcro' undoes this transition narrative and creates a speculative reality in which corporeal presentation is left more open. The 'many options' allowed by velcro give rise to a play of subtractions and additions that are possible, not in the sense of being unrealised hypotheticals but in the sense of being new abilities explored by the narrator ('I can' rather than 'I could'). In the short space that it occupies, the story carries the narrator across temporal locations: a past moment of decision, an imagined future, a present in which they can or do act, a past childhood body, and a more recently past teenage point of view. This movement mirrors the agile transformability of the body conferred by the velcro, which can give rise to gendered readings (presumably, if the breasts are 'over the ribs' or 'left at home') but also new human shapes (breasts over 'forehead' or 'ears'). Recalling the ethics of t4t, we can ask who will make these readings – who is the narratee of the story? Someone who, like the teenage narrator and their friends, would think that 'trans women have the most of all worlds' – or someone who, like the present narrator, 'knows better now'? Or is the text to be read ironically, baiting us to engage and release our expectations about transness?[4] What looks and does not look 'alien' to the narrator inhabiting this body introduces both clarification and confusion about whose gaze is invoked. The ambiguity of what exactly constitutes a 'better' knowledge, and the possibility of having 'the most of all worlds', are especially ideas that continue to be interrogated throughout the collection, as the author takes on (or velcroes on) the embodiments of other trans and cis men and women, as well as non-binary and non-gendered narrators and characters, who may or may not have the author's same body parts, corporeal presentation, gender identity, experiences, or views.

As anticipated, 'The Sweetness' is one of the stories that most overtly thematises the inhabitation of multiple bodies. The first word of the narrative is 'Bodies', and the subject who observes and narrates these bodies – of men entering a bathhouse – is eventually located as standing apart from them, unobserved in turn. When the narrator finally makes eye contact with another character, we begin to glimpse a level of insight into the minds of others that goes beyond ordinary focalisation. Accessing the perceptions of the boy whose eyes he looks into, the I tells us with certainty, 'To him, my car smells like money' (65). As the narrator enters the bathhouse himself, he experiences the physical mingling of men, who are initially 'bulky and separated, not having shed their identities yet with their clothes', but are eventually 'dimmed into each other' and have 'no single edge' (65). His own identity is in turn refracted and fragmented by 'many mirrors' (67). As it turns out, losing oneself among the bodies of others has a particular significance for the narrator, who has a supernatural ability he calls 'flashing' or 'flipping' that allows him to enter the minds of others and read their thoughts and embodied perceptions. Although it has some tragic consequences – the narrator explains that he caused the death of his lover by flipping into him while he was driving a car – this ability is ultimately framed as a gift of radical empathy. When the bathhouse is raided by a group of policemen, the narrator realises that he has 'flipped' into their leader and out of his own now unconscious body. This new body, Ray, initially immerses the I into homophobic and violent feelings. However, it turns out that the I can probe deeper into Ray, find his loneliness and disavowed desire for men, reach the 'places that were soft' (80). Able to manoeuvre Ray into rescuing his unconscious body but ultimately realising that they are both going to die in the fire that now engulfs the bathhouse, the narrator chooses in their last moments to love him, addressing Ray in the second person: '*I'm going to haunt you*, I told him' (80).

In its creation of an I that is separate from others but at the same time blends with them and feels through them, 'The Sweetness' can be read as materialising some of the operations that narrators perform. The ability to know and perceive from within multiple bodies is in fact rendered through what mostly looks like ordinary focalisation or free indirect discourse. For instance, the way in which we learn Ray's thoughts does not in itself betray that some supernatural ability is involved:

> Arrogant militant perverts. This was galling to Ray. He should have gone military, but what was the point? [...]
> Men fought for God and country. They protected their families. They strove to be heroes. They didn't suck other men's dicks.
> I felt Ray think that very clearly. (74)

This passage is not particularly dissimilar from one that we would receive from a heterodiegetic narrator focalising through Ray, only the last sentence making the operation of 'feeling Ray think' more explicit and thus less familiar. In addition to characterising narrators, acts of 'flashing' and 'flipping' into bodies can also symbolise more broadly some gendered experiences or desires. While the I of 'The Sweetness' seems to be a cis man and only inhabits other men's bodies, 'Rent, Don't Sell' introduces the idea of body swapping as a speculative solution for (gender) dysphoria. The protagonist Nok, a cis woman, works at a gym that allows clients to lend their body to trainers who exercise it on their behalf. Having lost a hand and finding the missing body part painful, Nok fantasises about being able to keep one of the bodies she trains, any body that would be 'whole' (43). However, simple desires to discard one's body for a supposedly better one are challenged when Nok meets Natasha, a trans woman who swapped her old body with a trans man but now feels less like herself: 'The estrogen's great. Dream come true. [...] But when I look in the mirror, it's someone else's reflection' (47). As Natasha decides to get her old body back and transition the 'old fashioned' way (47), her story adds meaning to the supposedly separate text of 'The Sweetness', which the reader encounters a few pages later, shaping a complex understanding of what it means to want to transcend one's body.

While fantastical abilities are only involved in a few stories from the collection, most of them negotiate transforming bodies. In 'You Wouldn't Have Known', an unnamed trans man recounts his experience of gender confirmation surgery at a Canadian clinic. This experience is collective, as the narrator is housed alongside other patients, all trans women. The story dwells on corporeal details about the narrator's appearance, the procedure to remove his breast tissue, his recovery from surgery, the vaginoplasties undergone by the others, and a sexual encounter with another patient. While this bodiliness ostensibly contrasts with the elusive ease of 'Velcro', there is a similar concern with making visible a space of in-between-ness that is erased by conventional trans narratives: 'Nothing that happens here matters. It'll collapse into a sentence—that time I went to Canada for my surgery' (156). During this time in which 'nothing matters', narratives of the self are negotiated intersubjectively. The story in fact opens with the narrator's gender being read by others: 'We're sitting in the commons when Annie says I look like a man. She says it like this: "They did a good job with her. She looks just like a real one"' (147). As Annie's daughter, Lisette, corrects her mother on this misgendering, the narrator remains silent as readers work to locate the appearance and gender of the I. But if being seen from the outside leaves one at the mercy of the narratives of others, it can also become a t4t space of gender validation. The narrator's view of Lisette, for instance, tells us what she looks like through a specific counter-lens that goes against cisnormative frameworks: 'A thin blonde beard dusts her lower features. There is nothing unfeminine about this. With the hair, her face is soft, softer, even, and it took me a moment to remember that most women don't grow facial hair' (165). As the story ends with Lisette's mother saying to her, after a vaginoplasty, 'It looks just like you gave birth' (168), the text works not only to affirm the characters' gender but to re-signify what it means for a character to appear textually like a woman or a man.

Taking on a different body, in *Invasions*, is sometimes desired and sometimes imposed, sometimes possible and sometimes impossible, sometimes resulting in isolation and sometimes in connection. Unnamed first-person narrators in particular create a space of trans-inhabitation between genders, between bodies, between self and other, and between a character and the author who says 'I' through them. Narratees are also similarly involved; this is most explicit in 'Transmogrification', which is written in the second person. The first paragraph, especially, could maintain for many the illusion that the 'you' is the person reading these words:

> You wake up one morning to find your body larger and hairier than you recall. Your hands seem twice – more, three times! – their normal

size, and your knees creak when you move. Your stomach, no longer pale and distended, is thick with muscles and fat. (81)

Because the text explains how 'your' body is new and unfamiliar, anyone who has hands and knees and whose stomach is currently pale and distended could be addressed by the narrative. Gradually, we learn specificities about this character that stop the effect of a second-person address: 'You went to bed as a six-year-old girl' (81). In a way that is similar to 'Velcro', the story plays with bodily changes across the binaries of natural/unnatural, real/imagined, realistic/fantastic:

> Your mother warned you that before you turned into a grown-up, your body would go through a series of strange and unappealing changes. She did not elaborate, but it stands to reason that becoming a middle-aged man is yet another step in the path to womanhood. (81)

This take on Kafka's *Metamorphosis* could function as a parody of cisnormative views that exaggerate and reify the gender binary: the idea of a man in a dress is for instance invoked as the protagonist worries about their upcoming ballet recital. At the same time, as the character comes to experience hormonal changes (they 'should be crying' but 'feel rage' instead) and changes in how others react to them (84), the story also reads as a genuine reflection on gendered embodiment. Like 'Velcro', this brief text asks questions that reverberate through other voluntary and involuntary embodiments in the collection.

Finally, transcending the body in *Invasions* does not always entail the taking on of multiple bodies. The narrator of 'Invasion' – a title that invades the other stories as its plural is used to designate them all – mostly withdraws from legibility while retaining substance as an I. Of this I, we know that they have a lover (only called 'she') and that they perform certain ordinary tasks, but we have no description of their appearance, which is only vaguely glimpsed through clothes – 'the cuff of my jeans', 'my boots', 'my jacket hiked to show vulnerable flesh' (145). If, in order to create a homodiegetic narrator that escapes gendered classification, 'a considerable degree of information might have to be omitted' (Lanser, 'Sexing' 88), a short story may just be short enough that these omissions do not appear remarkable. However, the I of 'Invasion' is surrounded by other narrators who have more 'visible' bodies, which are, moreover, often misread in what their appearance might tell us about the person within. This creates both the absence of a pattern according to which readers would guess the identity and visual presentation of the narrator – in the collection, we have seen different genders, different races, ages, and sexualities, as well as both trans and cis narrators – and the multiplication of possibilities, since no option is particularly precluded. The characterisation of the narrator in 'Invasion' further contributes to an unfixed identity: as we learn nothing very specific about their habits or tastes, we are also told that they are somewhat hazy and interchangeable in the eyes of their lover. The latter is in fact absorbed in an abstract and self-centring love, as the narrator explains: 'I—the object—was an axis on which her feelings could turn' (Gimpelevich, *Invasions* 146). Thematically, the story also engages with shapelessness through ambiguous reference to an alien invasion that is currently taking place but that has been easily integrated into the characters' routine. The narrator explains of the aliens that '[w]hen they died, they lost their structure. Live ones shifted and changed shape, growing larger and sharper than bears, flattening to slip under doorways' (145). The flexibility of corporeality and movement that is explored here can be taken broadly as characteristics of this narrator, and perhaps of (trans) narrators in general.

In line with these concerns with flexibility and shapeshifting, I read the textual bodies and voices of *Invasions* as engaged in a trans-inhabitation that approximates 'horizontal metalepsis'. This term normally designates the 'transmigration of a character or narrator into a different fictional text' which 'involves the transgressive violation of storyworld boundaries through jumps between ontologically distinct zones or spheres' (Alber and Bell 168). However, in this case metalepsis occurs through relaxed boundaries and less clear transmigrations. In fact, there are no explicit instances in which a character from one story reappears in another. Instead, my suggestion is that the individual entities that form a short-story collection by the same author are not 'ontologically distinct zones' to the same extent as narratives that are published separately. Their relationship, as they are bound between the same covers and separated by titles, is one of ambiguous touching. But it is precisely without the ingredients that define metalepsis (clear boundaries and their violation) that some of its transgressions occur and are even a structural feature of a collection of this kind. An illustrative example is a text that I have discussed before in 'Adaptation as Queer Touching': Rose Troche's film *The Safety of Objects* (2001), which adapts a 1990 collection by A. M. Homes of the same name. The film takes different characters from separate short stories and merges them together into a smaller cast, telling a unified story about them; the collection is treated as if it was a continuous narrative about the same few families in the same neighbourhood when in fact it comprises stories that were written and published at different times about different characters. It is not difficult to imagine an adaptation of *Invasions* that might do the same: aided by the recurring theme of body swapping and breaching of corporeal boundaries, a similar permeability may apply to the singular narratives, which could be imagined to occur in a shared world and even be about the same characters, especially when the latter are not named. Crucially, an unnamed 'I' appears in multiple stories, which means that the possibility that this is the same character is never definitively precluded. Although I admit that this may be an imaginative leap on my part, the properties of first-person narration permit this leap.

If we allow this transgression, the withdrawn corporeality of the 'Invasion' narrator can be given meaning through the statements of another (or maybe even the same) ambiguously gendered I, from a story called 'Eternal Boy': 'I preferred to show nothing of myself, to manipulate expectations [...] Ambiguity meant safety to me—gendered or otherwise' (137). This is only one in a plurality of desires, needs, and experiences that take shape across the separate stories of the collection when it comes to embodiment, disembodiment, visibility, and mixing with others. Shifting from the very embodied to the barely embodied, from the mobile to the trapped, from men to women to boys to girls and more, *Invasions* enacts trans-inhabitation thematically and formally. The choice of independent publisher Instar Books, who 'do not believe that genre distinctions are meaningful' and specialise in trans and digital literature, further signals a desire to explore and transgress classificatory boundaries (Instar Books). In the collection (and perhaps in any collection of this kind), the author temporarily 'velcroes on' different bodies, voicing characters who sometimes do the very same. The multiplication of bodies, as well as detaching the I from the visible substance it is tethered to, is never given a definitive meaning, value, or moral by Gimpelevich. The idea of 'flipping into' the body of a bathhouse raider shares some of the violence of this raiding, an invasion of safe spaces. But through Nok and Natasha's desires for body swapping, and eventual realisation that no absolute wholeness is possible, the taking on of a new body takes on a new connotation. The inexplicable transmogrification of a six-year-old girl into a middle-aged man asks further questions about the limitations and opportunities of severing the body from one's sense of self, and the embodiments of the past from the embodiments of the present. And the stories that are explicitly about being trans and about being read as gendered suggest that the transformability of the body, the splitting of the self, and the defamiliarisation of what it means to be corporeal are experiences not confined to speculative realities.

## Alison Rumfitt: Voicing the house

So far, I have discussed the material effects of trans literature as opening up and confounding hegemonic understandings of bodies and narrative, as well as carving a Trans4Texts space in which identity and stories can be communally re-signified. Alison Rumfitt's fiction is invested in these material effects too, but its functions also pertain more specifically to horror genres.[5] The author's second book, *Brainwyrms* (2023), appears on its publisher's website alongside quotations that call it an 'infestation' and an 'infection', with the promise that it will 'slither inside unsuspecting readers and lay eggs there' ('Brainwyrms'). And in the case of Rumfitt's earlier novel *Tell Me I'm Worthless*, this invasion of readers' bodies is figured as a haunting: in place of the dedication, the author writes, 'SORRY FOR LETTING YOU HAUNT THIS BOOK'. As was the case for Emezi and Gimpelevich, haunting and possession are mutual: one is not only haunted but haunts. And readers are not simply addressed, they are implicated by the text, drawn into it and made part of it. Other paratextual material adds to this suggestion: one of the epigraph quotations is from Isabel Fall's short story 'I Sexually Identify as an Attack Helicopter' (also known as 'Helicopter Story'). Published in *Clarkesworld Magazine* in January 2020, this story sparked an internet controversy that reveals much about the literary world that trans authors like Rumfitt find themselves having to navigate. Reappropriating as its title a phrase used in far-right online forums to mock trans people, 'Helicopter' was accompanied by a minimal author biography which did not mention that Fall was a trans woman. While initially praised for its exploration of queer gender, the story quickly attracted criticism for being transphobic; harassment of Fall and her forced outing as trans led to the story being taken down, and the author reportedly experienced intense dysphoria, and later detransitioned, following reviews of the story which said that 'Fall must be a cis man, because no woman would ever write in the way she did' (St. James). *Tell Me I'm Worthless* evokes this event by often blurring the distinction between those who voice violence and those who are the target of it, calling readers as participants in the harm done to characters and authors.

The haunting we do in this novel is the haunting of a house: the story centres on Albion, an evil building that absorbs and infests the thoughts of those who come near it. The text's narrator(s) often remind readers of their involvement in this dynamic: 'You, too, are implicated in its presence. Don't forget that. You, me. Those you love [...] Your housemate and your lover and your Queen. Your MP and your favourite author' (232). As the name suggests, the House is a fairly explicit metaphor for Britain, which is also the setting of the story. I choose the ambiguous term 'Britain' here for a reason: uneasy boundaries between the locations of England, Great Britain, and the United Kingdom are the result of the colonial oppression that *Tell Me I'm Worthless* reveals as infecting Albion. The novel focuses primarily on two characters, Alice and Ila, who have visited the House together with a third friend (Hannah) and they are now haunted by the memory of their time there. Each thinks that she has been the victim of sexual violence by the other; Alice, who is trans, remembers her friend's sudden brutal transphobia, and Ila, who is Jewish and Pakistani, witnessed Alice's racist and anti-Semitic hate. Bearing wounds carved in the House, Ila has now become an anti-trans activist and Alice obsesses about returning, eventually managing to convince Ila to do so. Even aside from Albion itself, the text is continually preoccupied with dwellings: descriptions of houses and flats, their locations, and their room configurations are prominent. British spaces often appear delineated in a disordered manner, in opposition to 'American cities' which 'are structured with intention':

> Grids of right angles, impossible to find yourself lost in, surely. Here the cities are mistakes, towns which grew too big and so conjoined with other towns, swallowing all the villages and the countryside around them whole in their desperate need for more space. (86)

Locating oneself in Britain entails 'finding yourself lost', and the embodied identities of characters also have jagged edges and hunger for more room.

Haunting inside and outside the text is shaped by its political context, one in which violence inhabits spaces from national borders to privately owned land and brick. The flat in which we find Alice at the beginning of the novel is introduced (through her first-person voice) as a hateful place. Initially, we are given vague explanations about this:

> Rooms sit and stew. They take the things you do in them. Their walls soak up every action you take between them, and those actions become part of the bricks and the plaster. Maybe I made it hate me. I can be hateful, to myself and to others. (8)

But, while Alice attributes the oppressive atmosphere of her rooms to her own hateful thoughts and actions, it is also evident that these are to be understood in a longer collective history. The political meaning of haunting is made clear through the narrator's reflection that '[t]he less income you generate, the less rooms you can have in your flat, the thicker the air, the more hateful the atmosphere' (8). Capitalist exploitation and social inequalities are sources of haunting, as Alice learns when asking strangers on the internet if they have experienced haunting: 'many of the people who answered said that their places of work were haunted [...] and every big imposing house in the country has people working in it' (9). Through this reasoning, Alice attempts to convince the narratee, equated with a sceptical reader, that the fear and oppression that lingers in certain spaces has a material explanation: 'You can tell me that ghosts aren't real all you like, but rooms are real, they have real walls with angles that hold suggestions cut deep into the blueprints' (33). As hate circulates between subjects shaped by violence and the rooms they inhabit, the novel's hauntings take on various meanings: repression of a shared imperialist consciousness, residues of brutalised and forgotten bodies, and the accumulated actions of individuals who are threatened and threaten others in turn. Alice's position as a narrator is from the start the double role of subject, releasing some of this hate into the world, and object of a social environment that pins her in certain places; she is responsible for her actions, but she is also moved by forces beyond her control.

The absorbing and disseminating of evil occurring via the House is at once metaphorical of the nation's history and a specific supernatural dynamic pertaining to this fictional place. The novel invokes a tradition of horror literature which, as Andrew Hock Soon Ng puts it, 'has demonstrated time and again that evil infesting lived space is almost always perpetrated by humans': in this dynamic, the lived space, in turn, 'will henceforth emanate certain qualities that adversely affect any subject who encounters it' (441). Ng's suggestion that, in considering these haunted settings, we should not 'privilege the figurative role performed by architecture' but also 'address its material implications' (442) seems to be heeded by Rumfitt, as *Tell Me I'm Worthless* never definitively settles haunting as metaphorical or literal, imaginary or 'real'. Echoing Gothic fiction more broadly, the novel explicitly references *The Haunting of Hill House* (30), *The Turn of the Screw* (9), and Angela Carter's 'Bluebeard' (145). Mirroring *Hill House* in particular, this text locates a source of horror in finding that the House has agency, and that the pain and cruelty within one person can breach the boundaries of their body and consolidate into an entity that spreads them on to others. In this process, the space that is supposed to be static and impartial is itself a live body that acts and is acted upon, becoming a nexus for trans-inhabitation. As *Tell Me I'm Worthless* eventually describes the visit to the House by the three friends, it features scenes that leave no doubt as to the extent to which the House is a living being, and one with bad intentions: 'Hannah put her hand out to the wall, and was shocked to find that it was now *warm*. Warm and alive. [...] There was a movement, from deep within the House. Shifting in and out. Deep breaths' (180). With the uncanniness of a warm breathing building, the text raises questions about how embodied subjects haunt and are haunted, how they can be safe from invasion and release their ghosts.

Among the unhealed social wounds that plague Rumfitt's contemporary British setting, transphobia features prominently, reflecting the political reality at the outset of the 2020s. As a result of her memory of being sexually assaulted by Alice in the House, and the scars that prove it, Ila has begun campaigning against trans rights and speaking publicly about how trans people pose a threat to cis women. After a first chapter narrated by Alice, a chapter called 'Ila' focalises through this character as she approaches a meeting of anti-trans organisers and is blocked by trans protesters, who are described in this passage as 'imposters in the guise of women' (39). The narrator guides the reader to adopt Ila's gaze as the trans women chanting on the street are reported as looking grotesque: 'They look like little girls who grew up very suddenly and very wrong' (38). Even if Ila's free indirect discourse forces a trans-hostile lens on the scene, this viewpoint still allows a criticism of the group of women 'protecting sex-based rights' that Ila is joining: as the only person at the meeting who is not white, '[s]he wonders sometimes if she is being tokenised and used as a shield against accusations of racism from the trans crowd' (42). The events following the meeting also contribute to casting doubt on the motivations and the integrity of women defending female-only spaces, as one of them assaults Ila in a women's bathroom. As an even more explicit undermining of Ila's view that it is the presence of trans women that make her 'unsafe' (46), the narrator goes beyond Ila's thoughts and perceptions to reveal that a trans woman was in the stall next to her in the bathroom of the meeting venue, while Ila 'hadn't noticed, or cared' (46). This woman, Gemma, is in fact at the meeting as a 'mole' and none of the participants have noticed that she is trans (44). While the narrator of this chapter, then, takes on a transphobic voice – in a way that recalls the reappropriation of an anti-trans phrase in the title of Fall's 'Helicopter Story' – it also allows hesitations and contradictions, and shows a larger context that is visible through its third-person omniscience.

Alongside the 'Alice' and the 'Ila' chapters, the novel features chapters entitled 'House'. In accordance with the idea that '[w]hen the House speaks, it comes from no mouth' (128), the identity of the narrator in these chapters is ambiguous. Albion itself does seem to have a 'voice', which intrudes in italics in the other sections and addresses the characters. But in the 'House' chapters, it is an external narrator who takes us through the building's history repeatedly and non-chronologically. Before the House was built, '[t]he ground that they grew it on was all wrong. Far beneath the earth, corpses lay which were older than God, and so when they raised the House it was already there in a way, fully formed, ready, ravenous' (143). After a series of violent and unhappy owners (who both affected the House with their thoughts and were affected in turn), the House is now abandoned, causing mysterious murders, suicides, and disappearances nearby. But the effects it casts are also unequal:

> There are some who immediately feel safer, knowing that the House is there, and there are some who do not. For someone to be comfortable, another has to be uncomfortable. For someone to feel safe, another has to be unsafe. [...] For someone, the majority, to prosper, another has to... well. I think you understand what I am saying, and why. (Rumfitt 61)

To mirror the building's own refusal to contain its effects within its borders and walls, the text trans-inhabits narrative boundaries here with a sudden address from an I to a you, implicating different subjects in the fictional and non-fictional 'someones' and 'others' who are agents and victims of injustice. During the main characters' visit to the House, we also learn that the walls have writing on them, graffiti and carvings, literally inscribing a multiplicity of voices into the building (176). As the text asks its central question – 'How easy is it to slip, unthinking, into ways that the house wants you to be?' (130) – this House is to be understood as a web of voices in tension with one another, pulling in different directions.

In the 'House' chapters and beyond, the text juxtaposes and ultimately blurs the boundaries between subject positions, shifting voice and focalisation from the perpetrators of violence to the victims of this violence, from the person being addressed to the person speaking. This is thematised when Alice reflects on being interpellated by hateful words:

> On a fetish forum I wouldn't be able to find again, I came across a long, repetitive string of German words when looking for people with sissy fetishes [...] when I read it, I felt – I became sure – that the author was addressing me and only me. (67)

As the novel reproduces this string of words, run through 'the automatic Google translation tool' (67), readers are also offered the unsettling opportunity to identify with the words, to become 'stuck in this pervert's fantasy' (70). The sex work performed by Alice echoes the dynamics of these fetish forums: as she is asked to read a script that a customer wrote addressing himself and shaming himself for 'dreaming of being a girl' (76), Alice cannot detach herself from the effects of the words, which make her feel the shame that the script is supposed to elicit in the listener. She attempts to distance herself from the text but does not quite succeed: 'I say what he wants me to say, but automatically. I don't think the words. They just happen, they come out of my mouth, and the shame and the disgust wash over me until I can't take it anymore' (76). In the same way as they seep in and out of the walls of the House, hateful narratives permeate the subjects adjacent to them – those who utter them, those who are the target of them, those who ask for them, those who impose them. As the words spoken by Alice in this scene include the phrase 'You are worthless' (76), the title of the novel is infused with the same ambiguity – who is telling, and who is asking to be told, 'I'm worthless'? What are the causes, and the consequences, of speaking and seeking hateful words?

Ila's hostility toward trans people is eventually implied to conceal a similar overlap of subject and object. In one of the chapters that focuses on her, Ila is reading online posts about women whose spouses came out as trans women, which are reproduced in italics in the text. As if they were recollections prompted by this reading, two paragraphs in brackets follow, to describe, first, Alice shaving her facial hair as a teenager, and, second, a parallel episode from Ila's adolescence:

> (When Ila was about sixteen, a girl in her maths class made fun of her for her darker facial hair. Ila cried when she got home, the girl had called her a man... she looked in the mirror and saw a man, in a kind fantasy, looking back at her. [...] She got out of the shower and tried to shave her face. (117)

The narrative begins to deal with Ila's own masculine identification at the same time as it explores her anger toward the trans community, setting up a clear connection between the two. Being a divided subject, who does not know or acknowledge parts of oneself, is equated to haunting, and the novel's main source of fear is not only the invasion of the self by others, but also of the self by the self:

> In the mirror Ila can see that she is a haunted house. She does not possess herself; her traumas sometimes come and peer out of the windows of her eyes and that is very frightening. I can see you there. I know you are inside. (128)

Up to this point, the chapter has occasionally switched to first-person narration in italics to signal the voice of the House, who is speaking to Ila and trying to lure her back. Here, without italics, this voice has fully intruded into that of the third-person narrator (who may or may not be linked to the author). And whoever or whatever is 'inside' Ila has become the narratee. Rather than revealing a fixed logic or a specific structure of speakers and addressees, these shifts in voice show that characters who attempt to consolidate their identities do so in the midst of clashing voices and political and affective chaos, both external and internal.

The tensions that haunt Alice and Ila's environment come to a climax in the epilogue of *Tell Me I'm Worthless*, which follows a boy who lives in a flat that has been built on the ground where the House stood. Having been radicalised into the far right through exposure to his dad's conservative views, online forums, and more generally Albion's aura that continues to emanate from this location, the boy detonates a bomb at a Pride parade attended by Alice and Ila, the latter now out as trans and called Harry. This ending is actually anticipated as one of the paranoid visions experienced by Alice early in the novel, in which she sees 'two trans people walking together bold and defiant but then a bomb explodes next to them and their brains and their limbs scatter over the streets like snow' (17). These visions, however, are implied to be not Alice's own fantasies but those of another, by whom she is afraid of becoming possessed. At the point in which this vision appears, the novel is describing Alice's paranoia about the poster of a singer that she has put up in her room coming alive and attacking her:

> maybe he would do it with his fingers, pushing his thumbs into my eyes, *last truly British people*, and when he is done with my eyes he would grab my mouth and put his words into it, *panic on the-*, whilst images of imagined atrocities that he has made up play into my head. (16)

As the fragments of song lyrics in italics identify the singer as Morrissey, known for voicing far-right views, the text physically stages the fear of being infected and invaded by the hate of others. In a sense, the bombing of the Pride parade seems to be one of the 'imagined atrocities' being 'made up' by the figure in the poster. In Alice's fantasy, what 'might happen if he comes to me' is that she will be unable to 'speak words that are not his, or think thoughts that are not his' (17). By the epilogue, then, who is imagining and speaking the events of the novel?

By insisting on the idea of taking on and taking over the voices of others, Rumfitt gives the impression that the text is brought into being not through a single agency but through the force of collective political tensions. Contradictions are often unresolved in the text: even the central problem that divides Alice and Ila, that of who was the subject and who was the object of violence in the House, is left open as the text splits into two columns describing alternative versions of events (Rumfitt 192–7). The chapter in which this occurs is accordingly entitled 'Alice and/or Ila' (182), and the doubled narrative is introduced by the third character: 'Hannah saw what happened next. One instance with one eye, and one with the other. The room split in two as she looked on, helpless and trembling' (192). Before this, the authorial voice has already posed the resolution of diverging narratives as an explicit political and creative question:

> Now, if three girls enter a house and only two leave, who is to blame? And if both girls tell a different story, but you read online that you have to BELIEVE WOMEN, what do you do? Do you decide one is a woman and one isn't, so you can believe one of them but not the other? Or the most *intersectional* one? [...] So, you go online and find an 'intersectionality score calculator' on the internet. You use it to work out who is more oppressed. (144)

In this metafictional reflection about character, Rumfitt invokes the irreducible complexities of a world formed of multiple and entangled vectors of oppression. The lives of trans people, the novel suggests, are shaped by the web of inequalities inherent in British society and its violent history of managing bodies and borders. As the narrative ends (before the epilogue) with a chapter called 'You', voicing various characters and weaving cultural references that have appeared throughout the book in a stream of consciousness, a certain catharsis seems to be achieved by letting Albion's malevolent thoughts play out on the page, leading to Alice and Ila saying that they love each other and exiting the House for the second and last time.

It is difficult to establish what happens to the characters in this text: social horrors, supernatural horrors, and imagined horrors are blended. Even if someone might be hallucinating, this is a shared hallucination with material consequences. *Tell Me I'm Worthless* refuses to settle boundaries between a first person and its others, transness and its others, one body and its others, and enacts a trans-inhabitation of all. The House functions as repository and amplification of traumatic events, hateful thoughts, injustice, and self-loathing – larger than the narrative participants (including readers) who come into contact with it. Hannah's absence and disappearance in the narrative – a chapter with her name, narrating the first visit to the House, focalises her thoughts for the first time toward the end of the novel – resists interpretation and impedes closure further. The text alludes to this when Ila attempts to narrate what happened in the House at the meeting of anti-trans organisers:

> silently, [she] apologises to Hannah for omitting her entirely. Hannah complicates things too much. Ila is telling the truth, everything she is saying is totally real to her, but to mention Hannah... it would overwhelm the story. Untether it from reality. (47)

Readers of the novel eventually learn that the House has killed Hannah by shaping her body into a swastika – a symbol whose literality paradoxically eludes reading. If authorial voice can be said to intervene in the text (and I have implied that it does), it introduces more confusion than it dispels. This is the case because it is mainly invested in interrogating readers: 'Are you a bad person, or do you just have reasonable concerns, are you a bad person, or are you just asking questions?' (212). Throughout the text, we are asked to probe our own complicity in the oppression of others, including at times these fictional characters. The question of trans embodiment runs through these concerns. The text voices the ways in which transness – both in how individuals experience it and in the public narratives that circulate about it – is connected to matters such as colonial histories, racial inequalities, and the uneven ground on to which houses are built and inhabited.

### Tell tale signs

The first-person narrators I have discussed in this chapter are ones who trouble – like ghosts – the spaces they are supposed to occupy: singular I, embodied I, gendered I, and narrating I. Trans-inhabitation is given shape through images of haunting, possession, invasion, ambiguous dwelling, and self-multiplication, which question the wholeness of the embodied self and the goal of finding a home in cisnormative systems of understanding. Being haunted, split, or separated from the body are recognised as affective experiences that come with both pain and possibility. As much as bodies are traversed by ghosts and disjunctures, there is connection and healing to be found in recognising the breaking apart inherent in the putting together of identity. Trans authors, in exploring these dynamics thematically and formally, reveal the multiplicity and fluidity of all human embodiment from the vantage point of a subject position that sees itself or is seen as particularly engaged in processes of transformation and re-signification. The question of re-narrating trans stories, which was centred in the texts I discussed in Chapter 1, here finds itself complicated by the fact that the I who tells and retells is manifold, fragmented, and extended across multiple locations. While this was often the case in Chapter 1 as well, especially through the juxtaposition of experiencing-I and narrating-I, future I and past I, and versions of the I that are articulated for different audiences and contexts, the multiplication of the self is particularly explicit here. As soon as they present an I, *Freshwater*, *Invasions*, and *Tell Me I'm Worthless* produce the presence of others beside it, by using plural first persons, multiple singular first persons, third persons, and, importantly, voices that call into question the boundary between these categories. These others inhabit the body with the I, interpret and shape the body of the I, and coexist alongside the I as its shadowy doubles. Italics and chapter (or story) divisions initially signal these changes in voice, only for these divisions to be abandoned, collapsed, or blurred. The result is a complex representation of trans corporeality across each text and a trans-inhabitation of narrative spaces.

Emezi's negotiations with the pains of being embodied take place through their protagonist's coming to terms with their identity as ọgbanje. Hinting metaphorically at the cultural dislocation of a Nigerian author in the US and resonating with trans concerns about not drawing conclusions from what is visible, the ọgbanje exceeds these symbolic connotations and comes to constitute a metaphysical subjectivity through which *Freshwater* firmly establishes identity as plural. This plurality is mirrored formally by the text, through a narrator that is multiple (the We) and multiple narrators that are one. As the novel's narrators trap and are trapped in each other, free and are freed by each other, a non-binary identity is inscribed on the body and in the text as a tension between and beyond available categorisations. Multiple subjects of multiple genders also come into contact in Gimpelevich's collection *Invasions* – this time, separate identities are explored in ontologically distinct stories but inform one another and can even be imagined to bleed into one another, transcending the borders of each individual text. The book explores the permanence of the I as its body(es) transform, not only as grounded in the experience of passing and transitioning but also as a speculative possibility occurring in new realities. Literalising some of the ways in which all narrators take on the interiorities and exteriorities of others, the narratives of *Invasions* fluctuate between more and less visible, more and less embodied, more and less gendered narrators, to create a collective and multi-voiced textual corporeality. An invasion of bodies also occurs both within and around Rumfitt's novel, as the text proposes to haunt (and be haunted by) its readers in the way in which the house of Albion does with those who come near it, absorbing and amplifying their cruellest impulses. Engagement with horror tropes allows for an exploration of British anxieties around bodies and borders, gender and violence, through narrative strategies that confound subject and object: adopting transphobic gazes but keeping them at a distance, flipping the 'I' and the 'you' of shaming speech, unsettling vectors of harm, and letting the thoughts of the House (which are in turn the thoughts of a collective history) seep into the voice of other narrators.

The embodiments that 'appear' to readers in this process are glimpsed from various angles: through the voice of a trans narrator describing themself, through an accumulation of reported movements and sensations (sometimes contradictory), or through the gaze of others – accessed through focalisation, free indirect discourse, or dialogue – which provides gendered readings of the body of the I. But, regardless of the formal choices employed to convey characters' corporeality, trans authors of written texts are in control of the level of (metaphorically) visual access that readers have to this corporeality. This is important in a political context in which being trans and being seen carries substantial risks. Bringing readers and narratees into this situation prompts the question: to whom is visibility granted or denied? Malatino's theorisation of 't4t' describes the liberatory possibilities of embodied existence in a space without cisnormative intrusion, and he asks, 'What does it mean [to] lack scripts, expectations, and assumptions for t4t intimacy? What possibilities inhere in the space of such unscriptedness?' (654). In literature that is mainstream to the extent that books that have reached publication are, a carefully restricted audience that would allow a complete lack of expectations and assumptions is not possible and often not desired.[6] But a certain unscriptedness when representing the body is still opened up by these texts, through bloody but cathartic corporeal reshapings (in *Tell Me I'm Worthless*), the exploration of the joys and perils of body swapping (in *Invasions*), and the spiritual identification with ọgbanje (in *Freshwater*). The textual bodies produced by Emezi, Gimpelevich, and Rumfitt are elusive and ambiguous as they are expansive and imaginative, exploring corporeal possibilities such as the tensions between competing agencies in the marble room of a mind, the flipping of the self into someone else, and the seeing of one reality with one eye and a different one with the other. As I move on to consider how trans narrators negotiate audiences who are expected to doubt their truths, worlds, and values, the matter of which bodies are shown, to whom, how, and why remains vital.

## Notes

[1] Among different versions used in English, I adopt the spelling of ọgbanje used in the novel.

[2] The ọgbanje sometimes refer to Ada as 'the Ada'. In some parts of my discussion, such as this one, I refer to Ada as 'she', as this is the pronoun used by the We for their human incarnation. However, as the novel progresses, Ada is consolidated as a subject with agency to identify as neither male nor female, and I use 'they' to refer to this character accordingly. Of course, as I attempt to make these distinctions, trans narratives continue to resist them.

[3] There is a case to be made that the pronoun 'they' is particularly appropriate for Ada and the author themself, as they identify as a 'we'. The use of this pronoun for non-binary identity could then be linked to the multiplicity of genders that one is, or in between which one is.

[4] With this 'us' here, I am to some extent implying 'cis readers such as myself', but I leave this position open to trans-inhabitation by others.

[5] A small portion of this analysis appears in Pellegrini, 'Temporalities Beyond Transition'.

[6] Within the category of texts that are mainstream enough to have reached publication there are of course significant differences. For instance, the success of *Freshwater* and the relatively small distribution

of *Invasions* entail different audiences, very likely varying the number of readers who are already familiar with, or open to, exploring imaginative possibilities for trans embodiment. However, in this book, I tend to take for granted that a published work always expects to reach audiences with diverse experiences, biases, and knowledges, to whom these radical reimaginings of gender and the body are sought to be made intelligible or available.

Chapter 4

# Trans Narrators and Reliability: Claiming Authority in Marginalised Realities

When a human narrator says 'I', this inevitably signals some limitation on their knowledge and their ability to perceive and assess their world: they are constrained by their bodies, their situated consciousness, their feelings and biases. When the narrator who says 'I' is trans, however, the ordinary dose of scepticism elicited by expressing a subjectively experienced truth risks being significantly amplified. This is because an element of their circumstances that is so fundamental as to be encoded in the grammar of many of our languages – their gender – is under contestation in cis culture. As Faye eloquently puts it,

> Cis men and women have the immeasurable benefit of never being thought to be mistaken, deluded or deceptive about this very fundamental fact about their personhood. That means that, in many contexts, they tend to be automatically credited with more authority, insight or expertise on both their own identity and on trans people's identities than trans people themselves are. (xvii)

A suspicion toward the speaker's expertise about their own reality is heightened in the case of trans children and youth (and non-adult narrators make two of the cases I discuss in this chapter), as well as for subjects whose authority is already seen as compromised, for instance because of their race or socioeconomic status. In this context, telling the truth, making things clear, gaining trust, and presenting an intelligible narrative are complicated endeavours, often requiring at least partial adoption of dominant discourses and epistemologies that could invalidate the very realities a trans narrator strives to convey. Obfuscations, equivocations, contradictions, and avowals of unreliability can then become ways out of this bind. As Lavery argues, 'a love of common sense, of plain speaking, of telling-it-like-it-is' is the reactionary posture of populist, far-right, and anti-trans agents (231). Against this, she values 'the position of the person who knows the truth very well, and takes pleasure in the beauty of invisible finery even so' (231). Alternatives to coercive modes of 'telling-it-like-it-is' are offered by the three texts I explore in this chapter: Jordy Rosenberg's fictional auto/biography *Confessions of the Fox*, Juno Dawson's young adult (YA) novel *Wonderland*, and Beckett K. Bauer's short story 'Notes from a Hunter Boy: As Filed by Girtrude the Librarian'.

With renounced reliability, I name a set of intentions and effects in the use of unreliability by trans authors, such as showing the impossibility of speaking 'reliably' in a world that is hostile to trans people, claiming the right to be unreliable in a society that demands simplistic fixities, and defamiliarising taken-for-granted truths. When unreliable trans narrators are employed for these purposes, we are faced with a bonding unreliability, one that encourages sympathy, and even care, for the unreliable narrator. Phelan's typologies of bonding unreliability can be seen to apply to the narratives I discuss here. For example, 'literally unreliable but metaphorically reliable' narration ('Bonding Unreliability' 226) is employed by Rosenberg when under- or misreporting details about the trans protagonist's body to show that not knowing can sometimes paint a more accurate picture than knowing; Dawson's narrator can be said to engage in 'sincere but misguided self-deprecation' (229) when she assumes that others will reject her when they learn she is trans (while in fact they already know that she is); and profound truths about gender are revealed by Bauer through 'naïve defamiliarization' (229) of systems of classification. The mapping of the operations of trans narrators on to these existing narratological models shows that these models retain the power to describe the forms that renounced reliability takes, but the work of trans authors is needed to illuminate key aspects and contexts of the signalling and attributing of unreliability. These three texts can even be read as each focusing on a particular axis of unreliability (Phelan, *Living*, 52): *Confessions of the Fox* is especially concerned with lies and the muddying of fact, *Wonderland* with hallucinations and the distortion of perception, and 'Notes from a Hunter Boy' with misjudgements deriving from an unfamiliar value system. Across and beyond these distinctions, constructing narrators whose identity resists cisnormative impositions shows that speaking the 'plain truth' is the privilege of those whose authority to do so is already recognised. But as unreliable as these narrators may be at any point, they are ultimately to be trusted when it comes to the reality of their gender.

In discussions about unreliable narrators in narrative studies, unreliability is at times something that is brought to the text by audiences (any narrator could be considered unreliable depending on any one reader's views) and, at others, something intentionally and formally signalled by the text (through contradictions and discrepancies designed to indicate that a narrator's willingness or ability to report and judge things correctly is compromised). Both are relevant in the discussion that follows. In fact, renounced reliability describes a situation in which awareness that trans narrators will be deemed unreliable by some readers, no matter how trustworthy and self-aware the text presents them to be, influences the way in which trans authors deal with narrative reliability in the first place. In the most basic sense, renounced reliability involves constructing a trans narrator who has flaws and limitations, rejecting the responsibility of dealing with the audience's assumptions about the reliability of trans people as a whole. Writing without an awareness of these assumptions in the current moment seems possible but rare, as Freddy McConnell comments in an interview with Peters about her bestselling novel:

> The truth is, back in 2018, she did not write *Detransition, Baby* with much awareness, let alone consideration, of 'the trans debate' being stoked in very different ways on either side of the Atlantic. 'At the time, when I was writing [...] I was just thinking about what was going to be funny for my friends and what was pertinent to our lives.'
>
> It sounds like a common and reasonable mindset for an author. Yet I, as a trans journalist and writer based in the UK, am taken aback. Is she really telling me there was recently a place and time when trans writers could forget about seeing themselves as politicised and instead operate with total creative freedom, simply as writers? ('Torrey Peters')

A desire to forget those readers who do not trust what trans subjects have to say is certainly felt in contemporary trans literature; at the same time, many trans narratives still foreground the question of who has the power to attribute or possess reliability, authority, expertise, and the ability to accurately perceive the world.

## Jordy Rosenberg: Declining to describe

The blending of genres, forms, and styles in trans literature is a phenomenon that I have touched on, especially in its function of layering temporalities that interrupt and disrupt each other, and of multiplying and fragmenting embodied narrators.[1] In the case of *Confessions of the Fox*, I am especially interested in how authority and reliability are distributed and attributed across the fictional and non-fictional discourses that are invoked, reproduced, and parodied by the text. This novel's popularity – it was shortlisted for multiple awards and recognised as one of the best books of 2018 by numerous publications – suggests that its central preoccupation with the production and reception of trans stories resonates widely in the contemporary moment. Rosenberg's role as an English Professor at the University of Massachusetts-Amherst and as a trans man also becomes relevant in relation to questions of authenticity and expertise that are asked by the text: readers may in fact seek authorial reassurance both that any historical knowledge gained from the text is legitimate and that the experiences of gender variance depicted are reflective of reality. The text, however, prompts us to investigate why and how we seek these reassurances. The novel's eighteenth-century setting gives rise to emulation of the styles and conventions of various documents belonging to non-fictional genres that lay claim to a truth – from biography to annotated editions to scientific papers. As the notion of 'truth' is contested when it comes to trans identities, the text is concerned with which and whose truth is being mobilised for what aims, interrogating the ideological discourses that produce the meaning of bodies and the ordering of reality in the first place. Rosenberg's academic and political investments in Marxism are reflected in the novel's understanding of transness in relation to the history of capitalist violence. As the author argues in his afterword to Jules Joanne Gleeson and Elle O'Rourke's *Transgender Marxism*, 'trans people have long been a fixation, scapegoat and target for convulsions in the mode of production, the organisation of space, and the social world' (Rosenberg, 'One Utopia' 288). *Confessions of the Fox* explores how subjects who exist as this 'fixation, scapegoat and target' cannot and will not speak in ways that conform to hegemonic paradigms for telling the truth.

In order to ask whether the narrator of *Confessions of the Fox* is reliable, which I maintain is a relevant question when it comes to this novel, we first need to establish who this narrator is. The novel blurs the boundaries between homo- and heterodiegetic narration, and cannot be said to have a 'trans narrator' in the sense of a single trans character who says 'I' – though it does have one in the sense that there is a trans-inhabiting (multiple, moving) narrating voice. The text consists of a fictional found manuscript, telling the story of eighteenth-century celebrity thief Jack Sheppard as a trans man. While Jack's life is narrated largely by a heterodiegetic narrator, the document is repeatedly called an autobiography and speculated to have been authored by its protagonist. It is also framed by a foreword, extensive footnotes, and an additional note to readers in the first-person voice of Dr Voth, an American historian, also a trans man, who finds and annotates the manuscript in the present. The fictional paratext constitutes a narrative in itself: Voth recounts episodes of his own life while performing his role as editor. While he initially attempts to verify the 'authenticity' of the manuscript, he comes to reject this practice as the narrative progresses and he discovers that it may have been authored collectively in a discontinuous manner. While a single narrator whose (un)reliability we can assess may be difficult to identify, there is certainly an overall renunciation of reliability in *Confessions of the Fox*, formally and thematically. Even without particular certainty about the ultimate agent responsible for this narrative (in its accumulated layers), the question of whether this narrative is reliable can still be asked.[2] The doubt that the text intentionally casts on its own claims ends up pointing to different sources of intention, from Jack Sheppard as a potential intra-diegetic author, to Dr Voth as narrator of his own footnotes, to unknown editors who have altered the manuscript in untraceable ways, to Rosenberg himself. Against desires to categorise the text in neater ways, these different entities blend into each other.

There is a shift, in the novel, from a situation in which a subject (Dr Voth) is in the position to observe and judge an object (the manuscript, but also Jack's body) to a situation in which Jack, Voth, and other textual participants exist in non-hierarchical relation to each other. This shift goes hand in hand with the progressive displacement of the question of whether the manuscript conveys the 'truth' about the historical figure of Jack Sheppard. Voth admits in the foreword that he is 'ashamed' of having once been interested in the question '*Is the manuscript the authentic autobiography?*' (Rosenberg, *Confessions* xiii). The question of the text's authenticity seems then to be tied to whether Jack may be the author of it, making it an 'autobiography' despite the way in which it refers to Jack in the third person; this is also the position of the publisher, a shady organisation called P-Quad, who are interested in marketing the manuscript as the *'earliest authentic confessional transgender memoirs known to history'* (121). Voth's belief that Jack is the teller of his own story often appears to result from the manuscript's ethical treatment of its protagonist, which indicates an author who intimately understands how Jack would want to be rendered visible to readers. This ethical treatment consists in practices of omitting, hiding, and refusing to expose. For example, Voth remarks on 'the excision of what appears to be Jack's given name (P– )' in favour of affirming his identity as Jack (16), and on 'the elegant declining-to-describe' employed when it comes to discussing certain parts of his body (109). Such narrative acts of omission counter a history in which gender-variant subjects have been dispossessed of their bodies and defined against their will, and are therefore an indication of a sympathetic author/narrator. Ultimately, Voth realises that the document's proof of authenticity does not lie in verifying its authorship by a single individual, but in its capacity to mobilise affects and experiences that connect a multiplicity of people excluded and exploited by the same systems.

In this context, the text's acts of underreporting are to be read as heightening its credibility (as a document of trans truth and as the narrative of an agent who knows what they are talking about) rather than undermining it. Dr Voth's numerous footnotes affirming that one detail or another points to the authenticity of the manuscript show that this authenticity is mostly found in the narrator's refusal to expose Jack in a way in which he would not want to be exposed. Additionally, the editor's affective relationship with the manuscript, for instance his 'jealousy' at Jack's capacity to be vulnerable with his lover, is enlisted as another sign of its 'authenticity', intended as a capacity to resonate with certain readers (91). This hints at a reframing of the question of truth and accuracy, signposting Voth's conclusion that the manuscript is authentic not because it conveys a historical truth about a particular person but because it depicts erased experiences that the editor and others can recognise as akin to their own. A chapter inserted by Voth in the manuscript itself – entitled 'Reader!' – explains his realisation that Jack's story is not 'exactly a singular memoir' but a sort of 'collective diary-keeping' (259). This is indicated by anachronistic references and passages that turn out to be quotations from later texts, which reveal to Voth that the manuscript is made up of layers of corrections and contributions by marginalised subjects and political groups throughout history. This realisation brings with it a shift in the purpose of editing. Initially, Voth edits the text for a publisher who is interested in the manuscript's status as a memoir – and his affective relationship with the text can still be enlisted for this purpose, since it signals a relatable experience. However, the discovery that the text constitutes 'collective diary-keeping' brings about the decision to steal the manuscript and continue editing outside of the framework of verifying Jack's identity for the publisher. The manuscript's value lies not in its capacity to document the truth in a way that P-Quad can understand and exploit for profit, but rather in its inaccuracies and contradictions, insofar as they lead to the discovery of a deeper and more elusive truth about community and resistance.

In his status as a fugitive, Voth, like the rogues and outlaws that populate Jack's story, embraces the untrustworthiness attached to this role, celebrating a refusal to comply with corporate and institutional economies of knowledge and displaying a freedom to elude explanations and, possibly, to invent. After stealing the manuscript, Voth seems to have found a place for himself and the text that is 'very far away', not 'primarily in terms of space' but also in the sense that he is 'living at a different timescale' (266). This place is populated by 'friends' who are 'archivists of us' and 'were once us' (267). The extent to which descriptions of this place are to be taken at face value is never entirely clear, as we know that Voth needs to conceal his location in order to avoid being traced. He describes the archives as a 'colossal library in chitin, spiderweb and glass that sprawls at the edges of the floating alleys of the central square' (267). This fantastical description could be taken as figurative (a poetic veiling), literal (taking the novel into the realm of speculative utopian fiction), or an invention intended to be believed (sending those with the wrong intentions on a futile chase). There is, above all, an indication that the way of living and knowing that Voth has discovered cannot be expressed in a language understood by (all) readers, as we are embroiled in the history that the archivists have managed to leave behind. An underlying reliable message stands through these equivocations: that 'there is no trans body, no body at all' outside the legacy of '[s]lavery, surveillers, settlers and their shadows' (315), and therefore no truth can be uttered that is not marred by this legacy. Some radical break with who 'we' are now is required in order to recover a history of the body as 'love's inscription' instead – a history of fighting against erasure and violence, one made up of 'fragments of a life untethered from this world, messages from a future reflected to us like light off broken shards' (315). To access such a history and such a future, 'reality' may not be enough.

As much as the text recognises a 'profound lacuna in the records', which 'cannot simply be filled' but 'must be encountered head-on as constitutive of the archive as such' (31), it often casts the discovery of the manuscript as a restoration of marginalised characters' authority over their own narratives, which gives hope for retracing what has been written over by violence. The historical figures of Sheppard and his lover Bess are given a voice that, in the world of the novel, is constituted as potentially 'truer' than any previous version. A chapter of the manuscript is narrated by Bess in the first person and features no footnotes by Voth, except for one at the very end stating: 'Reader, please forgive the radio silence. I'm not in the habit of interrupting women when they are speaking' (198). This indicates that the rest of the manuscript, which has a heterodiegetic narrator, makes it somewhat easier or more appropriate for Voth to intervene in a way that does not feel like 'interrupting' someone who is speaking. Since Jack does not speak as an I in the novel (aside from some brief passages of interior monologue), it is perhaps for this reason that Voth appears initially more comfortable with discussing the authenticity of the text's claims about him. The presence of both Jack and Bess in the manuscript is also remarked upon by the editor as revealing 'details that are not given in any of the other records': Jack is a trans man and Bess has South Asian heritage (56). This prompts him to conclude that this text is 'either the most or the least authentic Sheppard document in existence' (27). The notion that a narrative could be either the most or the least authentic version of reality, because of its variation from the norm, draws attention to some of the paradoxes of trans storytelling. Renounced reliability results from this paradox, as the text sets aside the question of what may or may not have happened to validate the affective and political reality (within and outside the novel) of its speaking subjects, whom it takes care to 'not interrupt' whenever they articulate a first-person narrative.

On the other hand, the interruptions represented by the footnotes show the outside interests that encroach upon Jack's narrative and that threaten to participate in the character's erasure the more they purport to want to make him visible. As Gil Mozer argues, 'the amalgamation of fictional biography text and fictional peritext' in *Confessions of the Fox* constitutes 'a visual and narrative model of the ways in which the contextual paratext of trans stories [...] [is] at times intrusive into trans lives themselves' (191). This 'contextual paratext' that intrudes on trans narratives, made up of the 'many voices, markets, and industries involved in the public-making process' (187), influences both a text's reception and an author's anticipation of that reception. Awareness of this contextual paratext leads to the difficulty described by McConnell for trans writers to 'forget about seeing themselves as politicised' ('Torrey Peters'). A prominent voice interrupting the narrative in this novel is P-Quad's marketing director Sullivan, whose emails are reported in all capitals in the footnotes. In the most illustrative example of an interference that struggles to be shut out of trans stories, Sullivan demands the use of clearer language, asking Voth to 'SPECULATE' when information is missing about characters' bodies (Rosenberg, *Confessions* 137). When Bess and Jack encounter a scientific text that mentions 'sexual chimeras', which are implied to be sex- and gender-variant individuals, the manuscript is supposed to include 'a painted illustration' for this entry, but Voth notes that 'the original author' has replaced it with an 'abstract page' (134) – the same abstract page that readers of *Confessions of the Fox* can see on page 133.[3] As the text hints at some similarity between what is represented in the scientific text and Jack's own anatomy, Sullivan insists: 'WE REQUIRE *SPECIFICITY* AS TO THE MEANING OF SEXUAL CHIMERA [...] READERS NEED TO BE ABLE TO VISUALIZE' (132). The demand to render the body intelligible for a cis audience ultimately leads to Voth rebelling through renounced reliability: not only does he provide nothing but avoidances on the question of the illustration, but he also refuses to use his own historical expertise and knowledge of gender-variant embodiment to give Sullivan authoritative answers.

The question of whether Voth is withholding the real illustration, as Sullivan believes, is clarified later, as the editor confesses to an act of lying:

## Trans Narrators and Reliability    147

> Incidentally, I need to make a confession: the footnote on page 251 contains a number of partial and necessary lies. [...] when I said I had sent him the missing page of the manuscript, containing an illustration of Jack's genitalia, what I actually did was Google 'waterlogged slug'. (272)

The fact that Sullivan's request for clarity on trans bodies has been satisfied by the picture of a dead slug can only be admitted, and reliability restored, when the footnotes are protected from the eyes of P-Quad, following Voth's escape. At this point, the latter explains that he has 'no idea if this page ever existed – and, if it did, at what point it may have been removed' (272). While in order to discover this lying we need a retrospective admission, Voth's refusal to use his expertise for the aim of providing definitive answers is a kind of unreliability that can be detected right away. This refusal too occurs in relation to trans embodiment, when the manuscript describes a mastectomy performed on Jack:

> SULLIVAN: EVER SEEN ANYTHING LIKE THIS?
> ME: In person? I'll reserve comment.
> SULLIVAN: IN LITERATURE OF THE PERIOD.
> ME: I am aware only of a similar operation performed nearly a century later on Frances Burney (1812). Although also performed without anesthesia, the operation was to remove a tumor.
> SULLIVAN: ANYTHING PERFORMED FOR THE PURPOSES OF GENDER TRANSITION?
> ME: Even if I said it was the only such record I've ever seen, what with everything we've already agreed on re: Mignolo and the 'epistemic disobedience' that *is* the archive (we've agreed on this, right???) – it wouldn't really mean anything. (146)

This dialogue, reported in a footnote without further commentary by the narrator, withholds this clarification from us as it does from Sullivan. Whether this form of elliptical speaking undermines the trustworthiness of Voth in the eyes of any given reader or not, the situation stands that we are never given a definitive answer. The novel is instead invested in interrogating why and how the question is being asked.

Overall, Dr Voth is constructed to be a bonding narrator whose motives for obfuscating the facts – to reveal the murky processes by which narratives about trans bodies are constructed by forces that work against their interests – are endorsed by the novel. But omissions about gender or refusals to clarify corporeal details are not read by everyone for their underlying reliable message, and are sometimes construed as unnecessary or malicious obstructions. I mentioned in my introduction how some reader reviews of a contemporary novel that omits the sex of its narrator (*The Lauras*) express irritation at an inability to be 'sure':

> regardless of what Alex identifies with and what pronoun Alex uses, Alex was born with anatomy of one gender and I wish the book had at least described which that was. [...] I wasn't a big fan of that approach, only because it left me wondering and I never received any answers which is always frustrating for me. (Jordan)

The novel, and the author, are cast by this kind of reaction as unreasonably stubborn, concealing information that is, and should be, available to everyone. Anticipating a similar frustration from readers (given voice in the text itself by the character of Sullivan), *Confessions of the Fox* doubles down on omissions, refusing to give Jack up to a cis gaze. Voth's footnotes draw attention to words that have been erased from the manuscript, such as Jack's former name. The description of a sexual encounter between Jack and Bess is also illustrative of the text's erasures:

> So to put it plainly there was a—
> —But language fails here—
> —Perhaps a ...
> ... *Transfixing Shape?*
> —blooming thick at his nethers.
> In any case, not the arborvitae of other coves—the ones possessed by childish glee. This was something else.
> Less a—
> or, rather, more a — (201)

We have seen this gesture of creating gaps with Alabanza, in Chapter 2, who claimed the power to name and not name, showing a similar impossibility and refusal to 'put it plainly'. What Voth calls the 'elegant declining-to-describe' (109) enacted by Jack's manuscript is a gesture whose author is not easily identifiable: whether it is the 'original' author of the text (maybe Jack himself) or subsequent authors/editors, someone always protects the body from the curiosity of readers.

Rather than rendering Jack's gender and embodiment illegible, however, the novel establishes a different kind of textual legibility, one in which 'not telling' tells as much as telling does, if not more. In the same way, the text's notion of authenticity moves away from ideas of accuracy and objectively verified truths. In the world in which this novel is published, discourses of factuality and scientific proof are often instrumentalised to invalidate trans identity. Renounced reliability is a refusal to participate in truth-telling in these terms, while still articulating a reliable message. Committing to what Snorton calls the 'political and ethical imperative to the right to opacity' (11), the text imagines the lost voices of marginalised subjects and accords to them the agency to speak or, crucially, not speak. The effects of becoming visible and legible are shown to depend on whether this visibility is desired or enforced. For instance, at the start of the novel, Jack craves more intimacy with Bess in spite of his fear of showing his body to her, as he does not want to 'retreat to [...] the wretched unseenness to which he'd become accustom'd' (Rosenberg, *Confessions* 68) – but the body that Bess sees is not displayed for readers. On the other hand, Voth describes his own sexual encounters in detail, and explains: 'I'm more than happy to go on at length about my prodigious genitalia. But there's a difference between a confession one wants to give, and one that is taken' (109). The distinction between a showing/telling that comes from an I who has control over what is revealed and one for which this is not the case is also tied to the status of Jack's manuscript as 'confessions'. When he is arrested by the police who ask for his 'confessions', Jack remarks that his 'tales are for rogues only' (83). Voth's theft of the manuscript – as well as the acts of omission, veiling, and metaphorical transfiguration performed by the text – indicates that some details are indeed 'for rogues only'. Those who can access Jack's tale as intended are those who understand it without an expert explanation, do not need help to visualise, and can suspend a demand for transparency.

In its negotiation with concealing and revealing, resisting and confessing, escaping and reaching out, Voth imagines different narratees at different times, and Rosenberg different readers. The audience of the text(s) is understood to possess different levels of understanding and ability to decode narrative obfuscations, and both the novel as a whole and the footnotes in particular speak for those who will hear. As Voth ambiguously explains, 'I'm editing this for *us* – those of us who have been dropped from some moonless sky to wander the world' (166). The novel's narrative agents insist on the question of who can and should claim the authority, or renounce the entitlement, to see and to speak. The attribution of reliability, whether in the sense of the trustworthiness of a narrator or the credibility of a claim, is both deliberately hindered by the text and one of its explicit thematic concerns. Against the acts of surveillance perpetrated by eighteenth-century police and land surveyors – as well as by twenty-first-century academic management and corporations who are out to exploit a new trans visibility – multiple characters give up the 'opportunity' to tell their story to those in power, but still use textual means to express solidarity with, and protect, each other. *Confessions of the Fox* performs ethical gestures to shield Jack from an invasive and punitive gaze and shows that sex and gender as fixed, coherent, and self-evident notions are dependent on a history of violence against bodies perceived as deviant. In the novel, declining-to-describe, omissions, and creating space for others to speak are political acts that do not always have identifiable authors – a number of intra- and extra-diegetic writers, editors, and readers form a virtual community based on empathy and care. As a trans scholar, Rosenberg simultaneously holds and renounces authority over the subject of his book: while his own lived experience of transness and knowledge of history mark him as an expert on the text's topic, the novel invites a questioning of the kind of expertise we seek from both academic authorities and members of marginalised groups, showing that whenever the assessment of another is sought to verify a subject's own knowledge of themselves, it is usually wielded as a means to discipline them.

### Juno Dawson: Loosening control

As is the case with *Confessions of the Fox*, texts that negotiate the agency, authenticity, and trustworthiness of a trans narrator prompt a consideration of the identity of the author, which comes to matter in relation to the questions that are tackled intra-diegetically.[4] By the time of *Wonderland*'s publication, Dawson was already an award-winning YA author, well known in the UK and internationally. Her cultural prominence has now grown even further: her first book series aimed at adult readers, *Her Majesty's*

*Royal Coven* (2022–), is a bestselling success; she is a high-profile popular culture commentator as the host of podcasts on *Doctor Who* and *Sex and the City*; and her non-fiction work on LGBTQ+ education for teenagers, *This Book Is Gay* (2014), has attracted right-wing attacks on schools and libraries in the US and Ireland (as is often the case, queer and trans visibility goes hand in hand with becoming the target of hostility and violence). When Dawson came out as trans in 2015, she was already a popular writer, and is considered 'the first Young Adult author in the United Kingdom to come out as transgender' (Williams). In her autobiographical book *The Gender Games* (2017), Dawson reflects on her pre-transition career:

> Until I announced my transition, the question I was asked at events more than any other was 'How do you write such convincing female characters?' I swear it wasn't anything I intentionally did – I was just writing myself into stories, and I am a girl. (126)

Three years later, when *Wonderland* featured her first trans narrator, the shift from voicing a girl to voicing a trans girl brought to the narrative fore reflections on authority and reliability linked to the experience of being trans in public. As the novel's narrator, Alice, experiences modern-day versions of the social puzzles from *Alice in Wonderland*, she struggles to both gain control over her mental health and relinquish the need to control how others see her; throughout, she is 'backed' by Dawson's commanding presence as a cultural leader in challenging dominant social forces to loosen their own control over young trans subjects.

While the narrators of *Clean* (2018) and *Meat Market* (2019) – the novels that precede *Wonderland* in Dawson's 'London Trilogy' and similarly explore the violent and nihilistic world of a glamorous elite – are also young girls whose agency is compromised, Alice's voice seeks to be heard in a context in which her very existence is at risk, as the erasure of trans rights, and especially of trans children and teenagers, is a dangerous reality. In 2020, the same year in which this book was published, the judgement on the *Bell v. Tavistock* case in the UK became national news: the ruling restricted the ability of young people under sixteen years old to consent to puberty blockers as treatment for gender dysphoria, resulting in the NHS suspending access to trans children's healthcare. When *Bell v. Tavistock* was overturned in 2021, the Appeal

Court deemed that the earlier judgement had 'undermined the entitlement of children under the age of 16 to make decisions for themselves' to the extent that, when seeking treatment for gender dysphoria, they would be 'treated differently from others in their age group seeking medical treatment' (Siddique). But this attempt to restore young people's ability to consent to treatment was not the final word on trans youth's agency in the UK, as 2024 saw the publication of the final report on the Cass Review, an investigation into healthcare for trans children commissioned by NHS England which has led to fears that gender-affirming care will be further threatened. The report implicitly frames being trans as an undesirable state to be avoided if possible, and explicitly expresses concerns that children may be influenced by social media to falsely believe that they are trans.[5] Dawson's own reaction on the day of the final report's publication expresses the hope that this will be taken as an opportunity to take trans youth seriously instead:

> I think you would have to really stretch to believe that this is reporting there is no such thing as a trans child or that some children are not experiencing gender dysphoria [...] it can be so hard when [...] some really transphobic people are taking this report as a major win. (Dawson, 'Cass Report')

The context of Dawson's writing, then, is characterised by widespread belief that teenagers are incapable of realising they are being manipulated by others or unable to know and articulate their gender identity, with the result that they are consistently blocked in their path by adults who exaggerate the dangers of trans-affirming care (for instance through misreporting on the effects of puberty blockers or on the easiness with which they are prescribed). Creating an authoritative young trans narrator who knows herself and is able to assess her reality (while also undergoing the kind of medical treatment that is the subject of much scaremongering) is an ethical imperative that Dawson takes seriously. But where does this leave us in terms of reading Alice's unreliability? Somewhat surprisingly, the novel begins by establishing that Alice cannot fully trust her own mind. Before the main plot begins – with Alice's quest to track down her missing schoolmate Bunny at a party filled with enemies who look down on her because of her *nouveau riche* status – the narrator explains that she is considering interrupting her medication against the advice of her therapist. After a suicide attempt, Alice has learned that she cannot always trust herself: 'Sometimes I *think* I want to die. I *don't*, it's a convincing lie, but that's what my brain is telling me' (*Wonderland* 28). By now, however, she feels like she is 'starting to *know my own brain*': 'If I can tell the difference between what's real and what isn't, I don't really want to spend the rest of my life taking medications' (29). When travelling to the isolated country estate where the party is taking place, Alice realises that she has in fact not taken her medication that morning and has also forgotten to bring it with her, suggesting that the ensuing weekend (the majority of her narrative) may bring back a situation in which she cannot tell 'the difference between what is real and what is not'. Other sources of unreliability are introduced too: Alice's 'body dysmorphia' is invoked to ask us to distrust her descriptions of herself (116) and the 'link between psychosis and marijuana' is mentioned in anticipation of her smoking some (38). But while the text continually draws attention to the ways in which Alice's perception may be altered, it ultimately communicates reliably about the reality of many things, including her gender.

In a society in which trans youth (and trans people in general) are often seen as being deluded or confused about their gender, it might seem that the text is leaving room for condescending adults to rule that, if Alice's brain can tell her 'lies', she may also be wrong about being a girl. Instead, allowing a trans girl to be an unreliable narrator shows that the novel is not prepared to make compromises to render Alice more legible to potentially suspicious audiences, thereby affirming her gender in defiance of the narratives that these audiences may wish to construct. Renounced reliability, in this case, takes the form of claiming the freedom to be unreliable in human ways without one's identity as a woman needing to be called into question. Even the scene in which the main villain of the story accuses Alice of being wrong about herself turns out to be a moment that affirms her gender: 'There's nothing special about you, is there, Alice? [...] It's all a façade and there's nothing underneath. You're... just a girl' (256). This is still hurtful for Alice because her social anxieties hinge on both being and not being an ordinary girl – not interesting enough or not girl enough. To resolve the former fear, the plot reveals her intelligence and resilience in the manner of other outcast or wallflower narratives. But being 'just a girl' is also what alleviates the latter fear. When the narrator explains that taking oestrogen did not put a stop to her depression, she realises that nothing, including her unhappiness, negates who she is: 'What did I think was happening inside the head of a common-or-garden girl? Pink kittens? [...] Because I had always been a girl. A very poorly girl' (224). Despite these reassurances, however, Alice is convinced that her peers will reject her once they learn she is trans: this is framed alternately as something she is unreliable about and as a reasonable concern. When this character thinks that everyone is out to get her, in one sense she is being paranoid, but, in another, she is understandably cautious. In this way, the text simultaneously bears witness to real hostility against trans people and offers hope that violence and gender invalidation are not the only possible responses one can expect from others.

Aside from the doubts that the novel casts on Alice's perceptions, the most unreliable readings of herself and of what her schoolmates think of her are formally separated from the main narrative by the use of italics and by the attribution of these claims to a version of her called Other Alice. Before the party, this separation is at its strongest, even as Alice's insecurities begin to surface in relation to a sexual encounter with Bunny. We learn that the two, previously only acquaintances, spent the night together in a hotel after a chance encounter, and that Alice's feelings for Bunny are partly what motivates her investigation of the missing girl. As the narrator reflects on Bunny leaving the hotel room without saying goodbye, some self-deprecating thoughts intrude but are quickly dismissed:

> *She came to her senses. Why would she want to be with you, you're–*
> I shake the thought off immediately. (25)

The hint that Bunny may have fled because Alice is trans is clearly marked as a train of thought that is not to be trusted. As the withdrawal from antidepressants worsens on the second morning of the party, the voice in italics, attributed to Other Alice (the lying part of herself she should not listen to), gets louder: '*Everything you are is embarrassing. You're no fucking girl, you're a man. You're disgusting, you will always be a*' (154). Despite finding it more difficult to interrupt these sentences, the main voice of the narrator still regains authority over reality to tell herself that 'there's something wrong with my brain. They haven't quite worked out what, but sometimes it makes me see and hear things which are not there. There is no such thing as Other Alice' (155). However, the perspective of Other Alice cannot always be kept at bay and is sometimes adopted as the narrator's own, leading to unreliable claims such as 'Other Alice is right. Normal love is for normal people' (203). The persistence of the protagonist's self-loathing cannot solely be imputed to a representation of teenage insecurity or clinical depression – after all, Other Alice is articulating views that trans girls hear and read about themselves every day.

In letting the narrator claim that 'Other Alice is right', reliability is renounced not defiantly this time, as a rejection of cis norms, but to show the impossibility of keeping anti-trans discourse from creeping into perceptions of oneself. It is to offer hope against this crushing reality that the novel takes care to provide moments of gender affirmation for Alice – though it is ultimately the realisation of her own strength, rather than the gaze of others, that restores her energy to fight and heal. These moments of gender affirmation take the form of a series of reveals that Alice's peers already know that she is trans, which cast doubt on her interpretation of their rejection of her. The first of these surprises is delivered by twins Jeremy and Jonty, who invite wandering Alice to join them in a hot tub, and are later discovered to have drugged her without consent with a plan to sexually assault her. The unambiguous condemnation of these characters' ethics adds a complicated layer to their validation of Alice as a girl, which consists in confirming that she is 'hot' and advising her to '[o]wn' the 'whole trans thing' (116). The twins' assertion that '[e]veryone knows' (117) that Alice is trans and yet they still include her in the misogynistic 'ranking system' (116) used to judge girls at their school creates a tangle of feelings that Alice has to carefully parse:

> It's not ideal, but whoever outed me has kind of saved me a thankless task, I suppose. It's a lie of course. It stings like vinegar. I quietly relished the fact that I thought I was 'passing' as a cis girl. It's a guilty badge of honour and I don't want to lose it. Heavens, being trans is complex. (199)

The fact that people know that she is trans and this is 'not the end of the world' (118) is not accompanied by straightforward relief as it does not erase the risks that girls (trans or not) face, and as Alice cannot help but internalise a system of norms that values 'passing'.

This means that assessing which of her thoughts are 'lies' is once again no simple endeavour.

In the narrator's comment that 'being trans is complex', I also see a metafictional nod to the presence of the author and her aims. In fact, the non-discovery of Alice's secret is often framed in explicitly narrative terms, calling attention to the constructedness of the text. When Maxim, a more sympathetic character than the twins, also shows desire for Alice and explains that he already knows she is trans, he invokes a specific kind of text in asking, 'Was it meant to be a big plot twist?' (197). Some readers may recall here narratives that do construct the reveal of a trans person's body as a 'plot twist', against which many trans writers protect their own characters. The mention of a twist signals the text's awareness of its audience, who are also somewhat didactically addressed by Maxim's next question to Alice, in response to her voicing the desire to be 'a normal girl': 'What makes *normal girls* normal?' (197). In this context, Alice's anticipations of what others will think of her (sometimes proven to be unreliable) mirror the author's anticipations of her readers' existing knowledge and judgement. These anticipations are explicit in a non-fictional text like *The Gender Games*, in which Dawson interrogates us directly: 'It boils down to one yes/no question: do you think I'm a man? [...] Fundamentally I *don't* think I'm a man. Nor was I ever. Hopefully I've convinced you of that now' (201). In *Wonderland*, the presence of an author who hopes that most readers will be 'convinced' that Alice is a 'normal girl', even if the character herself does not always believe this, becomes a less overt communication, happening behind the narrator's back – to use a common expression to describe narrative unreliability. To admit uncertainty and to show the sway that transphobic narratives have over Alice works to strengthen, rather than undermine, this message, as it creates a realistic result of the relentless effect of voices asking trans people to doubt themselves. The designation of the book as YA fiction should also be kept in mind, as the author's care for young readers who may be trans or questioning their assigned gender necessitates clarity about when Alice is misguided and when she is not.

Dawson's presence is felt throughout the unfolding of the fictional events. The chapter titles especially display a slippage between Alice's 'I' and an external agent. While titles like 'I Just Had Sex with Maxim Hattersley' (193) are clearly in Alice's voice – to the extent that the narration in this chapter continues from the title and starts with 'And very nice it was too' (193) – titles like 'Address for Alice' (51) regard the protagonist in the third person, and ones like 'I Would Advise Against "And It Was All a Dream"' (270) express specifically authorial concerns. The result is that an author or author-like entity accompanies Alice in her journey. When clarifying her capacity to take care of herself, the narrator explains, 'That's the thing with being trans, I always assumed everyone would leave me once they saw me for what I was, so I got very good at looking after myself. Well, until I couldn't' (147). In creating such a character, an author who aims to do justice to young and trans people can be imagined to feel a sort of ethical duty to 'watch over' her. When Alice takes her clothes off in front of Maxim, for instance, she reports, 'I stand before him, offering up my cursed body like some sort of curio' (199). Despite the narrator's self-deprecating view of her own body as something grotesque to be 'offered up' for the curiosity of others, she is still protected (or protects herself, and the two options are never quite distinct in the first person) from the gaze of readers, as the parts of her body that most catalyse her worry are never described to us. Even when Alice is unkind to herself, then, the author is not. But the latter does not take narrative agency away from her young protagonist either – Alice is predominantly the one in charge of what and how to narrate, as seen when she delays the story of her transition until a character explicitly asks for it, warning that it is not 'some inspirational TED Talk moment' (223). In her backing of Alice, Dawson honours both the fact that the character can 'take care of herself' and the fact that she is in need of support.

Questions of safety and trust are also at the centre of the novel's depiction of drugs. In one sense, drugs are shown to influence the narrator to the extent that her perceptions cannot be trusted, and that she needs in-story characters who possess greater lucidity to watch over her in the way that I have argued the 'author' also does. This is the case with both prescribed and recreational drugs, and more than once Alice emphasises the similarity between antidepressants and substances like MDMA, which both 'puppeteer the serotonin and dopamine in your brain' (71). But being controlled by chemicals also characterises her brain drug-free. The text shows Alice having a panic attack on the boat that takes her to the party, and dwells on how the faces (and intentions) of the attendees become distorted due to the 'adrenaline' flooding her body (73); later, as she watches Maxim sleep after sex, she reminds herself that his attractiveness can probably be attributed to an 'oxytocin hangover' (201). At the same time as the text indicates that there is no such thing as uninfluenced human perception, Alice rationally enumerates the hormones and substances that skew her ability to process and interpret reality. And even after she drinks tea spiked with 'magic mushrooms', the text asks us not to dismiss everything she sees. When she spots a silhouette resembling Bunny, the narrator asserts that 'It's real. I swear it', later adding the caveat 'if I can trust my two eyes' (104). As she chases Bunny in the woods, readers are presented with obviously unreliable descriptions of the trees: 'Knots blink open to reveal wet eyes, and bark lips part with stringy saliva' (105). However, several chapters later, it turns out that Bunny really was there. We may have surmised this by assessing the improbability of hallucinations so soon after drinking the tea, but one can never be sure how time passes textually, especially in a novel like this one, which also foregrounds the strangeness of time. Ultimately, the representation of drugs aids the thematic concern with relying on oneself, being mistaken, and being believed. As was the case with Alice's assumption that she would be rejected by anyone who learns that she is trans, her narrating mind on drugs is both misled and grasping a kernel of truth.

Being controlled by drugs – sometimes taken intentionally, sometimes entering her system against her will, and sometimes reluctantly accepted as necessary – is only one of the ways in which Alice heads toward unplanned destinations. Although the first chapter is entitled 'Alice's Inescapable Fate' (5) – signalling again the presence of an authorial voice behind the narrator – it is unclear what this fate is, as various factors that will shape her story (such as her transness, her suicide attempt, her difficulties integrating with her peers, and Bunny's disappearance) are all mentioned here in a discussion with her school's principal. And this inescapability could also refer metafictionally to the necessity of following the beats of the adapted story. As Alice feels carried along in different directions without being able to decide where she is going, loss of control is something mostly feared but occasionally desired. After the text moves her away from her comfort zone, it makes particular reference to vertical movements such as falling down, falling in, coming up, and growing up. At a climactic point, this vertical movement is even signalled typographically by blank space arranged between sentences to mimic falling (269).

Sometimes, Alice can choose her movements; in the same way, she also occasionally takes on the manipulation of her narrative's temporality that is often the prerogative of the authorial figure, such as when starting a chapter with 'let's wind it all back' (193). Mostly, however, progressions, regressions, rises, and falls are experienced reluctantly, and Alice notes demands imposed externally: 'Come up, fall down. Everyone wants me in a different direction so it seems' (141). But the shaking loose of linearity ultimately increases her ability to pick desired directions, recognising when to hold back and when '[i]t's time to let myself fall' (68). Without going as far as suggesting that a loss of agency can be empowering, the novel creates a temporary space of disorientation (culminating in a literal maze in the final act) in which Alice can lose and then find herself.

Even if readers have failed to detect Alice's unreliability from clues such as other characters' reactions, the separation between her thoughts and those of Other Alice, and the directing of narrative attention to drugs, mental illness, and other perception-altering circumstances, the end of the novel sees the character finding her way by retrospectively understanding a past misreading:

> A couple of years ago, I got lost in myself. I feel a little bit closer, now, to finding my way out. I forget that, when I was a very small child, I did something incredibly strong, and then somehow managed to convince myself I was weak. (283)

While not all doubts about what Alice experienced at the party are resolved – the book concludes with her telling a friend, 'when *I* know what happened, you'll be the first to know!' (278) – what the text clears up is how misguided she was in believing that her transness makes her less of a girl and less of a strong, loveable, and dependable person. Renouncing reliability, in this case, consists in showing how reliable self-reporting is compromised by trans-hostile discourse. We can see the kind of discourse that drowns Alice's voice in a chapter in which she does not speak but simply reports a series of questions asked to her in a bathroom:

> 'How did you know?
> 'Do you think children really know when they're that little?'
> 'What if you change your mind?'
> 'Are you a girl now?' (227)

At the same time, to renounce reliability in this novel also means to claim the right to create a complex and flawed young trans narrator, who does not have to always be 'certain' to prove that she should be listened to when it comes to her gender. The contextual paratext of Dawson's own speaking on issues such as the Cass Review and the proposed ban of discussions about gender identity in schools,[6] as well as her role as YA writer and former teacher, helps us understand that her presence behind and 'above' Alice is a caring one, seeking to protect and embolden the voice of her protagonist.

## Beckett K. Bauer: Misleading familiarity

'Notes from a Hunter Boy' is another text that uses a young narrator to explore the realities of transness through forms of renounced reliability. Unlike Dawson, however, Bauer is an elusive authorial figure, the only one I engage with in this book who has no other publications (at least under this name) and has minimal online presence, mostly centred on writing music. The context of the story's publication, however, helps position it in specific ways for an audience. Bauer produced this text for Fitzpatrick and Plett's anthology *Meanwhile, Elsewhere: Science Fiction and Fantasy from Transgender Writers* – I mentioned this collection in my introduction, and Gimpelevich, one of the authors discussed in Chapter 3, is one of its contributors. In an interview, Fitzpatrick explains the knotty relationship between this volume and a tradition of feminist speculative fiction. Firstly, *Meanwhile, Elsewhere* aims to recover and sustain the 'submerged history of trans SF/F writers' (Fitzpatrick and Plett, 'Interview'), and this is signalled by its dedication to trans author Rachel Pollack, 'who's been doing this for over forty years'. At the same time, the anthology recognises a connection with 'second-wave feminism, which had all these very political SF/F writers coming out of it [...] Ursula Le Guin above all' ('Interview'). Finally, it also aims 'not just to emulate but also to reclaim feminist SF/F traditions that often have been, as with Joanna Russ, quite hostile to trans people' ('Interview'). This triple relation to the genre's history – uncovering, connecting, subverting – results in preoccupations with bodies, social hierarchies, and the politics and affects of marginality that, like the worlds depicted in the stories, are both familiar and novel. When first-person narrators are present in this collection, they could be encountering the unknown for the first time or presenting it to readers as a matter of course. In some way, both are the case with 'Notes from a Hunter Boy'. The author's biography included in the anthology states that '[t]hey are interested in all kinds of liberation, especially kids' liberation' (443). Imagining the liberation of children not only from identity categories used to order the world of the Hunter boys, but also from those used to order our own, this text invites us to question the truths we take for granted.[7]

Following Fitzpatrick and Plett's hope that *Meanwhile, Elsewhere* will 'act as both an escape from the current world and a manual for your own possibilities' ('Afterword' 440), 'Notes from a Hunter Boy' blends elements that remind us of the constraints of the 'current world' and elements that lead us away from it – but it is not always easy to tell the two apart. The text comprises journal entries by Malkim, a boy growing up in a nomadic group of Hunters in an imagined society called the Gostayan people. While the narrative uses the words 'Men' and 'Women' as well as masculine and feminine pronouns, it gradually becomes clear that these distinctions are not made on the basis of anatomy or reproductive roles. There are no Women in Malkim's group, and he mentions that individuals belonging to this category exclusively live in cities. At the same time, he discovers that some of the boys in his group can be 'eggy' and some can be 'semmy', meaning that they can either produce ova or semen (Bauer 185); some boys have 'globs' (breasts) and others do not (179). Finally, in a short 'Translator's Note' that follows Malkim's journal entries, it is made clear that the 'Gostayan people, of course, have no concept of gender as we know it' (192). The translator has instead, somewhat arbitrarily, chosen Men and Women (and the associated pronouns) to translate a distinction so important for Malkim's people that it 'exists in their *language*': the distinction 'between people who live stationary lives' (called Women in the text) and 'people who wander the wild' (called Men) (192). If readers are looking for 'men' and 'women' in the story, therefore, they will find themselves misled: these terms, as the translator confirms, do not indicate what we may assume they do (a type of body or gender presentation). What appears to be a society that makes a strict distinction between two genders in the way that we do is revealed to be making a different distinction altogether, meaning that both wanderers (Men) and dwellers (Women) have the same diverse range of bodies.

While this social organisation will seem unusual to most (if not all) readers, this is all that Malkim knows – but he is also still in the process of learning it. Although he reports sincerely about his experiences and what he understands about his world, he is unreliable to the extent that he is a naïve narrator: as a child, there are a number of things that he has been sheltered from or that he does not grasp, which readers can instead recognise. Early in the text, it becomes clear that the Commanders who are in charge of the Hunter group have been giving the boys an incomplete and misleading education on sexual reproduction.[8] While Malkim is familiar with 'groping' (180) as a way to experience pleasure with another boy, a scene in which he sees for the first time two boys have penetrative sex reveals a misunderstanding:

> I would have ignored them except at second glance it looked like their gens were touching. I flattened myself to the ground to watch, holding my breath for the catastrophe to rain down on them. [...]
> Later I told Zak about it and he also said I must've seen wrong. 'Nobody touches gens,' he said. 'They wouldn't dare.'
> 'They were,' I said. 'Snake in a hole.' (180)

Here, the narrator lacks knowledge about his world, being unaware that having penetrative sex is not dangerous in itself, and that Commanders are referring to the risk of pregnancy when they warn the boys about it; at the same time, he also lacks knowledge about 'our world', in that we normatively call people with vaginas girls and not boys. While his former misunderstanding is meant to be corrected, the latter is not – it is our misunderstanding (that of cisnormative readers) that is to be corrected. For the community of authors, readers, and editors that exists around this narrative, there is nothing unusual about boys having vaginas – if a reader finds themself alienated by this, this is a sign of the marginalisation of trans people in our world.

As the text progresses, Malkim ends up questioning the strict separation of Men and Women in his own society – but, even before he begins to do so, he challenges our categories too. His unreliability about his own world, coupled with his lack of familiarity with the world of readers, ultimately urges us to unlearn the norms by which we deem others unreliable: which ones are the narrator's misreadings, and which ones are our own? The combination of a naïve narrator with a speculative world produces an unstable hierarchy of knowledge between narrator and reader: Malkim knows more about his reality, which is new to us, but the audience imagined by the text is supposed to know more about the characters' bodies than the narrator does. This gives rise to complex defamiliarisation effects that can be seen, for instance, in Malkim's encounter with a boy from a group of itinerant Players:

> He was pleasant to look at, a bit older than the elder boys, with full globs and faint hairs over his scarlet lips. But he was softer than any Hunter-boy I'd touched—his face shone smooth, Womanish even, unweathered by the wild. (184)

In this description, a reader is required to negotiate a growing understanding of what Man and Woman mean in the text and the impulse they may have to identify the sex and gender of this Player according to our own rules (or, to use the story's terms, whether the Player would be 'eggy' or 'semmy' and how his appearance may be influenced by this). There are multiple ways in which this passage invites us to read gender: the Player has breasts, a smooth face, faint facial hair, lipstick; he is referred to as a boy, like everyone Malkim meets in the wilderness; and he is considered 'Womanish' by the narrator, but the reason for this is not any observable phenotype but a soft face as the sign of being unexposed to the 'wild'. As we try to piece together what counts as a Woman and what counts as a Man for Malkim, we may find that we need to turn that same question toward ourselves.

In 'Notes from a Hunter Boy', the gaze of someone who lives in an environment different from the reality of most readers works in tandem with the gaze of a child, creating multiple distortions of the social order that end up communicating reliable messages about gender. Renounced reliability is aided by renounced familiarity to instil a productive confusion around how we sort individuals into identity categories. Reading speculative fiction raises particular questions in relation to (un)reliability: which statements about a world, event, or society should be mistrusted – because of a narrator's deception or lack of understanding – and which are simply unfamiliar but to be taken at face value? While he may not grasp some things like pregnancy, Malkim is not construed as 'wrong' when reporting about who is a Man and who is a Woman – he is operating according to what is true in this alternative social arrangement, and we have to accept that gender works in this way in this particular time and place. But, when we accept that, we may cease to see the necessity of it working in any specific way that we have been taking for granted. Ideas of familiarity are central to theorising science fiction, from Sarah Lefanu's assertion that the genre offers the 'twin possibilities' to 'defamiliarise the familiar' and to 'make the familiar new and strange' (21), to Simon Spiegel's argument that the primary formal operation of '*sf*' is not to '*estrange the familiar*' but to make '*the strange familiar*' (372). Bauer's story invites questioning of what this term means: is what is 'familiar' to Malkim supposed to be familiar to us? The answer is yes for some of us, especially for those who already live with an understanding of gender that is at odds with 'our' cis world. And while Malkim is not a visitor in this 'strange' time and place and is at home there, he is also discovering its rules gradually, just like we are, and sometimes he actually needs to catch up with what readers already know. As for form, the story certainly naturalises novelty by making it seem realistic and plausible, but it also proceeds to subvert this with the Translator's Note.

The Translator's Note that closes the story is shorter than a page, but it prompts a rereading of the whole text. If Malkim was already unreliable due to his limited knowledge, learning about the translator's choices casts doubt on the capacity of any claim in which Men and Women are mentioned to function as 'true'. By this point, these terms have lost most of the meaning we would have tried to attribute to them according to our own norms, but readers may still think that the social arrangement of the Gostayans has something to do with gender. And it does, to the extent that 'gender' also starts to lose its meaning. Girtrude the librarian – a narrator more reliable than Malkim in terms of the knowledge they possess but one who is admitting to having deceived us – explains that their 'mailbox has been flooded with complaints' regarding their decision to translate the two most essential Gostayan social categories as Men and Women (191). However, they explain, 'my specialty is language, not anthropology; and the Gostayan language poses a problem that can only be resolved with "he" and "she"' (192). Because of the Gostayan marking of the identities of wanderers and stationary people in pronouns and word endings, Girtrude has equated these categories to the ones that, in English, also produce a linguistic distinction. But this new narrator clarifies that the 'Gostayan people, of course, have no concept of gender as we know it – or hundreds of genders, as some scholars argue,

Trans Narrators and Reliability 165

pointing to the Jobs that shape their lives' (192). Upon reading the Translator's Note, we may now realise that this story had nothing to do with gender after all – but does it not? If it has to do with taxonomies for categorising humans and with differences that are associated with behavioural and appearance traits (making the Player 'Womanish' because his face is smooth and he spends more time sheltered from the elements), then it does have to do with gender. In the gesture of familiarisation that is this translation – as it makes Malkim's world more understandable to us – a defamiliarisation of our own world is effected.

The story's last word is given to Girtrude, who frames their deception as somewhat unintentional, or as a risk they had not considered: 'If I misled you, mapping gender onto an arbitrary distinction, so be it. Of course I have never met dear Malkim the Hunter-boy, but some of his descendants have assured me they find our distinctions equally arbitrary' (192). In my view, the translator comes across as having knowingly tricked the intradiegetic reader, now feigning surprise at their confusion – as the author has also done to those who may have similar 'complaints'. If this is the case, Girtrude renounces reliability in the sense of that playful rejection of truth-telling norms that catches the reader in their frustrated desire for a clarity that gender does not have. The underlying reliable message here, of course, is that gender is in a sense 'mapped onto arbitrary distinctions'. In featuring translation, the text taps into larger concerns in science fiction (especially by marginalised authors) with the cultural colonisation of alien societies and the domestication of what is other. The matter of gendering Malkim and his fellow Hunters recalls for instance the evolution of experiments with non-binary identities in Le Guin's *The Left Hand of Darkness* or Piercy's *Woman on the Edge of Time* – the feminist tradition that Fitzpatrick identifies as one to both build on and take to task. Le Guin's negotiations with the pronouns used for the Gethenians, a population whose ambisexual reproduction leads to the absence of binary gender in their society, are documented in her essay 'Is Gender Necessary? Redux' (1989). Across multiple revisions of this piece, she defends and then questions the decision to use he/him pronouns for the Gethenians, and discusses using she/her in an edited version of a short story set in the same world; a later story, 'Coming of Age in Kharide' (1995), features a Gethenian narrator who explains their reasoning for picking each character's pronouns. Piercy, instead, uses the invented non-binary pronoun 'person/per', an approach that is taken up in some of the stories from *Meanwhile, Elsewhere*; while most authors use the now common they/them, Sybil Lamb's 'Cybervania', for instance, uses '-' as a pronoun, in phrases like 'a pic of "-"self' (209). 'Notes from a Hunter Boy' similarly problematises the attribution of gender through language, and hints at the impossibility of ever doing this 'accurately'.

Regardless of whether we read Girtrude as deliberately creating confusion about gender, reliability is renounced first with Malkim's narration, in the sense of giving a naïve narrator free rein to denaturalise those arrangements of people and language that are deemed 'normal' at the expense of trans lives. As he struggles to learn what separates Men and Women, Hunters and other Jobs, boys who are 'eggy' and those who are 'semmy', he in fact mimics a very familiar process: the more or less conscious learning of the rules of gender, which may seem particularly difficult to those who less easily fit the category they have been assigned. The notion that there are individuals with penises capable of inseminating and individuals with vaginas and wombs capable of becoming pregnant is constructed as a surprise for the narrator. The first inkling of this arises when he is given a 'calmshirt' to support his growing breasts (179). He then begins to notice that some older boys and adults have breasts and some do not, realising that his body will grow to match some of them more closely than others. Worried that having one type of body will ensure better success as a Hunter, he becomes obsessed with reading anatomy:

> I've been staring around, at gens when they're out, and bodies if not, because even under our winter layers you can tell, sometimes, or guess, once you know the clues. I know the others' bodies, I see those shapes every day of my life; but now it's like they're whispering to me in a secret language [...] And when I'm alone I conjure pictures in my head of every Man who's crossed my path, thinking back for globs (because they mean MILK!), or voices (I don't know why), or hair sometimes (though not on your head, and not the color, nor the color of your skin, as far as I can tell). (187)

Instead of beginning the narrative with a gaze that already reads bodily 'clues' as part of a binary system of gender, the text presents a narrator who needs to actively learn this gaze: in doing so, it shows that this lens is anything but natural or inevitable.

Equally as complex as the matter of whether Malkim is unreliable, and which truths exactly he is supposed to learn in order to be less so, is the question of whether Malkim can be considered trans, and according to what parameters. Initially, we are led to believe that Malkim is trans in our world's sense: he has a body that would be assigned female but is considered a boy. However, this is significantly complicated by the differences between the Gostayan categories and our own, by what we learn about the translation, and by the narrator's questioning of all the rules and distinctions that he is beginning to learn. According to the dominant understanding of bodies and social roles among the Gostayan people, there is no 'mismatch' between Malkim's anatomy and his categorisation as a Man. And, as it turns out, the latter term simply means a person whose life is spent nomadically, which does not presuppose any particular genital or hormonal arrangement as the most suited to this category. In this sense, having breasts/a womb and being a boy is not a state of affairs that would warrant the label 'trans'. But how should we interpret the moment in which Malkim imagines being a Woman? This occurs during a performance by the Players, in which one of them is acting as a Farmer (a Job for Women, since it requires settling). As the narrator reports that 'She (he) couldn't have been a Woman but I was almost fooled' (182), he finds the Player's identity as a Woman so convincing to prompt a change of pronouns. Later, as the Farmer grows a plant, Malkim fantasises about doing the same: 'I imagined green things sprouting up around me [...] I imagined staying... and waiting... and going home, under solid stone, to wait... from now until my skin shriveled' (182). In this passage, what is described is both familiar and unfamiliar: the words 'Man' and 'Woman' invoke a trans experience despite how obviously ill-fitting our own meaning for them is, and Malkim's sincere but naïve attempts to learn the rules of his world result in him wondering how crossable the boundary between the two identities is.

On the other hand, the narrator's desire to be a Woman seems to be contradicted by the fact that his assigned role of Hunter (a Job for Men) is not one that the narrator questions. In fact, he persistently worries that he will be excluded from this category, and confirmations by others that '[t]hey assigned you to be a Hunter because they saw a Hunter in you' are welcomed by him (187). Malkim's fears evoke the spectre of our patriarchal society, as they centre on the dreaded possibility that his anatomy could determine his destiny – even though the Gostayan meanings of Man and Woman do not coincide with ours (or do they?). After reassuring himself that many of the best Hunters have breasts like him, he concludes, 'I suppose they must get in the way sometimes, but then, so do turned knees and balls and shaky hands' (180). But his capacity to become pregnant continues to pose concerns in terms of his ability to be a Man: 'I just didn't see how I was fit to be a Hunter if any stupid Human with an extra finger of flesh could make me fat, slow, delicate, perhaps even kill me, force me to a city and who knows if I'd return?' (187). In reasoning that gestating a child would entail slowing his movements and eventually stopping in a city to give birth, Malkim shows that having a womb may 'force' one to be a Woman – returning us, through unfamiliarity, to familiar territory. Ultimately, Malkim can be considered trans in two partially overlapping and partially contradictory senses: in the first, because he displays a wish to transcend the role designated as Man in his language, hinting at some forbidden desire to do what Women do (in his world); in the second, because, despite reassurances to the contrary, he believes that his 'eggy' body will be an impediment in his Manly occupation of Hunter. The first notion of transness is a moving between or being at the margins of the normative categories of the Gostayans; the second echoes what readers may recognise as 'our' gender dysphoria. More generally, both situations evoke the pains inflicted by the gender binary in the story's extra-textual context, linking trans and cis experiences.

Through Girtrude's unreliable translation, Malkim's own uncertainty and misreadings, and the confounding ways in which the text seems to sometimes match and sometimes depart from our dominant and resistant understandings of gender, the text manages to produce effects that are to be taken as its reliable message. Although the translator assures us that the Gostayan people have 'no concept of gender as we know it' (192), our two worlds do not always seem at odds. Readers of this text are situated in a history in which movement and dwelling, activity and passivity, hardness and delicacy (the characteristics used by Bauer's story to distinguish those called Men from those called Women) are already gendered: women are confined to the domestic and men explore and endure the outside, or, conversely, women are exchanged and men are rooted in their owned territory. Through a play of similarities and differences between intra-textual and extra-textual norms, some conventional notions of transness are defamiliarised:

for instance, Malkim's initial attraction to being a Woman does not correspond with a desire to change certain parts of his body, but a wish to remain within the category of Man he has been assigned does. And even when we learn that his world includes some 'holy Betweeners' who cease wandering for long periods but are still considered nomadic (188), there is no inkling that any dissatisfaction with the categories of Man and Woman will lead the protagonist to this non-binary path. Bringing the focus back to us, Girtrude's postscript foregrounds the impact that Malkim's diary has on audiences, displacing the question of his particular identity in favour of highlighting the very process of reading identity. Interpreting the protagonist's unreliability on questions of sex and gender proves a complex task, as he is both an authority on what distinguishes Men and Women in his world and still uncovering information about sexed bodies already familiar to us. As the narrator undermines his own authority on the former matter by learning that, after all, we might be 'all like Women and Men combined' (188), he also undermines ours by prompting us to consider the same. While the reliability that comes with knowing how gender categories are supposed to work undoubtedly comes with power, it may be productive to renounce it, unlearning the rules that those in charge have taught us to follow.

## Show and tell

The realities that the narrators of *Confessions of the Fox*, *Wonderland*, and 'Notes from a Hunter Boy' set out to describe are ones that have precarious epistemological status: a remote past depicted in a forgotten manuscript, about which a disobedient professor thinks he is intuiting an important truth; a secret party that promises an escape from ordinary life, infiltrated by an outsider who must navigate real and imagined dangers; and an unfamiliar society in an unknown time and place, seen through the eyes of someone sheltered from adult knowledge. But in addition to the uncertainties that inevitably attach themselves to many statements made in these narratives, the way in which each narrator's gender is at odds with cisnormativity creates additional effects in relation to the question of (un)reliability. The existence of trans subjects, intra- and extra-textually, is often itself deemed unreal, as transphobic discourses that infect most discussions of gender in the contemporary moment position these subjects as being deceptive, mistaken, or confused about a fundamental aspect of their reality. Trans authors cannot help but be aware of suspicious audiences, and this awareness leads them to simultaneously affirm their narrators' prerogative to tell the truth and refuse to do so in a way that would satisfy those readers who benefit from the structures that these narrators are trying to challenge. In fact, to 'tell the truth' in such terms would mean to sacrifice necessary nuance, as Alabanza suggests when reflecting on their impulse to 'explain': 'I found myself wondering which people are afforded the ability to question themselves, to interrogate their feelings and write their reality, without the end goal being the understanding of a certain group of people' (7). The choice to write fiction also enters into this dynamic, as it moves away from an imperative to narrate the self for the curiosity of others, which was met with frustration by the authors I have discussed elsewhere in this book. Fiction as make-believe does not however undermine the truths that trans authors aim to convey, but rather communicates these truths through a play of invention and referentiality.

In a range of genres – historical metafiction, YA, science fiction, and more – Rosenberg, Dawson, and Bauer foreground questions of claiming and renouncing the authority to speak, the opportunity to explain, the space to make visible, and the ability to be certain. Bringing us back to some questions asked by the autobiographical texts from Chapter 2 – whom are trans narratives for and how to articulate reality through structures that are shaped by white, patriarchal, and scientific hierarchies? – Rosenberg's novel offers a reflection on historical knowledges about gendered bodies, affective relationships to the archive, and the erasures effected by capitalist interests in trans identity. Against violent forces who demand to see clearly and to learn the 'facts', *Confessions of the Fox* refuses to settle on the reliability and trustworthiness of narrators, authors, and various tellers, often filling the gaps with new gaps. The intrusions into trans narratives that are sometimes reported in the footnotes of *Confessions of the Fox* become particularly evident in the hateful voice of Other Alice in *Wonderland*. In this novel, anti-trans discourse is harnessed by the narrator's mind as a means to hurt her, compromising her reliability when she is led to believe that she is weak, worthless, or undeserving of love. Fighting for the right of trans teenagers to be heard, Dawson gives her young protagonist strength by showing her to be mistaken about the negative reactions she assumes others will have when they learn that she is trans, but also by allowing her to fall short of impossible standards of objectivity and certainty. 'Notes from a Hunter Boy' returns us to a playful baiting of readers into examining the gendered assumptions they bring to narratives, as it unsettles the linguistic distinctions that ground the text by revealing it to be a misleading translation. Even before this point, however, Bauer's naïve narrator confronts us with our misreadings alongside his own. Malkim's gaze defamiliarises our world, which sections off people and body parts in historically contingent ways; by enacting different separations, the text undermines the authority of those who fixate on rigid meanings in order to be able to 'tell it like it is'.

The escapes from logic and obfuscations of corporeality that characterise the narrators from Chapter 3 are also to be found in these texts. Narrative refusals are deployed not only against cis discourses but also against new trans normativities – as seen when Dr Voth declines to work for cis people to authenticate the trans identity of others, when Alice voices contradictory feelings about being objectified as a 'normal girl', and when Malkim fails to identify with the already labelled identity of the 'Betweeners' despite questioning his belonging to the other available options. The renounced reliability that these texts both thematise and enact formally can be described by using a number of categories and tools from narrative studies. For instance, its ambiguities can be further unpacked through Greta Olson's distinction between fallibility as a situational unreliability and untrustworthiness as a constitutive unreliability:

> To determine how fallible a narrator is the reader must ask to what extent the narrator mistakes the information he has access to and the perceptions he has. Does the narrator make these mistakes consistently, and can we imagine circumstances in which the narrator would report infallibly? (103)

Renounced reliability can mean writing and reading trans narrators who are fallible without becoming untrustworthy, or who are untrustworthy as a deliberate stance adopted out of rejection of constricting standards, including the imperative to be infallible. But trans studies is necessary, alongside narratological frameworks, to understand the ethical and political implications of these textual choices and their effects. Renounced reliability, like re-narration and trans-inhabitation, is the mobilising of a range of narrative operations for the purposes of representing marginalised lives, of entangling and disentangling the contradictions of gender, and of conveying the affects of living under cisnormative violence. And the underlying affect of renounced reliability, beyond dejection, frustration, and fear, is often the joy of hope. Despite many equivocations, Rosenberg richly imagines subjects shadowed by history, showing how they might care for each other through a loving gaze; Dawson gives young readers a trans protagonist who overcomes panic and rejection; and Bauer offers a space to play with identity that may transform our world too.

## Notes

1. An early version of this analysis appears in Pellegrini, '"Declining to Describe"'.
2. It is useful to recall Margolin's argument that, while the matter of the dependability or trustworthiness of a narrative originator may only be meaningful in certain cases, 'the (un)reliability of narrated and narration can be dealt with separately [...] even in the most impersonal of third person narratives' (37). This, for instance, takes the form of assessing whether we can 'count on' each narrative proposition 'to provide us with the kind of true or valid information regarding the narrative domain we expect from propositions of this type' (36). And of course the third-person narrative of the Sheppard manuscript turns out to be far from 'impersonal', meaning that the attribution of (un)reliability to the narrated and the narrating is always entangled with the credibility we ascribe to its authors and narrators, who in turn give readers a few reasons not to trust them.
3. In response to Sullivan's demand for an explanation of what sexual chimeras are, Voth replies that '[i]t ranges. Hermaphrodism, heteroclitism, clitoramegaly, an abundance of masculine passions in a ciswoman, etc.' (132). There is an indication that Jack recognises himself in the 'painted illustration', or otherwise establishes an affinity with it, but without any specifics as to what is being recognised.
4. A small portion of this analysis appears in Pellegrini, 'Temporalities Beyond Transition'.
5. As Cal Horton explains in an analysis of interim reports, the Cass Review ultimately deems the 'rejection of a trans child's identity as neutral and benign, requiring no evidence', while '[a]ccepting and embracing a trans child is viewed as more extreme and in need of

"high quality" evidence' (18). For further analysis, see McConnell's 'Hilary Cass's Proposals Are Mostly Common Sense. She Must Reject Anti-Trans Bias with the Same Clarity' and Pearce's 'What's Wrong with the Cass Review? A Round-Up of Commentary and Evidence'.

6   Dawson compares the 2024 proposal by the Conservative government to Section 28, which was active when she was in school: 'The result? A new generation of young people feel like outsiders at their own schools' ('Section 28'). This context is also valuable when approaching *Wonderland*, a novel that begins and ends in a school.

7   In discussing this text, I use the first person plural more often than usual to indicate sets of readers encountering the familiar and unfamiliar elements of the text – but I know of course that familiarity is relative. Some reference to 'our world' and to how 'we would read something' is necessary for my analysis, even though I acknowledge that readers have a diverse range of experiences. With 'our world' I refer to the current historical moment, and to the social environments of audiences that could be plausibly reached by this collection. Within this 'we', there will be readers who belong to queer and trans subcultures to different extents, who will be immersed in cis epistemologies with varying degrees of awareness or resistance, and who may or may not have a knowledge of other fictional or historical societies that are organised like the one in the text. Therefore, I strive to make clear in my discussion what kind of reader I am imagining each time I say 'we'.

8   The story appears at times to articulate a critique of this withholding of knowledge from young people, which recalls Dawson's efforts to combat silence about sex and gender in order to support queer and trans youth and make them feel less isolated. The Commanders' attitude toward sex is implicitly criticised when adults from another group scold them for allowing the boys to socialise unsupervised without knowing about contraception. Their dialogue is reported by Malkim who overhears snatches of the conversation, once again allowing readers to draw conclusions that he himself cannot yet reach (186).

# Conclusion: More than I

When considering the current flourishing of trans-authored literature and the ways in which mainstream culture has become more interested in gender-variant experiences, it is often tempting to invest in a narrative of progress, from past misunderstanding and discrimination to present belonging and respect. We see this rhetorical gesture in a recent Channel 4 documentary, 'Miriam: Death of a Reality Star' (2024). 'Death of a Reality Star' looks back on the life of trans model Miriam Rivera, who is perhaps most famous for starring in 'There's Something About Miriam' (2004): a controversial reality television show in which men competed to date her without knowing that she was trans, which ended with a shocking 'reveal' to the contestants and was accompanied by much public mockery and berating of its trans protagonist. As the documentary appears to pat itself on the back about how '[t]hankfully, there's more understanding of trans people today than when the show aired' (as a statement from the original show's creator reads in the concluding frame), it fails to address the wave of restrictions on trans rights and normalisation of transphobia that characterises our own time.[1] In fact, 'Death of a Reality Star' slips into many of the textual strategies that are part of the unethical treatment of trans subjects that it purports to critique. As Devon Price observes in a discussion about trans representation in the media, the focus on 'making people as individuals more visible', which characterised much public debate about transness in the 2010s, has not brought about the policy changes that would help trans people 'as a marginalised class': 'visibility is not necessarily liberation, a lot of times it's vulnerability and putting a target on your back'. With a documentary like 'Death of a Reality Star', the limitations of de-politicised trans visibility are evident – both in 2004, in a more 'clumsy' and overtly exploitative form, and today, as we rehash this recent history and congratulate ourselves on knowing better. In addition to providing a representative example of how trans lives are publicly negotiated at this particular historical juncture, discussing 'Death of a Reality Star' in this conclusion allows me to offer a brief glimpse of how re-narration, trans-inhabitation, and renounced reliability can help analyse media about trans people beyond written text, as well as critique media that is made about trans people in their absence, serving as a broad framework to approach issues such as time and change, first-person authority, corporeality and visual representation, and truth and deception.

Uncritical repetition, rather than re-narration, results from the insistence, in 'Death of a Reality Star', that past representations of transness are something that would 'not happen now'. Despite this avowed conclusion, the way in which the documentary reproduces footage of the infamous dating show reveals a desire to affect viewers in a similar way, and ends up exploiting trans people in the process. There is initially a self-awareness that would seem to approximate the re-narrations that I have discussed in this book: when footage from the 2000s is shown, this is often set up as a scene of rewatching, in which the clips play on a television or tablet that is in frame and sometimes specifically being watched by one of the interviewed subjects (some of whom are trans women). In a moment that shows an attempt to filter, critique, and reappropriate what is displayed, a montage of cruel and degrading jokes about Miriam is interspersed with an interview with trans presenter India Willoughby, who explains that seeing this backlash on television at the time delayed her own coming out. Aaron, one of the two contestants interviewed about their experience on the show, delivers one of the most explicit moments of distancing the present from the past: looking back regretfully at the anger and mockery that followed the revelation to the men that the woman they had been pursuing was trans, Aaron says, 'I would have never reacted the way I did then, now'. But this self-consciousness is mostly lost as soon as the 2004 show ceases to be the topic of the narrative, and the documentary delves instead into the transphobia and violence that Miriam experienced in her youth and up to her mysterious death sixteen years after 'There's Something About Miriam' aired. The sordid details offered to the audience and the scrutinising of moments of pain and vulnerability – which include footage of a trans friend of Miriam's crying upon being shown an article describing some of the abuses perpetrated by the same gang that might be responsible for her death – erase trans life by reducing it to tragedy for the consumption and shock of (cis) audiences. Even if we can consider the documentary as genuinely attempting a re-narration, this is done without consistently encoding this re-narration, as actual disruption and interruption of patterns, formally into the text.

What is the effect of accompanying verbal acts of distancing (by Aaron, Willoughby, and many other interviewees) with lengthy clips of 'There's Something About Miriam' and the comedians who parodied it, regardless of how many metaphorical and literal screens are placed between us and the scenes of the past? As the original show has now been removed from circulation by Sky, 'Death of a Reality Star' brings back its ghost and makes it flesh again. As the show's visual jokes alluding to Miriam's genitals are condemned, these images are still shown to us. Extensive discussion of how the crew, as well as the psychiatrist hastily hired toward the end of filming, were anticipating the 'reveal' of the final episode with considerable worry seems to take a stand against this sensationalistic trope; however, the majority of the documentary reproduces this exact structure, teasing the reaction of the contestants and inviting the audience to imagine just how bad Miriam's humiliation will be. As this tension builds, reminders are offered of Miriam's trans-inhabitation – her embodiment as a movement across, as an in-between-ness, as a site of multiplicity. But emphasising trans-inhabitation does not aim at celebrating the corporeal possibilities beyond fixed genders (even if this open-mindedness is sometimes touted as the original goal of the show), but instead serves the fascination of those who want to revel in her otherness. As the documentary reproduces a long scene from the show in which Miriam and a contestant are passionately kissing, a refracted gaze (of the other men in the scene, of the original viewers of the show, and of the viewers of the documentary now) is invited to contemplate the model's beauty and the supposed incongruity of this image with the 'something' that we 'know about her'. This knowledge means having privileged access to Miriam's body, access that the contestants are prevented from gaining. A crew member interviewed explains having been constantly on call for alerts from those monitoring the cameras, ready to intervene to make sure 'the barriers weren't broken'. And barriers between the bodies being filmed were as important to the show's premise as the barriers between male and female, which are reinforced even as they are apparently trans-inhabited.

Miriam's subjectivity in the long kissing scene is suppressed by an objectifying gaze, in contradiction with how the documentary now attempts to incorporate her first-person voice. An actor sometimes reads Miriam's written words, and her own recorded voice from the show, from other television appearances, and from her personal videos is played throughout. However, this voice has to vie for the viewers' attention alongside footage of degrading comments and images of demeaning newspaper headlines. Of course, the undermining of Miriam's agency and reliability mostly centres on The Secret (which is also the title of the first episode of the documentary, the second one being called 'The Truth'). On the one hand, the responsibility for hiding the truth is placed firmly on the side of the producers, and much is made of the contestants' legal action to stop the show from airing based on their lack of informed consent in what was filmed. However, the language used by the interviewees confounds how active a role Miriam is supposed to have played in this deception, painting her in turn as duper and duped. Her willing and enthusiastic participation in the dating show is remarked upon repeatedly, both by others and in her own words; however, it is evident that she can only act within the constraints of the job, which requires her to be unreliable. The psychiatrist interviewed states that he knew that Miriam's reveal speech was scripted because he 'overheard a conversation about how they would word it'; but regardless of who chose the words, he goes on to explain, 'she said them, so they became her words'. The most we get on this topic in the first person, from the actor who voices Miriam, is often again a reporting of the narratives of others: 'the media were all saying that I was wrong, tricking the boys'. Reliability is renounced here through the impossibility of Miriam articulating her own narrative about herself, in the absence of available cultural models according to which trans women are not hiding anything. The role of the deceiver is one in which she has been cast, and there is no language for her to be otherwise. As she ventriloquises a truth scripted by others, what becomes clear is the need to either more explicitly centre her subjective experience, acknowledge the irreparable loss of it, or recognise her choice to decline to speak further.

There would be much more to say about questions of form (the tensions and overlaps between documentary and reality television formats), temporality (historical shifts in trans representation, or the narrative layering of Miriam's past and interrupted future), embodiment (the use of photographs and clips to show bodies that change and/or are thought to 'conceal'), and reliability (the fragments of Miriam's truth, and the ways in which we are invited to trust some narratives over others). But what this brief discussion aims to highlight are further directions for applying and developing the concepts of re-narration, trans-inhabitation, and renounced reliability. The question of narrating agents remains relevant throughout. Between a production executive declaring that Miriam 'knew exactly what she was getting into and why, and she wanted to be part of it' and a contestant regretting that his lawyers used her as a 'pawn', how can Miriam speak in the first person? First-person voice will of course take different shapes in different media, and is sometimes difficult to circumscribe. What I have shown in this book is that, even in seemingly straightforward instances in which an 'I' tells a story from start to finish, other voices from within and outside the narrative self end up intruding and amplifying. This is manifested formally in choices that recur across the different texts I have discussed, such as the attempt to confine invasive narratives to italics or other graphically distinct forms, only to find these boundaries to be breachable; appeals to a 'you', alternately hostile and sympathetic, as a participant in narrative communication; or the use of dashes to erase descriptions of the body, a declining-to-voice that hints at what could be voiced or is usually voiced. But the nature of the 'I' as both multiple and unifying is only one possible site of exploration for the intersection between trans studies and narrative studies, which can lead to rich understandings of temporality, embodiment, and reliability in their formal and political dimensions.

In this book, I have considered a small number of post-2015 trans-authored prose narratives in English that use gender-variant narrators in the first person; many other texts remain outside the scope of my analysis and can further shape, enrich, and expand the ways of reading that I have developed here. For instance, popular trans narratives in other languages – such as Camila Sosa Villada's *Las Malas* (2019) and Chi Ta-wei's *The Membranes* (translated in 2021) – deserve and are gaining more critical attention. Just as trans cultural production in other languages, genres, and media is being and will continue to be analysed outside of this book, I hope that my conclusions support further work on what is 'more than I' – especially, taking trans narrative studies beyond the focus I have adopted here on autodiegetic narration and on individual identity. What does it look like to re-narrate, trans-inhabit, or renounce reliability without a first-person narrator? How are solidarity and relationality expressed formally? Such questions may be answered by a novel like Rivers Solomon's *An Unkindness of Ghosts* (2017), which reflects on gender, race, and community through multiple (and mostly heterodiegetic) narrators, a speculative but familiar world, and a thematic and linguistic focus on 'more than I':

> In my language, there is no word for *I*. To even come close, you must say, *E'tesh'lem vereme pri'lus*, which means, *This one here who is apart from all*. It's the way we say *lonely* and *alone*. It's the way we say *outsider*. It's the way we say *weak*.
> Everyone always wonders about *I love you*. In Ifrek you say, *Mev o'tem*, or, *We are together*.
> 'How do you say, *I'm tired*?' people ask.
> '*Ek'erb nal veesh ly*. The time for rest is upon us.' (317)

In this passage, the translation of 'I love you' into the non-hierarchical 'We are together' invokes the hope for a liberated collectivity, linking the ghosts of the past and generations to come, the embodied subjects that transcend into something greater than themselves, and all the loud or quiet voices that lend strength to this 'we', both inside and outside the novel.

When a trans narrator tells their own story for a public of any size, other subjectivities come into contact with it. My own cis subjectivity has mediated the narratives I have presented here, and a variety of voices filter, contextualise, and occlude Miriam's speaking in 'Death of a Reality Star'. In practices of t4t that I have mentioned in some chapters, gender-variant subjects carve a space to communicate to and for each other away from a normative gaze. Extending toward 'more than I', texts with third-person or multiple first-person narrators can show these dynamics of intersubjective refraction, amplification, and distortion that inhere in trans (and, in a sense, all) representations. In a novel like Nicola Dinan's *Bellies* (2023), for instance, alternating narration ends up showing us a trans character from the inside (as an I) and the outside (as 'he' and then 'she' for another I).[2] Alternating narration also structures work of popular fiction *Mad Honey* (2022); co-authored by cis writer Jodi Picoult and trans writer Jennifer Finney Boylan, this book offers a collaboration on the question of voicing and witnessing trans identity for a mainstream audience. And the novel that is considered to have 'changed the landscape of trans fiction—in part because it made no concessions to tourists' (Burt), Imogen Binnie's *Nevada* (2013), is written in the third person. Initially, the heterodiegetic narrator mostly reports the indirect and direct discourse of the protagonist, Maria, or adopts a clearly authorial voice, and therefore has both the agency and limitations of many homodiegetic narrators. Halfway through the narrative, there is a switch to focalisation through James, a character designated as 'he' who is questioning their gender. As soon as Maria enters James's life, however, the latter's gender is affirmed through her gaze, as her internal monologue is reported: 'I'm gonna talk to that girl and tell her that she's a girl' (187). While I have discussed extensively the agility of the 'I', other narrators and pronouns provide other freedoms and possibilities, which are deployed by trans literature to effect re-narrations, convey trans-inhabitations, and renounce reliability.[3]

Analysing trans narrators – narrators who are trans characters, narrating entities that function in trans ways, trans subjects who speak for themselves, and trans people who are asked to narrate – allows us to consider simultaneously the implications of saying 'I' for narrative and for trans studies. This non-gendered pronoun designates someone who can belong within, be outside of, or be at the borders of normatively defined categories, and these positionings can occur successively or simultaneously over the course of one narrative. The I is also a deictic term, and its referent can remain ambiguous (be any instance of the experiencing-I or the narrating-I) and exist across and between diegetic levels. First-person narration demands that attention be paid both to the stability and presence of the I (an embodied character, approximating an embodied person, from a group that is marginalised because of their embodiment) and to its slipperiness and multiplicity (an ambiguously referenced subject, and one who flits at the borders of the storyworld). When representing its bodies, times, and truths, the I affirms a substantial (visible and vocal) identity at the same time as it articulates something that is fragmentary and in flux. Temporality, embodiment, and reliability are three areas in which the investments of trans studies and narrative studies overlap – there are many more. As we continue to explore them, my suggestion is that analysis of trans narratives should at least attend to (1) the specific formal techniques and strategies employed by different texts to convey narratives of transness, and (2) the ideological positions and lived experiences of authors and audiences who do the speaking, the looking, the structuring, the imagining, the explaining, and the disrupting. And while the matter of defining contemporary trans literature may not settle on a definitive answer any time soon, what should remain uncontroversial is the duty to do justice to trans people in a world that often strips them of their agency, bodily autonomy, and narrative control.

### Notes

1. At the moment in which I am writing this, the past month alone has seen a flurry of activity and news, specifically on the subject of healthcare for trans youth. In the days leading up to the 2024 UK general election, the activist group Trans Kids Deserve Better occupied a ledge of NHS England's headquarters in London, responding to party leaders' stances against trans rights under the slogan of 'we are not pawns for your politics'. In Florida, a ban on gender-affirming care prohibiting puberty blockers for trans minors was ruled unconstitutional, giving a glimmer of hope as many similar bans are proposed and enforced across the US and Europe. Maintenance Phase, a popular podcast debunking health and wellness myths, released the last of three episodes analysing the methodological flaws of studies that are used to fuel anti-trans moral panic for tens of thousands of listeners.
2. I analyse this text and its intersubjectively refracted characters in more detail in 'When Narrative Studies Meets Trans Studies'.
3. Jonathan H. Grossman's analysis of Binnie's work offers a much more in-depth analysis of these effects, arguing that this author 'reinvents the fictional device of the unreliable narrator for a modern US trans community, marshaling the epistemology of fiction to expose the nonsense of solving, as if it were a problem, that human beings may be trans' (438). Grossman's discussion also resonates with the concept of renounced reliability that I have developed in this book.

# Bibliography

Aizura, Aren Z. 'Of Borders and Homes: The Imaginary Community of (Trans)sexual Citizenship'. *Inter-Asia Cultural Studies*, vol. 7, no. 2, 2006, pp. 289–309.
——. 'The Persistence of Transgender Travel Narratives'. *Transgender Migrations: The Bodies, Borders, and Politics of Transition*, edited by Trystan T. Cotten. Routledge, 2012, pp. 139–56.
Alabanza, Travis. *None of the Above: Reflections on Life Beyond the Binary*. Canongate Books, 2022.
Alber, Jan, and Alice Bell. 'Ontological Metalepsis and Unnatural Narratology'. *Journal of Narrative Theory*, vol. 42, no. 2, 2012, pp. 166–92.
Amin, Kadji. 'Temporality'. *Keywords*, special issue of *TSQ: Transgender Studies Quarterly*, vol. 1, nos. 1–2, 2014, pp. 219–22.
Anderson, Linda. *Autobiography*. 2nd edn. Routledge, 2010.
Anzaldúa, Gloria. *Borderlands/La Frontera: The New Mestiza*. Aunt Lute Books, 1987.
Awkward-Rich, Cameron. 'Anti-Elegy'. *The Rumpus*, 26 Apr. 2019, https://therumpus.net/2019/04/26/national-poetry-month-day-26-cameron-awkward-rich/. Accessed 15 July 2024.
——. 'Craft Capsule: Elegy'. *Poets & Writers*, 23 Dec. 2019, https://www.pw.org/content/craft_capsule_elegy. Accessed 15 July 2024.
——. 'Trans, Feminism: Or, Reading Like a Depressed Transsexual'. *Signs: Journal of Women in Culture and Society*, vol. 42, no. 4, 2017, pp. 819–41.
Balaguera, Martha. 'Trans-migrations: Agency and Confinement at the Limits of Sovereignty'. *Signs: Journal of Women in Culture and Society*, vol. 43, no. 3, 2018, pp. 641–61.

Bastian, Misty. 'Irregular Visitors: Narratives about Ogbaanje (Spirit Children) in Nigerian Popular Writing'. *Readings in African Popular Fiction*, edited by Stephanie Newell. Indiana University Press, 2002, pp. 59–66.

Bauer, Beckett K. 'Notes from a Hunter Boy: As Filed by Girtrude the Librarian'. *Meanwhile, Elsewhere: Science Fiction and Fantasy from Transgender Writers*, edited by Cat Fitzpatrick and Casey Plett. Topside Press, 2017, pp. 177–92.

BBC, 'Trans Women May Be Banned from Women's NHS Wards'. *BBC News*, 3 Oct. 2023, https://www.bbc.co.uk/news/health-66994133. Accessed 15 July 2024.

Bekhta, Natalya. 'We-Narratives: The Distinctiveness of Collective Narration'. *Narrative*, vol. 25, no. 2, 2017, pp. 164–81.

Bellot, Gabrielle. 'What Counts as Transgender Literature?' *Literary Hub*, 9 Dec. 2016, https://lithub.com/what-counts-as-transgender-literature. Accessed 15 July 2024.

Bettcher, Talia Mae. 'Trans Identities and First Person Authority'. *'You've Changed': Sex Reassignment and Personal Identity*, edited by Laurie J. Shrage. Oxford University Press, 2009, pp. 98–120.

——. 'Trapped in the Wrong Theory: Rethinking Trans Oppression and Resistance'. *Signs: Journal of Women in Culture and Society*, vol. 39, no. 2, 2014, pp. 383–406.

Bey, Marquis. *Black Trans Feminism*. Duke University Press, 2022.

Binnie, Imogen. *Nevada*. Picador, 2022.

Bornstein, Kate. *Gender Outlaw: On Men, Women, and the Rest of Us*. Vintage, 2016.

——. *A Queer and Pleasant Danger: The Inspiring True Story of a Nice Jewish Boy Who Left the Church of Scientology to Become the Lovely Lady She Is Today*. Beacon Press, 2012.

Boylan, Jennifer Finney. *I'm Looking Through You: Growing Up Haunted: A Memoir*. Broadway Books, 2008.

Bradway, T. 'Queer Narrative Theory and the Relationality of Form'. *PMLA*, vol. 136, no. 5, 2021, pp. 711–27.

'Brainwyrms'. *Cipher Press*, 2023, https://www.cipherpress.co.uk/shop/brainwyrms-pre-order. Accessed 15 July 2024.

Brooks, Peter. *Reading for the Plot: Design and Intention in Narrative*. Harvard University Press, 1992.

Burt, Stephanie. 'The Invention of the Trans Novel'. *The New Yorker*, 20 June 2022, https://www.newyorker.com/magazine/2022/06/27/the-invention-of-the-trans-novel-imogen-binnie-nevada. Accessed 15 July 2024.

Caracciolo, Marco, and Karin Kukkonen. *With Bodies: Narrative Theory and Embodied Cognition*. Ohio State University Press, 2021.

cárdenas, micha. *Poetic Operations: Trans of Color Art in Digital Media*. Duke University Press, 2021.

Carroll, Rachel. *Transgender and the Literary Imagination: Changing Gender in Twentieth-Century Writing*. Edinburgh University Press, 2018.

Chen, Jian Neo. *Trans Exploits: Trans of Color Cultures and Technologies in Movement*. Duke University Press, 2019.

Chu, Andrea Long. 'The Wrong Wrong Body: Notes on Trans Phenomenology'. *TSQ: Transgender Studies Quarterly*, vol. 4, no. 1, 2017, pp. 141–52.

—— and Emmett Harsin Drager. 'After Trans Studies'. *TSQ: Transgender Studies Quarterly*, vol. 6, no. 1, 2019, pp. 103–16.

Cousens, Emily. *Trans Feminist Epistemologies in the US Second Wave*. Palgrave, 2023.

Dannenberg, Hilary P. *Coincidence and Counterfactuality: Plotting Time and Space in Narrative Fiction*. University of Nebraska Press, 2008.

Dawson, Juno [@junodawson]. 'Babe, wake up! Section 28's back!' *Instagram*, 15 May 2024, https://www.instagram.com/p/C6-6al8gZ1S/?hl=en. Accessed 15 July 2024.

—— [@junodawson]. 'Because you all wanted my hot take on the Cass Report and what it means for trans youth'. *Instagram*, 10 Apr. 2024, https://www.instagram.com/p/C5ltTOOrVIE/?hl=en. Accessed 15 July 2024.

——. *The Gender Games*. Two Roads, 2017.

——. *Wonderland*. Quercus, 2020.

Derrida, Jacques. *Spectres of Marx: The State of the Debt, the Work of Mourning, and the New International*, translated by Peggy Kamuf. Routledge, 1994.

Dinan, Nicola. 'Trans Art and the Complex Politics of Representation'. *Dazed*, 6 July 2023, https://www.dazeddigital.com/life-culture/article/60276/1/trans-art-and-the-complex-politics-of-representation-bellies-nicola-dinan. Accessed 15 July 2024.

DuPlessis, Rachel Blau. *Writing Beyond the Ending: Narrative Strategies of Twentieth-Century Women Writers*. Indiana University Press, 1985.

Emezi, Akwaeke. *Dear Senthuran: A Black Spirit Memoir*. Faber & Faber, 2022.

——. *Freshwater*. Faber & Faber, 2018.

——. 'I'd Read Everything – Even the Cereal Box'. Interview by Arifa

Akbar. *The Guardian*, 20 Oct. 2018, https://www.theguardian.com/books/2018/oct/20/akwaeke-emezi-interview-freshwater. Accessed 15 July 2024.

——. 'Transition'. *The Cut*, 19 Jan. 2018, https://www.thecut.com/2018/01/writer-and-artist-akwaeke-emezi-gender-transition-and-ogbanje.html. Accessed 15 July 2024.

Faye, Shon. *The Transgender Issue: An Argument for Justice*. Allen Lane, 2021.

Feinberg, Leslie. *Stone Butch Blues*. Firebrand Books, 1993.

——. *Transgender Liberation: A Movement Whose Time Has Come*. World View Forum, 1992.

Fitzpatrick, Cat, and Casey Plett. Afterword. *Meanwhile, Elsewhere: Science Fiction and Fantasy from Transgender Writers*, edited by Fitzpatrick and Plett. Topside Press, 2017, pp. 439–40.

——. 'Meanwhile, Elsewhere: Talking to the Editors of a Trans Speculative Fiction Anthology'. Interview by Joe Macaré. *Truthout*, 20 Sep. 2017, https://truthout.org/articles/meanwhile-elsewhere-talking-to-the-editors-of-a-trans-speculative-fiction-anthology/. Accessed 16 July 2024.

Flood, Alison. 'Akwaeke Emezi Shuns Women's Prize over Request for Details of Sex as Defined "by Law"'. *The Guardian*, 5 Oct. 2020, https://www.theguardian.com/books/2020/oct/05/akwaeke-emezi-shuns-womens-prize-request-for-details-of-sex-as-defined-by-law. Accessed 15 July 2024.

Fludernik, Monika. 'Scene Shift, Metalepsis, and the Metaleptic Mode'. *Style*, vol. 37, no. 4, 2003, pp. 382–400.

—— 'The Category of "Person" in Fiction: You and We Narrative-Multiplicity and Indeterminacy of Reference'. *Current Trends in Narratology*, edited by Greta Olson. De Gruyter, 2011, pp. 101–43.

Freeman, Elizabeth. *Time Binds: Queer Temporalities, Queer Histories*. Duke University Press, 2010.

Funke, Jana. 'The Case of Karl M.[artha] Baer: Narrating "Uncertain" Sex'. *Sex, Gender and Time in Fiction and Culture*, edited by Ben Davies and Jana Funke. Palgrave, 2011, pp. 132–53.

Genette, Gérard. *Narrative Discourse: An Essay in Method*, translated by Jane E. Lewin. Cornell University Press, 1980.

Getsy, David J. 'Capacity'. *Keywords*, special issue of *TSQ: Transgender Studies Quarterly*, vol. 1, nos. 1–2, 2014, pp. 47–9.

Gimpelevich, Calvin. 'Among Men'. *Ploughshares*, vol. 47, no. 2, 2021, pp. 51–63.

——. *Invasions*. Instar Books, 2018.

Gossett, Che. 'Blackness and the Trouble of Trans Visibility'. *Trap Door: Trans Cultural Production and the Politics of Visibility*, edited by Reina Gossett, Eric A. Stanley and Johanna Burton. MIT Press, 2017, pp. 183–90.

Gossett, Reina, Eric A. Stanley and Johanna Burton. 'Known Unknowns: An Introduction to Trap Door'. *Trap Door: Trans Cultural Production and the Politics of Visibility*. MIT Press, 2017, pp. xv–xxvi.

Graham, Sarah. Introduction. *A History of the Bildungsroman*, edited by Graham. Cambridge University Press, 2018.

Grossman, Jonathan H. 'Imogen Binnie's Unreliable Narrators'. *TSQ: Transgender Studies Quarterly*, vol. 11, no. 3, 2024, pp. 435–57.

Halberstam, J. *Female Masculinity*. Duke University Press, 1998.

Hale, C. Jacob. 'Tracing a Ghostly Memory in my Throat: Reflections on Ftm Feminist Voice and Agency'. *'You've Changed': Sex Reassignment and Personal Identity*, edited by Laurie J. Shrage. Oxford University Press, 2009, pp. 43–65.

Halpern, Faye. 'Charles Chestnutt, Rhetorical Passing, and the Flesh-and-Blood Author: A Case for Considering Authorial Intention'. *Narrative*, vol. 30, no. 1, 2022, pp. 47–66.

Hayward, Eva. 'More Lessons from a Starfish: Prefixial Flesh and Transspeciated Selves'. *Women's Studies Quarterly*, vol. 36, nos. 3–4, 2008, pp. 64–85.

———. 'Spiderwomen: Notes on Transpositions'. *Transgender Migrations: The Bodies, Borders, and Politics of Transition*, edited by Trystan T. Cotten. Routledge, 2012, pp. 92–104.

Herman, David. *Narratologies: New Perspectives on Narrative Analysis*. Ohio State University Press, 1999.

Heyam, Kit. *Before We Were Trans: A New History of Gender*. Basic Books, 2022.

Horak, Laura. 'Trans on YouTube: Intimacy, Visibility, Temporality'. *TSQ: Transgender Studies Quarterly*, vol. 1, no. 4, 2014, pp. 575–85.

Horbury, Ezra, and Christine 'Xine' Yao. 'Empire and Eugenics: Trans Studies in the United Kingdom'. *TSQ: Transgender Studies Quarterly*, vol. 7, no. 3, 2020, pp. 445–54.

Horton, Cal. 'The Cass Review: Cis-Supremacy in the UK's Approach to Healthcare for Trans Children'. *International Journal of Transgender Health*, 2024, pp. 1–25.

Instar Books. https://www.instarbooks.com. Accessed 15 July 2024.

Irving, Dan. 'Normalized Transgressions: Legitimizing the Transsexual Body as Productive'. *Radical History Review*, vol. 100, 2008, pp. 38–59.

Jacques, Juliet. *Front Lines: Trans Journalism 2007–2021*. Cipher Press, 2022.
——. 'The I in Trans Genre: An Interview with Juliet Jacques'. Interviewed by Chiara Pellegrini. *TSQ: Transgender Studies Quarterly*, vol. 7, no. 1, 2020, pp. 105–13.
——. *Trans: A Memoir*. Verso, 2015.
——. *Variations*. Influx Press, 2021.
Jordan. Review of *The Lauras*, by Sara Taylor. *Goodreads*, 27 Dec. 2016, https://www.goodreads.com/book/show/42281796-the-lauras. Accessed 16 July 2024.
Lakoff, George, and Mark Johnson. *Metaphors We Live By*. University of Chicago Press, 2003.
Lamb, Sybil. 'Cybervania'. *Meanwhile, Elsewhere: Science Fiction and Fantasy from Transgender Writers*, edited by Cat Fitzpatrick and Casey Plett. Topside Press, 2017, pp. 200–24.
Lanser, Susan S. *Fictions of Authority: Women Writers and Narrative Voice*. Cornell University Press, 1992.
——. 'Queering Narrative Voice'. *Queer and Feminist Theories of Narrative*, special issue of *Textual Practice*, vol. 32, no. 6, 2018, pp. 923–37.
——. 'Sexing the Narrative: Propriety, Desire and the Engendering of Narratology'. *Narrative*, vol. 3, no. 1, 1995, pp. 85–94.
——. 'Toward a Feminist Narratology'. *Style*, vol. 20, no. 3, 1986, pp. 341–63.
Latham, J. R. '(Re)making Sex: A Praxiography of the Gender Clinic'. *Feminist Theory*, vol. 18, no. 2, 2017, pp. 177–204.
Lavery, Grace. *Please Miss: A Heartbreaking Work of Staggering Penis*. Daunt Books, 2022.
Le Guin, Ursula K. 'Is Gender Necessary? Redux'. *Dancing at the Edge of the World: Thoughts on Words, Women, Places*. Grove Press, 1989, pp. 7–10.
Lederer, Jenny. 'Exploring the Metaphorical Models of Transgenderism'. *Metaphor and Symbol*, vol. 30, no. 2, 2015, pp. 95–117.
Lefanu, Sarah. *In the Chinks of the World Machine: Feminism and Science Fiction*. The Women's Press, 1988.
McConnell, Freddy. 'Hilary Cass's Proposals Are Mostly Common Sense. She Must Reject Anti-Trans Bias with the Same Clarity'. *The Guardian*, 11 Apr. 2024, https://www.theguardian.com/commentisfree/2024/apr/11/hilary-cass-trans-children-review. Accessed 16 July 2024.
——. '"I Just Wanted to Write Something Funny for my Friends": Torrey Peters on *Detransition, Baby*'. *The Guardian*, 7 Oct. 2021,

https://www.theguardian.com/books/2021/oct/07/torrey-peters-trans-novelist-interview-detransition-baby. Accessed 16 July 2024.

McDonald, CeCe. Foreword. *Captive Genders: Trans Embodiment and the Prison Industrial Complex*, edited by Eric A. Stanley and Nat Smith. Expanded 2nd edn. AK Press, 2015, pp. 1–4.

Malatino, Hil. 'Future Fatigue'. *TSQ: Transgender Studies Quarterly*, vol. 6, no. 4, 2019, pp. 635–58.

———. *Trans Care*. University of Minnesota Press, 2020. *Manifold*, https://manifold.umn.edu/projects/trans-care. Accessed 9 Oct. 2024.

Margolin, Uri. 'Theorising Narrative (Un)reliability: A Tentative Roadmap'. *Unreliable Narration and Trustworthiness: Intermedial and Interdisciplinary Perspectives*, edited by Vera Nünning. DeGruyter, 2015, pp. 31–58.

Mattheis, Lena. 'Nonbinary Pronouns in Literary History: Queer(ing) Pronouns in the Works of Aphra Behn and Margaret Cavendish'. *Women's Studies Quarterly*, vol. 51, nos. 3–4, pp. 44–58.

Mejeur, Cody, and Chiara Pellegrini, editors. *Trans/forming Narrative Studies*, special issue of *Narrative*, vol. 32, no. 2, 2024.

Miller, Nancy. Preface. *The Poetics of Gender*, edited by Miller. Columbia University Press, 1986, pp. xi–xv.

'Miriam: Death of a Reality Star'. Channel 4, 2024, https://www.channel4.com/programmes/miriam-death-of-a-reality-star. Accessed 13 January 2025.

Mock, Janet. *Redefining Realness: My Path to Womanhood, Identity, Love and So Much More*. Atria, 2014.

Morgan, Hannah, et al. 'Attitudes to Transgender People'. *Equality and Human Rights Commission*, 10 Aug. 2020, https://www.equalityhumanrights.com/sites/default/files/2022/our-work-attitudes-to-transgender-people-august-2020.pdf. Accessed 15 July 2024.

Mozer, Gil. 'Transforming Paratext: A Transgender Touch across Time in *Confessions of the Fox*'. *Trans/forming Narrative Studies*, special issue of *Narrative*, vol. 32, no. 2, 2024, pp. 186–201.

Ng, Andrew Hock Soon. 'Conceptualizing Varieties of Space in Horror Fiction'. *The Palgrave Handbook to Horror Literature*, edited by Kevin Corstorphine and Laura R. Kremmel. Palgrave, 2018, pp. 441–56.

Nünning, Vera. 'Conceptualising (Un)reliable Narration and (Un)trustworthiness'. *Unreliable Narration and Trustworthiness: Intermedial and Interdisciplinary Perspectives*, edited by Nünning. DeGruyter, 2015, pp. 1–30.

Ogunyemi, Chikwenye Okonjo. *Africa Wo/Man Palava: The Nigerian Novel by Women*. University of Chicago Press, 1996.

O'Keefe, Tracie, and Katrina Fox, editors. *Finding the Real Me: True Tales of Sex and Gender Diversity*. Jossey-Bass, 2003.

Olson, Greta. 'Reconsidering Unreliability: Fallible and Untrustworthy Narrators'. *Narrative*, vol. 11, no. 1, 2003, pp. 93–109.

Page, Ruth E. *Literary and Linguistic Approaches to Feminist Narratology*. Palgrave, 2006.

Patrick, K. 'Notes on Craft'. *Granta*, 28 Oct. 2022, https://granta.com/k-patrick-notes-on-craft. Accessed 16 July 2024.

Pearce, Ruth. 'What's Wrong with the Cass Review? A Round-Up of Commentary and Evidence', https://ruthpearce.net/2024/04/16/whats-wrong-with-the-cass-review-a-round-up-of-commentary-and-evidence/. Accessed 17 July 2024.

——, Sonja Erikainen and Ben Vincent. 'TERF Wars: An Introduction'. *TERF Wars: Feminism and the Fight for Transgender Futures*, special issue of *The Sociological Review*, vol. 68, no. 4, 2020, pp. 677–98.

Peeren, Esther. *The Spectral Metaphor: Living Ghosts and the Agency of Invisibility*. Palgrave, 2014.

Pellegrini, Chiara. 'Adaptation as Queer Touching in *The Safety of Objects*: Transgressing the Boundaries of Bodies and Texts'. *Queer/Adaptation*, edited by Pamela Demory. Palgrave, 2019, pp. 107–20.

——. '"Declining to Describe": Intersex Narrators and Textual Visibility'. *Interdisciplinary and Global Perspectives on Intersex*, edited by Megan Walker. Palgrave, 2022, pp. 49–64.

——. 'Posttranssexual Temporalities: Negotiating Canonical Memoir Narratives in Kate Bornstein's *Gender Outlaw* and Juliet Jacques' *Trans*'. *a/b: Auto/Biography Studies*, vol. 34, no. 1, 2019, pp. 45–65.

——. 'Temporalities Beyond Transition: Form, Genre, and Contemporary Trans Novels', *Studies in the Novel*, vol. 55, no. 4, 2023, pp. 492–508.

——. 'When Narrative Studies Meets Trans Studies: Reflections on Methodology with *Bellies* and *Pew*'. *The Palgrave Handbook of Feminist, Queer and Trans Narrative Studies*, edited by Vera Nünning and Corinna Assmann. Palgrave, 2025.

Peters, Torrey. 'Seeing through a Trans Lens: Torrey Peters Pens "Detransition, Baby"'. Interviewed by Sam Sanders. *NPR*, 8 Mar. 2021, https://www.npr.org/2021/03/08/974705967/seeing-through-a-trans-lens-torrey-peters-pens-detransition-baby. Accessed 18 Oct. 2024.

Phelan, James. 'Estranging Unreliability, Bonding Unreliability, and the Ethics of *Lolita*'. *Narrative*, vol. 15, no. 2, 2007, pp. 222–38.

——. *Living to Tell About It*. Cornell University Press, 2005.

Price, Devon. 'How the Media Gets Trans Coverage Wrong | Medium Day 2023'. *YouTube*, uploaded by Medium, 19 Aug. 2023, https://www.youtube.com/watch?v=C2FGh9VB4xc&list=PLgtayi6nE1yk49tHO1GHJa8XU58y4GZMN&index=10. Accessed 16 July 2024.

Prince, Gerald. 'The Disnarrated'. *Style*, vol. 22, no. 1, 1988, pp. 1–8.

Prosser, Jay. *Second Skins: The Body Narratives of Transsexuality*. Columbia University Press, 1998.

Punday, Daniel. *Narrative Bodies: Toward a Corporeal Narratology*. Palgrave, 2003.

Pyne, Jake. 'Autistic Disruptions, Trans Temporalities: A Narrative "Trap Door" in Time'. *South Atlantic Quarterly*, vol. 120, no. 2, 2020, pp. 343–61.

——. 'Unsuitable Bodies: Trans People and Cisnormativity in Shelter Services'. *Canadian Social Work Review*, vol. 28, no. 1, 2011, pp. 129–37.

Roof, Judith. *What Gender Is, What Gender Does*. University of Minnesota Press, 2016.

Rosenberg, Jordy. 'Afterword: One Utopia, One Dystopia'. *Transgender Marxism*, edited by Jules Joanne Gleeson and Elle O'Rourke. Pluto Press, 2021, pp. 259–95.

——. *Confessions of the Fox*. Random House, 2018.

Rubin, Henry S. 'Trans Studies: Between a Metaphysics of Presence and Absence'. *Reclaiming Genders: Transsexual Grammars at the Fin de Siècle*, edited by Kate More and Stephen Whittle. Cassell, 1999, pp. 173–92.

Rumfitt, Alison. *Tell Me I'm Worthless*. Cipher Press, 2021.

St. James, Emily. 'How Twitter Can Ruin a Life'. *Vox*, 30 June 2021, https://www.vox.com/the-highlight/22543858/isabel-fall-attack-helicopter. Accessed 17 July 2024.

Salah, Trish. 'Transgender and Transgenre Writing'. *The Cambridge Companion to Twenty-First-Century American Fiction*, edited by Joshua Miller. Cambridge University Press, 2021, pp. 174–95.

Salamon, Gayle. *Assuming a Body: Transgender and the Rhetorics of Materiality*. Columbia University Press, 2010.

Seid, Danielle M. 'Reveal'. *Keywords*, special issue of *TSQ: Transgender Studies Quarterly*, vol. 1, nos. 1–2, 2014, pp. 176–7.

Semino, Elena. *Metaphor in Discourse*. Cambridge University Press, 2008.

Shenjé, Kuchenga. '"The Future Is Wide Open": How Trans Literature Came of Age'. *Penguin*, 15 Nov. 2021, https://www.penguinrandom

house.co.uk/articles/2021/11/trans-literature-history-future-stories. Accessed 17 July 2024.

Siddique, Haroon. 'High Court Ruling on Puberty Blockers "Based on Partisan Evidence"'. *The Guardian*, 23 June 2021, https://www.theguardian.com/society/2021/jun/23/high-court-ruling-on-puberty-blockers-based-on-partisan-evidence. Accessed 17 July 2024.

Smith, Jennifer A. '"We Shall Pass Imperceptibly through Every Barrier": Reading Jeanette Winterson's Trans-formative Romance'. *Critique: Studies in Contemporary Fiction*, vol. 52, no. 4, 2011, pp. 412–33.

Snorton, C. Riley. *Black on Both Sides: A Racial History of Trans Identity*. University of Minnesota Press, 2017.

Solomon, Rivers. *An Unkindness of Ghosts*. Akashic, 2017.

Spiegel, Simon. 'Things Made Strange: On the Concept of "Estrangement" in Science Fiction'. *Science Fiction Studies*, vol. 35, no. 3, 2008, pp. 369–85.

Spillers, Hortense J. 'Mama's Baby, Papa's Maybe: An American Grammar Book'. *Diacritics*, vol. 17, no. 2, 1987, pp. 64–81.

Stanzel, Franz K. *Narrative Situations in the Novel: Tom Jones, Moby Dick, The Ambassadors, Ulysses*, translated by James P. Pusack. Indiana University Press, 1971.

Stone, Sandy. 'The Empire Strikes Back: A Posttranssexual Manifesto'. *Camera Obscura*, vol. 10, no. 2, 1992, pp. 151–76.

Stryker, Susan. '(De)subjugated Knowledges: An Introduction to Transgender Studies'. *The Transgender Studies Reader*, edited by Stryker and Stephen Whittle. Routledge, 2006, pp. 1–18.

——. 'My Words to Victor Frankenstein above the Village of Chamounix: Performing Transgender Rage'. *GLQ: A Journal of Lesbian and Gay Studies*, vol. 1, no. 3, 1994, pp. 237–54.

——. 'Susan Stryker Discusses Trans Studies, Trans Feminism, and a More Trans Future with V. Varun Chaudhry'. Interview by V. Varun Chaudhry. *Signs: Journal of Women in Culture and Society*, vol. 47, no. 3, 2022, pp. 789–800.

——. 'Transgender Studies: Queer Theory's Evil Twin'. *Thinking Sex/Thinking Gender*, special issue of *GLQ: A Journal of Lesbian and Gay Studies*, vol. 10, no. 2, 2004, pp. 211–313.

—— and Aren Z. Aizura. 'Introduction: Transgender Studies 2.0'. *The Transgender Studies Reader 2*. Routledge, 2013, pp. 1–12.

——, Paisley Currah and Lisa Jean Moore. 'Introduction: Trans-, Trans, or Transgender?' *Trans-*, special issue of *Women's Studies Quarterly*, vol. 36, nos. 3–4, 2008, pp. 11–22.

Sundén, Jenny. 'Temporalities of Transition: Trans-Temporal Femininity in a Human Musical Automation'. *Somatechnics*, vol. 5, no. 2, 2015, pp. 197–216.

Thom, Kai Cheng. *Fierce Femmes and Notorious Liars: A Dangerous Trans Girl's Confabulous Memoir*. Metonymy Press, 2016.

Tobia, Jacob. *Sissy: A Coming-of-Gender Story*. G. P. Putnam's Sons, 2019.

Van den Bossche, Sven. '"How to Become a Rock": Non-Human Metaphors as Trans Paranarratives'. *Trans/forming Narrative Studies*, special issue of *Narrative*, vol. 32, no. 2, 2024, pp. 202–14.

Warhol, Robyn R. *Gendered Interventions: Narrative Discourse in the Victorian Novel*. Ohio State University Press, 1989.

—— and Susan S. Lanser. Introduction. *Narrative Theory Unbound: Queer and Feminist Interventions*, edited by Warhol and Lanser. Ohio State University Press, 2015, pp. 1–23.

Whitehead, Joshua. 'Why I'm Withdrawing from my Lambda Literary Award Nomination'. *Tia House*, 14 Mar. 2018, https://www.tiahouse.ca/joshua-whitehead-why-im-withdrawing-from-my-lambda-literary-award-nomination/. Accessed 17 July 2024.

Williams, Joe. 'International Best Selling Author Comes Out as Transgender'. *Pink News*, 24 Oct. 2015, https://www.thepinknews.com/2015/10/24/international-best-selling-author-comes-out-as-transgender/. Accessed 17 July 2024.

Winnett, Susan. 'Coming Unstrung: Women, Men, Narrative, and Principles of Pleasure'. *PMLA*, vol. 105, no. 3, 1990, pp. 505–18.

Winterson, Jeanette. *Written on the Body*. Vintage, 1992.

Young, Tory. 'Introduction: Futures for Feminist and Queer Narratology'. *Queer and Feminist Theories of Narrative*, special issue of *Textual Practice*, vol. 32, no. 6, 2018, pp. 913–21.

# Index

affect, 37, 40–1, 50, 75, 82, 92–3, 132, 134, 143–5, 172
Aizura, Aren Z., 30–1, 42
Alabanza, Travis
  cisnormativity, 5, 81–2
  editing, 80–1, 86–7
  memory, 49–50, 83–4
  transition, 78–9, 85–6
  transphobia, 50, 79–80
  uncertainty, 60, 86–7, 170
audiences, 5–6, 45, 52–3, 56–8, 81, 83–4, 98, 117–18, 124, 129, 133, 136, 140, 144, 146, 148–50, 153, 156, 165, 176, 179
authorship, 4–5, 58, 124–5, 133, 140, 146, 156–7
autobiography, 7, 66–8, 70, 78, 88, 90, 96–7, 98–9, 142
Awkward-Rich, Cameron, 37, 92–3

Bauer, Beckett K.
  bodies, 162–3, 166
  feminist science fiction, 160–1, 164–6
  gender norms, 161–3, 165–8
  naïve narrator, 162, 164, 168–9

Bettcher, Talia Mae, 2, 42, 54, 58–9
Bey, Marquis, 6, 13–14, 53, 103
bodies *see* embodiment
Bornstein, Kate, 9, 12, 60

canon, 4–6, 10–11, 44, 67–8, 89
community, 90, 92–4, 115, 143–4, 179

Dawson, Juno
  authorial presence, 150–2, 156–7, 160
  drugs theme, 153, 157–8
  girlhood, 151, 153–4, 156
  unreliable narration, 152–5, 157, 159
defamiliarisation, 75, 163–4, 168
Dinan, Nicola, 56, 179–80
disnarration, 44–5, 81–3, 86, 111

elliptical narration *see* gaps
embodiment
  and corporeal boundaries, 32–3, 36, 46, 102–3, 107, 115–16, 118–19, 123, 127, 167–8, 176–7

embodiment (*cont.*)
  and containment, 28, 34, 107–9, 116
  and multiplicity, 52, 102–4, 109–11, 113, 116, 118, 132
  and physical transformation, 73–4, 110–12, 117, 119–21, 166
  in narrative studies, 42, 50–2
  in trans studies, 36–7, 46–7, 50–3, 111
Emezi, Akwaeke
  challenge to binaries, 105–6, 111
  Igbo identity, 105–7, 112
  plural narration, 107–8, 110, 112–13
  space, 109–10

Faye, Shon, 15–16, 75, 138
Feinberg, Leslie, 8–9, 11, 28, 49
feminist narratology, 19–20, 39
film *see* visual media
first-person narration
  and ambiguity, 3, 94, 113, 116–17, 120, 123
  and authority, 2, 52–3, 145, 157, 169, 177–8
  and narrator/character distinction, 3, 47–9, 103, 114, 157
  and other characters, 93, 52, 110, 154–6, 159, 178–9
  and the pronoun 'I', 2, 47–8, 85, 107, 112, 123, 130, 180
fluidity, 17, 46, 53, 85, 107, 112, 117, 122
focalisation, 48–9, 116, 118–19, 128

gaps, 61, 86, 57–8, 92, 121–2, 143, 145, 147–8
genre, 45, 66–8, 74, 90–3, 95, 123, 124, 127
Gimpelevich, Calvin
  body modification, 116–18, 120–1
  disembodied identity, 121–2
  relational identity, 114–15
  transcending the body, 115–16, 118–19, 123

Halberstam, J., 17, 33
Halpern, Faye, 5, 57–8
Hayward, Eva, 36–7, 46, 103
haunting, 35–7, 61, 87, 104, 110, 118, 124, 126–7, 130
heterodiegetic narration *see* third-person narration
homodiegetic narration *see* first-person narration

Jacques, Juliet
  media, 69, 76–8
  memoir, 70–1
  self-reflexivity, 74–5
  time, 72–4, 76–7

Lanser, Susan S., 19–22, 52, 113
Lavery, Grace, 44–5, 49, 139

Malatino, Hil, 40, 50, 89, 115, 135
medicine, 2, 7–8, 43–4, 58, 71, 75, 111–12
metalepsis, 49–50, 96, 103, 122–3
metaphors
  for trans identity, 32, 87, 90–1, 97, 104, 106, 108, 127

in narrative theory, 30–2, 35
in trans theory, 16, 30–3, 36

narratee *see* 'you' pronoun
non-binary identity, 22, 33, 82, 85–6, 105–6, 165–6, 169
non-gendered narrators, 21, 57, 121–2
normativity, 13–15, 37, 44, 74–5, 82, 95, 105, 111, 121, 141, 164–5, 167

objectification, 14, 51, 114, 129–30, 142, 155, 157, 176–7
omission *see* gaps

Peters, Torrey, 6, 140
Phelan, James, 56, 61, 139
playwriting, 79
Plett, Casey, 6, 4, 160–1
plot, 39, 42, 76, 91–2
poetry, 6, 53, 93–4
Prosser, Jay, 8, 16–17, 31, 45, 58
Punday, Daniel, 42, 52

queer theory, 16–17, 20–2, 40–1

reliability
  and autobiography, 55–6, 142–4
  and care, 143, 145, 150, 156–7
  and messy truths, 60–1, 80, 83–4, 86–7, 142, 148, 165, 171
  and speculative reality, 90, 96, 117–18, 144, 162–4, 166
  and transphobia, 55–6, 58–60, 138–40, 144–5, 149, 153–6, 157–9, 177

and young narrators, 138, 151–3, 155, 162–3
Rosenberg, Jordy
  authenticity, 141–3, 145–6
  collective, 144, 149–50
  equivocation, 144–5, 147–9
  resistant truths, 141, 145–6
Rumfitt, Alison
  British context, 125–6, 131
  horror, 124, 127–8, 131–2
  inequalities, 126, 129, 132
  gender, 128, 130

Salah, Trish, 4, 10, 66, 88, 91
science fiction, 6, 9, 115–17, 124, 160–1, 163–6, 169
short stories, 68, 70, 121–3
Snorton, C. Riley, 14, 33, 149
spatiality, 16, 30–1, 33–5, 46–7, 93–4, 105–6, 125–7, 129, 168
Stryker, Susan, 11, 16–17, 38, 54

temporality
  climax, 39, 51, 72, 77, 131, 158, 176
  closure, 41–3, 72, 87, 95, 112, 132–3
  linear progression, 30–1, 39–41, 43–4, 67–8, 70–2, 77, 79, 85, 93
  order, 71–2, 80, 96, 159
  retrospection, 49, 73–4, 174–6
  slowness, 40, 72–3, 76
  sudden change, 12, 42, 73–4
television *see* visual media
third-person narration, 22, 50–1, 116, 119, 128, 131, 142, 179–80

Thom, Kai Cheng
 collective narrative, 92–4
 creativity, 88–90, 96–7
 endings, 95–6
 the fantastical, 90–2, 96
trans narratology, 11, 18–20, 23–4, 29, 54, 62–3
translation, 106, 161, 164–6

UK context, 7, 15–16, 69, 79, 125, 151–2
unreliable narrators *see* reliability

visibility, 14, 21, 51–3, 71, 104, 111, 120, 122, 135, 143, 146, 174–7
visual media, 50, 174–8

Warhol, Robyn R., 19–20
'we' pronoun, 107–8, 112–13
writing process, 53, 71, 75, 80–1, 86, 97

'you' pronoun, 84–5, 95–6, 120–1, 124–5, 129, 131; *see also* audiences